Migration and Identity in Central Asia

This book is an ethnographic and sociolinguistic study of Uzbek migrants in the capital city of Uzbekistan. The ethnographic details of the book represent post-Soviet urban realities on the ground, where various forms of belonging clash and kinship ties are reinforced within social safety networks. Theoretically, it challenges the existing theories of identity and identification which often considered the relations between 'We and They', taking the 'We' for granted. The book offers in-depth insights into the communication strategies of migrants, the formation of collective consciousness and the relations within the 'We' domain.

Constructed around contradictions regarding Uzbek identity and how various groups relate to one another as different ethnic groups, the theoretical argument of the book is built through such methods and analytical tools as strategic rhetoric and discourse analysis, communication and identity theories and the analysis of power and dependence.

The book will be of interest to students and scholars of Central Asian studies, migration studies and Central Asian culture and society.

Rano Turaeva is an Affiliated Researcher at the Max Planck Institute of Social Anthropology, Germany.

Central Asia research forum
Series Editor: Shirin Akiner

Other titles in the series:

Sustainable Development in Central Asia
Edited by Shirin Akiner, Sander Tideman and John Hay

Qaidu and the Rise of the Independent Mongol State in Central Asia
Michal Biran

Tajikistan
Edited by Mohammad-Reza Djalili, Frederic Gare and Shirin Akiner

Uzbekistan on the Threshold of the Twenty-first Century
Tradition and survival
Islam Karimov

Tradition and Society in Turkmenistan
Gender, oral culture and song
Carole Blackwell

Life of Alimqul
A native chronicle of nineteenth century Central Asia
Edited and translated by Timur Beisembiev

Central Asia
Aspects of transition
Edited by Tom Everett-Heath

The Heart of Asia
A history of Russian Turkestan and the Central Asian Khanates from the earliest times
Frances Henry Skrine and Edward Denison Ross

The Caspian
Politics, energy and security
Edited by Shirin Akiner and Anne Aldis

Islam and Colonialism
Western perspectives on Soviet Asia
Will Myer

Azeri Women in Transition
Women in Soviet and post-Soviet Azerbaijan
Farideh Heyat

The Post-Soviet Decline of Central Asia
Sustainable development and comprehensive capital
Eric Sievers

Prospects for Pastoralism in Kazakhstan and Turkmenistan
From state farms to private flocks
Edited by Carol Kerven

Muslim Reformist Political Thought
Revivalists, modernists and free will
Sarfraz Khan

Economic Development in Kazakhstan
The role of large enterprises and foreign investment
Anne E. Peck

Energy, Wealth and Governance in the Caucasus and Central Asia
Lessons not learned
Edited by Richard Auty and Indra de Soysa

The Politics of Knowledge in Central Asia
Science between Marx and the market
Sarah Amsler

The Economics and Politics of Oil in the Caspian Basin
The redistribution of oil revenues in Azerbaijan and Central Asia
Edited by Boris Najman, Richard Pomfret and Gaël Raballand

The Political Economy of Reform in Central Asia
Uzbekistan under authoritarianism
Martin C. Spechler

Turkmenistan's Foreign Policy
Positive neutrality and the consolidation of the Turkmen regime
Luca Anceschi

Religion and Security in South and Central Asia
Edited by K. Warikoo

Conflict and Peace in Eurasia
Edited by Debidatta Aurobinda Mahapatra

Social and Cultural Change in Central Asia
The Soviet legacy
Edited by Sevket Akyildiz and Richard Carlson

Leadership and Authority in Central Asia
The Ismaili community in Tajikistan
Otambek N. Mastibekov

National Identities in Soviet Historiography
The rise of nations under Stalin
Harun Yilmaz

Identity and Memory in Post-Soviet Central Asia
Uzbekistan's Soviet past
Timur Dadabaev

Migration and Identity in Central Asia
The Uzbek experience
Rano Turaeva

Migration and Identity in Central Asia

The Uzbek experience

Rano Turaeva

LONDON AND NEW YORK

First published 2016
by Routledge
2 Park Square, Milton Park, Abingdon, Oxon OX14 4RN

and by Routledge
711 Third Avenue, New York, NY 10017

Routledge is an imprint of the Taylor & Francis Group, an informa business

© 2016 Rano Turaeva

The right of Rano Turaeva to be identified as author of this work has been asserted by her in accordance with sections 77 and 78 of the Copyright, Designs and Patents Act 1988.

All rights reserved. No part of this book may be reprinted or reproduced or utilised in any form or by any electronic, mechanical, or other means, now known or hereafter invented, including photocopying and recording, or in any information storage or retrieval system, without permission in writing from the publishers.

Trademark notice: Product or corporate names may be trademarks or registered trademarks, and are used only for identification and explanation without intent to infringe.

British Library Cataloguing in Publication Data
A catalogue record for this book is available from the British Library

Library of Congress Cataloging-in-Publication Data
Turaeva, Rano.
Migration and identity in Central Asia : the Uzbek experience / Rano Turaeva.
  pages cm
  Includes bibliographical references and index.
  1. Uzbeks–Ethnic identity. 2. Ethnology–Uzbekistan–Tashkent.
  3. Group identity–Uzbekistan–Tashkent. 4. Ethnic relations–
  Uzbekistan–Tashkent. 5. Migration, Internal–Social aspects–
  Uzbekistan. 6. Tashkent (Uzbekistan)–Social conditions. I. Title.
  DK947.T87 2016
  305.809587–dc23   2015016284

ISBN: 978-1-138-91349-3 (hbk)
ISBN: 978-1-315-69142-8 (ebk)

Typeset in Times New Roman
by Wearset Ltd, Boldon, Tyne and Wear

Contents

List of figures	x
Acknowledgements	xi
Note on transliteration	xiii
List of abbreviations	xiv

Prologue   xv

1 Unmaking Uzbek identity and language   1
    In Khorezm *1*
    In Tashkent bazaar *1*
    Collective identity theories revisited *5*
    Constructivist or primordialist? *8*
    Uzbek ethnicity and sub-ethnicities *10*
    Doing fieldwork at home *12*

PART I
Uzbek identity   21

2 Making of Uzbek nationality   23
    Early history: were there Uzbeks in the past? *24*
    From tribes to nations *29*
    Creating Homo Sovietikus *33*
    Internationalisation strategies: population movements *38*

3 *De jure* boundary among Uzbeks; de facto *propiska*   48
    Propiska *policies: historical trajectory 50*
    Migration after the Soviet Union *51*
    Migration from Khorezm to Tashkent *52*
    Residential arrangements *63*

viii Contents

     'Propiska *is the first thing to do and organise before coming to Tashkent; otherwise you cannot come and live here*' 65
     Difficulties in being illegal residents 72
     International migration within one country 78

PART II
Identification and communication 85

4 Linguistic means and rhetorical strategies in identification processes 87
     The Uzbek language and its dialects 90
     Status and role of the official Uzbek literary language in comparison with Uzbek dialects 92
     Contexts of communication 94
     Impact of linguistic differences on 'We' and 'They' 100
     Defining 'They': group names and stereotypes 105
     From rhetoric to identification 110

PART III
Identification and belonging 119

5 Who is a Negro and who is not? Sub-ethnic groups of Uzbeks: Khorezmians and others in Tashkent 121
     Uzbeks and Uzbek sub-ethnic groups: introduction 122
     Defining the 'Other' 125
     Performing the Other 127
     Identity markers 130
     Marriage strategies as contexts of relevance in politics of belonging in Tashkent 135
     Defining the 'We' 138
     Making of 'We and They' 146

6 Networking strategies of migrants: Khorezmian community in Tashkent 150
     Finding the right partner: Sayora and the brides' school 152
     Forms of socialising 159
     Institutions of support 165
     Institutionalisation of patrons and clients or ethnic entrepreneurship 171

PART IV
Identification and interdependence   179

7 '*Ipsiz boglanib qalmaq*' or bound without ropes: interdependence in Khorezmian migrant communities in Tashkent   181
   Kichkina *and* katta *Khorezmians 182*
   Socialising duties and responsibilities 194
   Concluding theoretical discussion: power relations and dependence theories 196

Epilogue   207

8 Identity theories revisited: relations of 'I and We' vs 'We and They'   209
   We vs Others: de jure *boundaries 210*
   We vs Others: identification and communication 210
   Who are We and who are the Others? 211
   The relations of I and We: identification and bonding 212

   Index   215

Figures

1.1	Fruit seller in a bazaar in Tashkent	2
2.1	Borders of Turkestan and its ethnic composition at the time of the Russian conquest	30
2.2	Today's Central Asia and former Turkestan borders	30
2.3	Population movements during Soviet rule: to Central Asia	39
3.1	Preparing rice for the sale in the bazaar: Khorezmian rice traders in Tashkent, 2005	57
3.2	Male *mardikor* bazaar, 2006	74
4.1	Spatial location of Uzbek dialect groups and other Turkic languages and their mutual influence	91
4.2	Linguistic map showing territorial distribution of the groups of dialects in the territory of Uzbekistan	92
4.3	We and They distinctions among Uzbeks	109

Acknowledgements

This book is based on the dissertation I wrote under the supervision of two professors, Prof. Dr. Wolfgang Klein and Prof. Dr Guenther Schlee. I would like to express my gratitude to them for their support and tremendous academic input into my work. This project would not have happened without the generous institutional, financial and administrative support of two institutions: the Max Planck Institute for Social Anthropology in Halle (Germany); and the Max Planck Institute for Psycholinguistics in Nijmegen (the Netherlands).

My great appreciation is addressed to the IT department, administrative and library support teams of the Max Planck Institute for Social Anthropology, without whom this work would have been difficult to finalise. Among others I appreciate the patience and support of Oliver Weimann and his IT team, Anja Neuner and Anett Kirchhof for their library assistance, and Kathrin Niehuus, Janka Diallo and their administrative team.

My sincere thanks go to my colleagues and friends who have helped me find my way through the jungle of life in Halle as a newcomer and foreigner. Their intellectual support was also vital for the successful conclusion of this project. Among others, I wish to mention here the late Irene Hilgers, Michaela Pelican, Markus Hoehne, Dereje Feissa, Nina Glick-Schiller, Steve Reyna, Johan Rasanayagam, Felix Girke, Sophie Roche, Rita Sanders, Anita Schroven, Madeleine Reeves and Peter Finke.

I would like to express my gratitude to Billy MacKinnon, who was not only a friend but was also patient enough to do the language editing of my dissertation. Markus Hoehne also engaged with my writing and helped me to clarify my position in countless discussions over the past years. My dissertation also benefited from the academic colloquia and seminars at the Max Planck Institute in Halle, which were partly self-organised and partly organised and led by John Eidson and Joachim Görlich. John's and Joachim's input, as well as the discussions in these seminars and colloquia, forced me to rethink my material and sharpen the line of argumentation. Additionally, John Eidson engaged with my work more than could be expected and gave me valuable tips in numerous discussions.

I wish to thank my family, including my husband Markus Hoehne, my daughters Feruza and Fatima Maria, my son Ali Johannes, my sisters Muyassar and Muhabbat Turaeva and my parents and other siblings who supported me in difficult times and shared happy and sad moments. Without them I would never have managed to complete my PhD and later this book.

I am grateful for all my informants in Uzbekistan for their trust and openness. With many, I was able to keep good relationships throughout the time of fieldwork and to the present.

Note on transliteration

There is no clear agreement on the transliteration rules within the studies of Central Asia. The region was influenced by Russian language policies including change of script and other linguistic conditions peculiar to the region. This has led to inconsistencies in the use of geographic names and transliteration of local terms into Latin script. The recent change into a Latin script has not solved the existing confusion in transliteration rules.

In this book I have used the following method of transliteration: 'j' was used as [dj] as the first consonant in the word 'judge'; 'y' was used as [j] as the first sound in the word 'year'; Russian vowels such as Cyrillic 'е' have been transliterated in Latin as 'ye'; Cyrillic 'ю' as Latin 'yu', 'ё' as 'yo', 'я' as 'ya', etc. The same sounds in Uzbek have been transliterated following this rule.

I used diacritical sign ' mainly for Russian words or Russian borrowings such as *bol'*/pain, to express a soft consonant.

For the transcription of the lexemes (those within the square brackets) in the linguistic part of the book I followed the International Phonetic Alphabet to express the sound of each word or lexeme.

In the direct quotations and in the context where I have used the descriptions of other authors I tried to retain their way of using the local names.

I have used the Latin letter 'k' for the Uzbek equivalent 'k', the Latin letters 'q' for hard 'k', 'ğ', 'ö' and 'h' instead of 'kh'.

Generally I kept the transliteration close to the spoken version in order to keep it simple and enable smooth reading when it was not necessary to indicate specific phonetic features or other linguistic meanings.

Abbreviations

FB	father's brother
HB	husband's brother
HBW	husband's brother's wife
Kh	Khorezmian
MB	mother's brother
MBDS	mother's brother's daughter's son
MS	mother's son
Ru	Russian
Uz	Uzbek

Prologue

1 Unmaking Uzbek identity and language

In Khorezm

I am sitting in a café in Khorezm and having lunch with a very interesting 'collection' of people consisting of two men from the *Philarmoniya*, two others and their driver from the Prosecutor's Office, three male actors from the *Ogakhiy* Theater of Urgench in Khorezm, a Khorezmian writer of song lyrics and a stage director. We all are having a break from a preparation for the event called '*Vozrojdeniye Khorezmskih traditsional'nih pesnopeniy Bahshi i Halpa*' (Revival of Khorezmian traditions of *Bahshi* and *Halpa* singing).[1] The men from the Prosecutor's Office and an old man (an ex-prosecutor), along with their driver, were present at the event because the old man was a fan of traditional singing, and had financially supported the event. He wanted to have influence on how the event was staged and therefore spent time with the management team, most of whom were present at the lunch meeting. Having had some disagreements and other unpleasant discussions about the details of the event, the members of the group remembered that I was present and directed their attention to me. A man in his late forties, who was the most talkative in the group (a man from the *Philarmoniya*), looked at me and asked where I came from. I looked puzzled and said: 'From here, I am a Khorezmian.'[2] He said, 'No, no, where do you come from.' I was perplexed. He continued and requested, 'Say [erkœn]!' I repeated the word, and he insisted that I repeat it again, which I did. He said: 'Everything is clear.' I was astonished and asked what he meant. He said that I came from Urgench and had a Turkmen accent. I replied that this was correct and that my parents grew up in Turkmenistan.

In Tashkent bazaar

A young woman (Laziza,[3] 43) from Namangan region who lived for many years in Tashkent told me a story about her negative encounter with a female Tashkenti fruit seller. She described a Tashkenti fruit seller who had insulted another fruit seller from outside of Tashkent (a 'regional') in order to take away a selling place. Laziza[4] said:

2 *Prologue*

In the Chilanzar bazaar I had a very negative encounter between a fruit seller from a region and a Tashkenti woman who insulted her in the middle of the bazaar with bad words. [...] The *mestnaya* [the Tashkenti woman] verbally said '*Negrlar hamma yoqni bosib ketdi*' [Negroes have occupied everywhere here]. Then I interrupted by asking her why she was insulting her [a regional woman] and said that her being from Tashkent does not give her any rights to insult her [a regional woman] and being from another region does not make someone a Negro. I said that only because these 'Negros' work hard she makes money and eats fruits. In reply the local [Tashkenti] woman said without any shame in public that '*Ozi Negr bogannan keyin negrni himoya kiladi da*' [because she herself is a Negro of course she will defend a Negro]. I was shocked and I said that when she becomes sick she will come to me [the speaker was a medical nurse], a Negro, and I left.

These two dialogues took place in two different locales in Uzbekistan, situated a thousand kilometres away from each other. Different actors are talking about the same thing and asking the same question about identity, yet on a different scale. The questions all of them ask are: Who are the Others? Who are We? What is the difference between Them and Us? The dialogues show that individual actors communicate their identities in many different ways and use various rhetorical means to emphasise differences. The first example highlights 'micro-differences' among regional groups in Khorezm itself, and are related to local sub-dialect

Figure 1.1 Fruit seller in a bazaar in Tashkent.

variations within a Khorezmian dialect. The second example illustrates the ways identity politics evolve in Tashkent – namely with the use of racist terms, derogative names, other insults and conflicts among Uzbek groups in Tashkent (Tashkentis, Khorezmians, Bukharans, etc.). These conflicts and contradictions among Uzbeks challenge the often taken-for-granted Uzbek national identity. The main argument of this book is constructed around those contradictions to show how Uzbek groups relate to each other as different ethnic groups, which then raises questions about the complexities of politics of belonging and identification among Uzbeks.

I explore the dynamics of inter-ethnic relations among sub-ethnic Uzbek groups in Tashkent. To do this, linguistic means employed during the identification processes will be explored in a detailed manner. Besides this, I study interactions and communication practices of individuals and groups to decipher practices and representations of collective identification and to show the very making of the differences among the groups in question. I will use the terms 'group' and 'collective' interchangeably and am aware of the academic discussions and critical debate on the limitations of the use of these terms (see below). I will use these terms 'group' or 'collective' in the meaning of a collective of individuals and actors who share basic ideas of their similarity based on the place of origin, sharing similar or common culture, and the main criteria for a group or a collective, which is the feeling of *Gemeinsamkeit* as Weber (1968: 926) used it.

In social sciences, collective identities are usually considered as the relations between We and They. I argue that there is *not* only the domain of relations between *'We and They'* but there is also a domain which comprises relations between *'I and We'*. The latter has an important contribution to the processes of collective identification. In this book I consider both domains as relevant and present the relations and interactions within both domains to explain collective identification of various Uzbek groups in Uzbekistan.

The central argument of this book is that the communication and maintenance of collective identities constitute a dialectical process between two domains of relations, namely 'We and They' and 'I and We'.[5] Within this process, one finds, on the one hand, a collective identity as a process of a formation of the We with its own internal rules and principles of organisation, and, on the other hand, representations and communications of this collective identity in its relation to the relevant Other. I use the term 'dialectic' metaphorically to denote the relationship where two opposite sides are united through complex relationships that contribute to the constitution of the respective Other where one observes contradictions and struggles on both sides. In this process the two realms do not become just similar to the point of assimilation, but rather differences multiply, and things that were once insignificant come to become significant as cultural markers. In this process, the We-ness is redefined against the Other. Contradictions do not dissolve but rather take on a more complex character and this process is continuous This contributes to and develops lines of argumentations that have been pursued by Barth (1969, 1994) and others (Banks 2013; Brubaker

4 Prologue

2014; Candea 2010; Huntington 2004). I will do this by starting to look at the existing boundaries which delineate differences at various levels of social relations going from external boundaries to internal ones which make the We or a group. Formal boundaries, or what I called *de jure* boundaries, among Uzbeks are drawn by state policies such as *propiska*.

Propiska is a local registration system which is strictest in Tashkent, the capital city. All legal residents of the capital must have a *propiska* or official permission to reside in the city. The difficulties of obtaining a *propiska* have a number of consequences for the legal status of migrants to the city in both their working as well as their social lives. *Propiska* provides a *de jure* marker of 'otherness' among Uzbeks and mirrors to some degree the unequal distribution of resources and wealth that intensifies differences between Tashkentis (born holders of *propiska*/autochthons in the capital) and Others (allochthons in the capital). Theoretically, it is also relevant for the definitions of citizenship and national identity in general. I argue that *propiska* and other (internal) government directives and practices of state agents create the political field within which the frequently illegal migrants from the regions have to manoeuvre. Their everyday practices and strategies of 'survival' result in the formation of translocal networks (between the regions and the capital) and particular ways of social organisations of migrants in Tashkent. This provides the everyday-life basis for identity formation.

Khorezmian Uzbeks are the central focus of the book. Khorezmians are the most distinct Uzbek group among other Uzbeks besides the Tadjik-speaking 'Uzbeks' who come from Bukhara and Samarqand. The Khorezmian dialect is distinct from other Uzbek dialects both phonetically and partly semantically, which I briefly show in the linguistic part of this book.[6] Why did I choose Tashkent as a fieldwork location and not any other city? Tashkent is a very big city, with more than 2.5 million inhabitants (at the time of the research) that is situated very far from Khorezm (1,000 km), at the 'other end' of Uzbekistan. It is the city where most Uzbek citizens want to live as it offers better standards of living, good infrastructure and better job opportunities thanks to the centralised system of governance and resource allocation in Uzbekistan. This makes Tashkent a prime location for studying contact among various Uzbek groups. Life in Tashkent is, of course, somewhat different from an average life in any other region or town of Uzbekistan. However, it is not the aim of this book to bring forth examples of the average lives of Uzbeks. Rather, the aim is to explore the dynamics of contact between various Uzbek groups, which can only be observed in Tashkent. Tashkent provides ample opportunities to study such contacts for the reasons I just mentioned.

When I talk about Uzbek groups in this book, I mostly refer to Khorezmians, Tashkentis, Bukharans and Samarqandis, *Vodiylik* (those who come from the Fergana Valley) and other people who come from the regions of Surkhandarya and Qashqadarya. There are many ways to group people together. The question is from whose perspective the categorisation is made, and I will discuss this in the book at some length. I take the differences that actors themselves make as a starting point. I focus on how members of groups make sense of their 'We-ness' and how they define 'the Other'

This book not only contributes to the ethnography of Uzbekistan and Central Asia,[7] but also adds theoretically innovative insights into the studies of collective identification and communication.[8] It does so by combining socio-anthropological and sociolinguistic approaches that shed light on the communicative aspects of identity politics and dynamics of identification. Gumperz, Giles, Hymes and Fishman are among those who have written on these topics since the 1970s. I will discuss these works in Part II of this book, which will outline some sociolinguistic approaches to the studies of collective identification. Still, considerable work needs to be done in this field, and this book contributes to that.

Theoretically, this book benefited from an interdisciplinary approach to studying inter-ethnic contact and communication. For the theoretical framework of this book a range of traditions of thought and methods have been applied and consulted, drawing on sociolinguistics and the ethnography of communication, classical social anthropological theories of inter-ethnic relations and group formation, economic theories of rational choice and the so-called trader's dilemma, as well as psychological theories of bonding and dependence.

Besides making a theoretical and methodological contribution, I believe this book contributes to the social anthropological research on the region, which is a relatively new field for anthropologists. Since Soviet Central Asia was closed for any external research during the 70 years of Soviet rule, only a few foreigners had been allowed to travel to these regions; among these were Hughes (1934), Maillart (1934), and Bacon ([1966] 1980) (Kuehnast 2000: 103, 104). The ethnographic material I contribute to the regional studies includes thick description of travelling experiences of internal migrants and other nuances of internal migration, the patterns of which are comparable to those of international or transnational migration. My ethnography also includes both language material and other descriptions of how inter-ethnic relations are established and maintained in an urban context, in addition to case studies of three different institutions in Tashkent: a Khorezmian medical clinic, a Khorezmian brides' school, and a *propiska* office, including formal and informal businesses taking place within these institutions. This widens the horizon of the readers of this book, making it accessible not only to an academic audience but also to a lay reader who has an interest in this part of the world.

Collective identity theories revisited

The scholarly debate on identity and identification has been going on for several decades and it was even suggested to get rid of the term 'identity' and instead use the term 'identification' (Brubaker and Cooper 2000). Brubaker and Cooper (ibid.) argued that the term identity is a reifying term which should be rather studied through applying a processual approach and therefore the term 'identification' is more useful. However, this approach has been critically discussed

6   *Prologue*

particularly in the recent work on identity theory and collective identification (Donahoe et al. 2009). Below I will address this critical discussion by the authors.

Donahoe et al. (ibid.: 4) distinguished between collective and social identities. According to the authors, this distinction is a matter of perspective, and when studying collective identities an investigator starts with an individual in order to find out about his/her multiple affiliations.[9] The term *social identities*, on the other hand, refers to characteristics of individuals which results from social processes affecting the significance of the individual's position in relation to others, e.g., a mother, a wife, a teacher, etc. In studying collective identities, I take the definition by Donahoe et al. (ibid.: 2) as a starting point. They define collective identity as

> a representation containing – or seeming to contain – a normative appeal to potential respondents and providing them with the means of understanding themselves, or being understood, as members of a larger category of persons or as participants in a larger assemblage.

The authors distinguish identity and identification by suggesting that we consider the former as representation and the latter as process. Following Brubaker and Cooper (2000), I am keen to take a processual approach and use the term *identification* when I describe the processes of collective identification. However, I and others (Donahoe et al. 2009) believe that the substantive 'identity' is useful to indicate the types of identity that are the object of these identification processes. Without its object, these processes cannot take place.

Certainly, the wider socio-political and economic context of identification processes has a tremendous influence on identity formation. I will consider this context by providing historical and institutional background information particularly focusing my analysis on historical composition of local populations over a longer time, and current state practices of restricting mobility through the *propiska* regime. The former provided for de facto historical boundaries between the groups in question, whereas *propiska* delineated *de jure* boundaries between those groups.

The theoretical framework of this book is divided into three meaningful parts, introduced in Parts II, III and IV, concerning *identification and communication*, *identification and belonging* and *identification and interdependence*.

Identification and communication: We-codes and They-codes

To understand collective identities and identification processes it is crucial to analyse the ways identity is communicated to the significant Other. Features indicating similarities and differences are communicated between members of the groups in a language, which has to be analysed with a particular set of tools in order to understand the manner of communication, the quality of contact, and the strategies employed while sending messages to each other. Related to that, the question arises whether the relevant Other got the message or not. The question is whether communication or miscommunication took place.

Linguistic means and rhetorical strategies have recently gained importance in the study of inter-ethnic relations in urban contexts (Gumperz 1997). Their significance in the process of identification has been recognised. In the process of communicating identity and difference We-codes and They-codes are employed (ibid.). I discuss these codes in more detail in the linguistic part of the book (Part II, Chapter 4).

Any communication implies the exchange of information, which is interpreted differently depending on the context and considering the background of the interlocutors. I will follow Gumperz's (ibid.) interpretive sociolinguistic approach to shed light on the meanings of communicated identities and differences. The sociolinguistic analysis of the contact between the groups in question indicates the points of references to language choice and actors' preferences of belonging in relation to the Other. These aspects are depicted in Figure 4.3. The analysis of communication serves as the basis for further investigation of other variables contributing to the process of collective identification.

Identification and belonging: relations between We and They

Further analysis of the communicated content and the above-mentioned codes in identity politics among Uzbeks show the importance of belonging to a place. I discuss autochthony discourses among Uzbeks in Part III of the book. These discourses and practices of belonging to a place include the making and/or construction of 'home' by Khorezmians. This touches on discourses of autochthony and allochthony in Tashkent (Geschiere 1997, 2004; Jackson 2006; Nyamjoh 2005, 2007). Moreover, Cancea (2010, 2014), following Tarde's theory of possessions and associations, investigated the anthropology of belonging and identification. She skilfully showed how collective identities and belonging to a place are linked and offered a new perspective on studying identification and configuration of connections among individuals and groups.

Such variables as identity markers, including physical features, clothes, food, marriage strategies, as well as representations in the official sphere of identity politics in Uzbekistan – for instance at big concerts, national holiday celebrations and so forth – constitute the main plot of those discourses of belonging and identification in this book.

Identification and interdependence: relations between I and We

The relations within the We-domain, namely between 'I and We', is not considered at all in the literature on collective identities and identification which I discuss in Part IV of this book. I agree with Barth's (1969, 1994) argument that the 'We' is not a container consisting of cultural stuff that is ready-made for representation to the outside. Therefore, it is necessary to delve deeper into the We-domain and analyse this domain as a space which is constituted through a series of relations between 'I and We'. The process of the We-formation is continuous and thus the relations within a group (i.e. Khorezmians) are constantly renegotiated. These relations are themselves full of contradictions and lead to divisions within the Khorezmian community. These contradictions imply that the We should not be taken for granted and, rather, scrutinised and considered seriously when analysing group formation and collective identification.

The analysis of networking strategies within the group highlights the importance of differential access to resources and power. These differences contribute to the formation of patron–client relationships (and other dependencies), which overlap with kinship relations. In order to find the way out of this complex of networks and relationships with overlapping and cross-cutting ties, the focus on networks and marriage strategies among Khorezmians is important to consider in order to gain a better understanding of the formation of the We. Furthermore, understanding of dependencies and power relations such as patron–client relations where age and gender-based duties and responsibilities, among others, play their roles is crucial to the making and holding of the We together. In this context, I distinguish between bonding and identification. Schlee (2008) suggested that bonding exists often in the form of parent–child relations. Bourdieu (1977: 196) used bonding also to describe the relationship of 'a creditor and debtor, master and *khammes*'. In my work, I integrate both aspects, the emotional and economic, of bonding in the analysis of identification processes. The case of charismatic leaders of the Khorezmian networks and their private interests in keeping those networks in Tashkent, outlined in Chapters 6 and 7, serve as an illustration of how groups form and what holds them together.

Constructivist or primordialist?

The theoretical framework of the book outlined so far does not strictly follow one clear direction regarding the constructivist or primordialist, and some might even add instrumentalist, view on identity. I do not find these seemingly mutually exclusive approaches very helpful for a number of reasons. I will explain this by presenting some opinions expressed on these points by other scholars, as well as by giving some ethnographic examples.

Jenkins (2001: 4827) argued that the debate about instrumentalism and primordialism exaggerates the differences between 'for example, Geertz and Barth, and it does neither justice'. Authors attributed to primordial thinking about ethnicity are, among others, Geertz and Shills. However, Geertz (1963), for example, was misinterpreted and it is clear that he did not advocate a primordial view on identity but was interested in the perspectives of the people themselves on their identities. He found that in the emic view, identity is often perceived (and represented) as something 'given'.

In contrast, some Russian scholars proposed some genuinely primordialist arguments. Shirokogorov (2002), Gumilev (1989, 1994) and Bromley (1973, 1983) related *ethnos* to aspects of biology. Gumilev (1994: 42) argued that *ethnos* of human beings is the same as the pride of lions, [or the bond between the members] of a pack of wolves, and of herds of hoofed mammals. It is a form of existence of a [biological] species, [namely] *Homo sapiens* and its specimen, which is different [from other forms of existence or social organisation] both by social formations and purely biological characteristics that are races (*kakimi yavlyayutsya rassy*).

The main critique of this equation of race to ethnicity is that ethnicity is not a universal principle of organisation. There is no ethnic 'group', which has clearly delineated borders. This means, as Schlee (2008: 7) with reference to Elwert (1989: 445) argued, 'that we are not dealing with groups at all, but rather with a continuum in which the border between the "We" and "the Others" shifts depending on the point of view of the observer'.

The existing social, cultural and linguistic differences between Khorezmians and other Uzbek groups are instrumentalised in order to construct their collective identities and in this context the terms 'instrumentalised' and 'construct' are etic. Khorezmians, as well as other groups in Uzbekistan, essentialise the markers of their identity. Most of the 'raw material' used for the construction of ethnic and sub-ethnic identities in the country is based on biological reasoning. This makes the identities seem natural in the eyes of the actors themselves. In the case of Khorezmians, particularly their cultural distinction and references to their 'great past', buttress their argumentations about their identity. Frequently, members of sub-ethnic groups in Uzbekistan believe that their identity is biologically rooted, such as blood ties and physical features, among others. Therefore, emic conceptions of the actors' identities are largely essentialist. The most pronounced argument in this regard refers to blood and territory. When I would ask how one could become a Khorezmian, I often received answers such as 'one does not become a Khorezmian, one must be born one. One's umbilical blood must be dropped into the Khorezmian earth.' I would then often argue that according to this a non-Khorezmian mother or any parent might produce a Khorezmian by simply letting him or her be born in Khorezm. The Khorezmians' counterargument would follow that the child's ancestors (*ota buvalari*[Kh] 'father grandfathers') should also have been born in Khorezm. By contrast, when some of my Khorezmian informants started communicating with members of other groups in Tashkent they could easily construct and instrumentalise certain differences and become very flexible Different versions of the Khorezmian past were told, and other differences in culture and customs emphasised, in order to present an authentic story about their identity, deliberately omitting the major similarities and common past of not only Uzbeks but also all other Central Asians. Among the most pronounced differences, physical features were stressed which would immediately group all other non-Khorezmians, especially Tashkentis, as having mongoloid physical features. Khorezmians, in their own view, would be good-looking, tall with big, round eyes. Some even mentioned that in the past 'real' Khorezmians had blue eyes and blond hair. Khorezmians maintained that the real Khorezmians became mixed with Arabs and Turks and developed black hair and dark eyes, though one could still find those blond and blue-eyed Khorezmians in rural areas, if less so now in towns in Khorezm region. In practice, however, blond hair and blue eyes in rural Khorezmians are not considered to be attractive.

An observer can only take a note of these processes and analyse people's behaviour and their discourses as instrumental and constructed. In this context, linguistic strategies employed during the identification process are crucial in order to highlight that aspect. Selective reference to the past and use/disregard of 'culture' are the materials employed instrumentally in the construction process of the politics of identity and difference.

To sum up, actors are often primordialists in their understanding of their identities, which researchers rarely are. Thus, a second and closer look at, for example, Geertz's works reveals that there is a clear distinction between the emic and etic analyses of identities and meanings. In this book I try to 'walk the thin line' between the view from within (frequently characterised by pseudo-biological references to identity) and the view from outside (in which identities are socially constructed). My aim is to present the reader with as 'thick' description of dynamics of identification and identity issues as possible.

Uzbek ethnicity and sub-ethnicities

Following Barth, I approach ethnicity not as a property of a group, but rather as a property of relations among groups. This argument was subsequently developed by different authors who analysed the relationship between similarity (as the basis for identity) and difference (Banks 2013; Candea 2010, 2014; Jenkins 1996, 1997, 2001). The definition of ethnicity offered recently by Banks outlines much of what I would like to touch upon when talking about ethnicity in Uzbekistan. He defines ethnicity as 'a collection of rather simplistic and obvious statements about boundaries, otherness, goals and achievements, being and identity, descent and classification that has been constructed as much by the anthropologist as by the subject' (Banks 2013: 190). Schlee and others emphasised the strategic character of this relationship, inspired by economic theories of rational choice calculation of costs and benefits (Hechter and Kanazawa 1997; Schlee 2008:14). The situational aspect of ethnicity was theorised by Handelman (1977: 188), distinguishing between ethnic categories, ethnic associations and ethnic communities, emphasising the variation of the strength of ethnic identifications.

Against this background, the term ethnicity refers to perceived similarities and differences among groups on the basis of relevant markers, mostly stemming from the sphere of culture. It also shapes the rational calculations of costs and benefits by the actors involved. This last point, however, can easily lead to an over-emphasis of pragmatism and calculation on the side of the actors, without considering emotional aspects of social relations.[10] In this regard, the third part of the theoretical framework will particularly engage with the emotional and other ways of bonding that bind individuals together in interpersonal relationships. Looking at the mechanisms that hold the 'We' together is an important point to consider, namely between bonding and identification when studying collective identities.

This book explores different layers of the same Uzbek ethnicity by analysing the relations between sub-ethnic groups in Tashkent city where they come into contact with one another. While doing so I will touch upon the existing classifications or categorisation of these groups, and the names of groups and their pronounced differences. Furthermore, I will also highlight the meanings and 'feelings' behind that classification and finally their social organisation as collectives.

I will treat the term 'ethnicity' as an overarching concept that comprises multiple layers and levels of sub-ethnicities. Throughout the book I will use the term *ethnicity* in the meaning of sub-ethnicity towards Khorezmians and their relations with other Uzbek groups because I have little interest to engage in ethnic relations between Uzbeks and non-Uzbeks, which is a different scale of identification. The sub-ethnic differences between Uzbek groups do not necessarily contradict the existing sentiments towards a unified Uzbek identity, or any other identities such as Muslim or even pan-Turkic feelings which might be relevant in other contexts of interactions with non-Uzbeks.[11] This might be different with Tadjiks, who most probably do not identify with Uzbeks, but that is out of my research focus and I do not have enough material to cover this aspect of Uzbek identity (Borovkov 1952).

Here, it is also necessary to mention the background of the ethnic groups in question. There were various groups, tribes, clans etc., which might have been involved in the process of an 'artificial' creation of the Uzbek nation. There have been critical discussions on ethno-genesis of Uzbeks as a nation. Abashin (2006), Kurzman (1999), Lubin (1981), and earlier Yakubovskiy (1941) have largely contributed to the discussion of ethno-genesis of Uzbeks. Sometimes the confederation of all or some tribes and clans can constitute a separate ethnicity. When an ethnic group is strongly bound to a territory and advances the political claim to have its own state, we talk about the formation of a nation in the ethnic sense (Guibernau 2004, 2013a, 2013b; Smith 1983). In the context where many different groups (tribes and/or clans) transformed into one ethnicity, it is very probable that this ethnicity comprises various levels and (sub-)scales of identification.

I argue that these divisions within one overarching ethnic identity (in my case, Uzbek) take place because ethnicity is not homogeneous in content and can have different layers. Ethnic identity is by its nature ambiguous. Sub-ethnicities within one ethnicity imply multiplicity and flexibility, as well as the situationality of collective identification. In spite of the impression given by some of the extreme advocates of the constructivist position, ethnic identity is not arbitrary. There must be some plausibility in the process of constructing identities (Schlee 2002, 2008).

In the case of Uzbek groups, claims differ in content and meaning as well as regarding the process of making differences. These inconsistencies create the taxonomy on the basis of which these groups relate to each other. The discrepancies or contradictions within this taxonomy are due to the fact that the position in the hierarchy might change depending on from whose perspective relationships are outlined.

Doing fieldwork at home

> Social scientists are human beings, and the object of their study is actions of human beings.
> (Coleman 1990: 16)

Locating the field, researching mobility

I did 13 months of anthropological fieldwork in Uzbekistan from September 2005 to October 2006, applying both classical anthropological research methods and others from sociolinguistics. In order to design and identify the 'borders' of the research in doing urban ethnography I consulted the works of the Manchester School (Mitchell 1969).

Sometimes the boundaries between anthropology and other disciplines blur since objects and ideas have become mobile, translocal and changing in the era of contemporary globalisation (Appadurai 1991, 1996; Gupta and Ferguson 1997). This directly challenges the definition of 'field', whether it is a territorially bound, small-scale location which is feasible to grasp for an individual ethnographer, or goes beyond a small village to a far larger domain which becomes more difficult to overview. Problematising fieldwork in the global changing world, Appadurai (1991: 191, 196 cited in Gupta and Ferguson 1997: 3) stated:

> As groups migrate, regroup in new locations, reconstruct their histories, and reconfigurate their ethnic 'projects', the *ethno* [italics in original] in ethnography takes on a slippery, *non-localized* [italics mine] quality, to which the descriptive practices of anthropology will have to respond. The landscapes of group identity – the ethnoscapes – around the world are no longer familiar anthropological objects, insofar as groups are no longer tightly territorialized, spatially bound, historically self-conscious, or culturally homogeneous.... The task of ethnography now becomes the unravelling of a conundrum: what is the nature of locality, as a lived experience, in a globalized, *deterritorialized* [italics mine] world?

Gupta and Ferguson (ibid.: 5) questioned the fields of the fieldworker anthropologist and proposed rather a commitment to the local and attention to the 'social, cultural, and political location' and 'willingness to work self-consciously at shifting or realigning our own location while building epistemological and political links with other locations'. They suggested 'location-work' to be 'the most innovative reconceptualisations of anthropological fieldwork practices'. However, what they rather suggest is not 'location-work' but actually the 'work of locating' the location of the episteme they mention (ibid.). To my mind, rephrasing existing terms is not so productive in the practical sense, although I fully agree with the arguments of the authors who point out the challenges for fieldworkers which have arisen with contemporary globalisation processes. It would be more productive to define the field of our fieldwork. My field was rather not limited or defined by territory or place in the physical understanding of the term but rather consisted of spaces determined by my research focus, namely the spaces where different Uzbek groups came into contact. The territorial boundary was a secondary aspect defined by those contacts and not the other way around.

Besides classical anthropological methods of participant observation, interviews and collecting autobiographies, I also used such methods as group discussions, travelling ethnography and ethnography of communication. Travelling ethnography involved boarding the most commonly used means of travel, hours-long informal conversations with passengers, interviews with drivers and participant observation during the travel. I was told several autobiographies on the way, mostly by women, as women take seats next to each other while men sit next to men. During travels on buses it is impossible to take any notes as the roads are bumpy and transport usually leaves late afternoon and it becomes dark after a few hours. All information received during travel was mind-mapped and noted later.

Ethnography of communication

I followed the suggestion of Hymes (1962, 1964) in doing ethnography of communication during my field research. Hymes (1962, 1964) drew attention to communication from a different perspective and contextualised language use by drawing several disciplines together. He argued for the necessity of introducing a revised and innovative methodology such as 'ethnography of communication' which would 'provide the frame of reference within which the place of language in culture and society is to be described' (Hymes 1964: 3). He defined the work of this ethnography within the boundaries of the community within which communication is possible; the boundaries of the situations within which communication occurs; the means and purposes and patterns of selection, their structure and hierarchy, that constitute the communicative economy of the group, are conditioned, to be sure, by properties of the linguistic codes within the group, but are not controlled by them.

Ethnography of communication, according to Hymes (1964: 2), deals with the 'studies [which are] ethnographic in basis, and of communication in the scope'. He argued that, methodologically, this means that the study of communication must take place within the social processes, situations and events, making use of linguistics and related disciplines, as well as entailing anthropological methods of participant observation and interviews, among others. On the basis of works pioneered by Hymes, Bauman and Scherzer (1974: 6), this field developed further into an 'ethnography of speaking' which enquired into 'the organization of speaking in social life'.

Many of my conversations and talks were informal and casual, and took place during various social events, in the homes where I was invited to eat, at pilgrimage sites, when waiting in the queue for a fortune teller or healer with my informants, in the bazaars when going shopping with informants or, if my informants were traders, when sitting next to them and selling rice, in people's offices during the day, and during hospital visits and sanatoria. There were also many interviews organised either in my place, my informants' places or in cafés. All interviews and conversations were either voice-recorded and transcribed, noted or mind-mapped. Linguistic terms and other phrases were systematically asked and explanations noted throughout the fieldwork.

*Rano-journalist and Rano-*Shurik

I did the fieldwork for this research *at home* in Uzbekistan. This, on the one hand, was very convenient; particularly as I myself had been an internal migrant as a Khorezmian in Tashkent in 2002. On the other hand, I faced the challenges of most native anthropologists concerning the questions of objectivity and keeping distance. I could deal with these challenges successfully because I was both a member of the group and yet a stranger. I was born in Khorezm but my parents had come from Turkmenistan, meaning we had no relatives in Uzbekistan. Second, I went to a Russian school and was socialised with Russian and Armenian friends. Since my extended family lived so 'far' away in Turkmenistan I did not become closely involved in the mundane affairs of extended family life in Uzbekistan. Furthermore, I entered the English philology faculty and continued my professional life engaging with American companies and working in an English-speaking environment. After I moved to Tashkent I pursued a career (which in itself is not usual for a young female Uzbek) without getting 'too much' involved with the existing Khorezmian networks. It was therefore something new for me to find out during the field research how Khorezmians organised themselves in Tashkent through various networks and events. Being a Khorezmian myself and a researcher at the same time had certain implications for the data I gathered.

Fieldwork in the anthropologist's own country became common after the early 1960s (Eriksen 1995; Jackson 1987; Mascarenhas-Keyes 1987). There are known advantages and disadvantages to doing anthropology 'at home'. The advantages concern native knowledge which is not available to foreign researchers, different status of a native researcher in a society and many other privileges of being native. A classical disadvantage is taking many things for granted – the so-called 'home blindness' (Eriksen 1995: 20). The latter, however, can be overcome by training and awareness of that disadvantage.

When I came back to my 'own' country to study my 'own' people as an anthropologist, I was perceived differently in different situations and by different people. For some people I was an ideal example of how to build an academic career. Professionally I was jokingly and also seriously compared to *Shurik*, who is a famous character in one of the classical humoristic Russian movies called

'Caucasian hostage' (*Kavkazskaya Plennitsa*). *Shurik* is an ethnographer and collects Georgian toasts. The story of the movie is about a bride kidnapping in Georgia and an ethnographer who comes from Moscow to Georgia to collect and collate drinking toasts. This movie was one of the classical Russian films that were frequently shown on TV all over the Soviet Union.[12] These classical movies were very popular among viewers of all ages. When people did not understand my activities, frequently somebody, who seemed to be more or less well-read, would be in the position to explain to others by comparing my work to that of *Shurik*'s by saying 'she is like *Shurik*'. Sometimes it was even understood literally and an informant would try to make great and memorable toasts so that I should write them down. In fact, it was also interesting how people rhetorically express themselves towards others, and how they send messages to one another by means of toasting when they get together.

For others I was a potential law-breaker and a bad example for their daughters. For security officers I was a potential threat and a spy. For many I was somebody who could be possibly benefited from, and for almost all I was both insider and outsider at the same time. This mixture of different perceptions involving suspicion, mistrust, threat and acceptance (sometimes very quick as I was taken for *ozlarimizdan/svoy* meaning: our own[13] member of the group), raised a great number of ambiguities on how to behave, and where and how to take a stand when doing this fieldwork.

The worst role ascribed to me was the one of a journalist. Whenever I mentioned the word 'interview' and used a voice-recorder, I was always taken for a journalist. Very often people would recognise me by the nickname 'Rano-journalist' that I had earned in many circles and networks of my informants, which carried negative connotations since the media is not free in Uzbekistan. Journalists are almost seen as foreign spies who were usually pursued by the authorities and called 'too much attention' to those individuals to whom the journalist had spoken. This fact has rightly been stressed by Rasanagayam (2003: 25–26) in the methodological part of his doctoral dissertation. He indicated that people avoid drawing the attention of officials because they do not want to get into any trouble with the state. People in Uzbekistan tried to avoid attention of any kind from state officials, not only because they did not want to be detected engaged in any illegal activities (non-payment of communal services, avoidance of taxes or some other petty crime) but there was also a belief that state officials were always 'hungry' meaning 'in need of bribes' and 'will always find something against a person if they want to'. Hence it was better not to be noticed in any official context, as to come to the notice of the authorities would mean to easily attract trouble. This was one of the main difficulties in gaining access to informants. Additionally, those involved with the state, such as state employees in relatively good positions, were extra careful and keen to avoid being caught in unpleasant situations (by having contact with a suspicious person like me) in order not to endanger their job.

To enter the everyday routine of people's networks required a great deal of participation beyond the limited role of an observer. Also, entering into some kind of relations of reciprocity was necessary, which was often quite demanding. Consequently it was challenging to keep the 'Faustian contract' and maintain the balance in the 'research bargain' (Loizos 1994 cited in Dudwick and DeSoto 2000: 14).

The most rewarding field experience was participation in a project of Khorezmian university students in Tashkent. The project was on presenting Khorezm region and its culture on the Khorezmian day at the University in Tashkent. I contributed with some funding as well as photos and video material taken during the event. It turned out to be a very big event, with a huge lunch served after the presentation, and a small concert featuring a famous Khorezmian singer.

In dealing with all of those networks I had to consider power relations and to find some kind of balance between them. Many times I had to cross boundaries which I would not have been allowed to do easily if I had not been a researcher. My activities included participation in men's circles and elder women's gatherings, as well as long conversations with both male and female elderly persons at events or in everyday interactions. If I had been a 'normal' young Uzbek woman I would have been expected to help in the kitchen instead of talking or sitting with guests, My practice of taking pictures and video filming was always seen as odd since this was usually men's work.

To sum up, I have introduced the reader to the basic challenges and dilemmas that I faced during my fieldwork. I also have dealt with my own role and the expectations different people in the field had of me. As the contexts and experiences during my fieldwork suggest, I gathered very rich data on travelling experiences and the lives and experiences of traders, construction workers, students, doctors, and so forth. I also had a close look at the social organisation of ethnic and kinship networks, patron and client relations in different contexts of private and public spheres, a brides' schools and a office issuing Tashkent *propiska*.

Notes

1 See a more detailed description of *halpa*s and other traditional male singers such as *bahshi*s in Khorezm in Turaeva (2008).
2 All translations of the cited scholarly texts as well as of interviews in languages other than English (Russian and Uzbek) are mine if not indicated otherwise.
3 All the names that appear in this book are changed in order to maintain anonymity of the informants. For the same reasons some details about the places and persons are omitted.
4 Laziza, 43, Tashkent, 15 August 2006.
5 I am aware of the complexity and abstractness of the term 'dialectics' and the whole philosophical discussion behind this term, which is often connected to dialectical materialism.
6 See Turaeva (2013, 2014a, 2014b) for a more detailed linguistic analysis of those differences.
7 Central Asia in geographical understanding of the region is a bigger territory than the region meant in this book. 'Central Asia' will be used to include only the territory

which was previously part of the Soviet Union: Kazakhstan, Uzbekistan, Kyrgyzstan, Turkmenistan and Tajikistan.
8 Before the end of Soviet rule it was almost impossible to do any kind of research in Central Asia. Consequently, there are very few ethnographic monographs on this region compared with Africa, for example, where most of the solid classical anthropological ethnographies were written over the twentieth century. Only after 1991 was research possible in most post-Soviet states. Recently, ethnographic work in Central Asia intensified. See Finke (2006) for dynamics of national identity in Uzbekistan, Kehl-Bodrogi (2006) for a rich ethnographic study of shrines in Khorezm region of Uzbekistan, Yessenova (2005) for rural and urban comparative ethnography in Kazakhstan, Kandiyoti (1998, 1999, 2002) on detailed ethnographies of rural areas in Central Asia and Turkey, Humphrey and Mandel (2002) on postsocialist ethnographies in general, Trevisani (2007, 2009) for an analysis of agricultural politics and rural life in Khorezm region of Uzbekistan, Baykal (2007) for urban ethnography in Samarqand in Uzbekistan, Reeves (2007) for a very detailed ethnography on border regions between Kyrgyzstan and Uzbekistan, McBrien (2007) for a study on gender and religion in Kyrgyzstan, Hilgers (2006) on religious conversion in Uzbekistan, Sanders (forthcoming PhD) on identity issues in Kazakhstan, and Ismailbekova (2012) for a biographic approach to studying political leaders in Kyrgyzstan.
9 In order to keep the text readable, the male form is used for pronouns if there is no particular other gender required.
10 Rationality has to be evaluated in its particular social context. It can be based on considerations that would not be accepted as rational by actors in other contexts.
11 See Finke (2006) for a detailed account of Uzbek national identity.
12 There were only a few TV channels available in Uzbekistan during the time of the Soviet Union; one or two local TV channels and several Russian channels. The national and local channels were considered to be boring. Most people watched Russian channels. International channels were not available and video players were prohibited under Soviet rule; see Ellen Mickiewicz (1988) for more analysis of television viewing in Soviet society during the late 1980s; see also McBrien (2007) for the role of TV viewing in post-Soviet Kyrgyzstan; see Kuehnast (2000) for her fieldwork accounts in Kyrgyzstan and how she was perceived by local women for whom she was an imaginary ideal Western woman and how she dealt with that situation.
13 *Ozlarimizdan* in Uzbekistan can be translated as 'from ours'; *svoy* is a Russian word translated as 'our own'. Both expressions are used in the meaning of 'a member of the group/insider'. The opposite word is '*chuzjoy*', a Russian word translated as 'a stranger'. The Uzbek equivalent would be '*begona*'. These two terms are used to denote 'an outsider'.

References

Abashin, S.N. 2006. 'Invitation to discussion', *Anthropology & Archeology of Eurasia*, 44 (4): 7–9.
Appadurai, A. 1991. 'Global ethnoscapes: Notes and queries for a transnational anthropology,' in Richard G. Fox (ed.), *Recapturing Anthropology: Working in the Present*. Santa Fe, CA: School of American Research Press, pp. 191–210.
Appadurai, A. 1996. *Modernity at Large: Cultural Dimensions of Globalisation*. Minneapolis, MN: University of Minnesota Press.
Banks, Marcus. 2013 [1996]. *Ethnicity: Anthropological Constructions*. London: Routledge.
Barth, F. 1969. *Ethnic Groups and Boundaries: The Social Organisation of Culture Difference*. Bergen: Universitetsforlaget. Allen and Unwin.

Prologue

Barth, F. 1994. 'Enduring and emerging issues in the analysis of ethnicity', in H. Vermeulen and C. Govers (eds), *The Anthropology of Ethnicity: Beyond Ethnic Groups and Boundaries*. Amsterdam: Het Spinhuis.

Bauman, R. and I. Scherzer 1974. (eds), *Explorations in the Ethnography of Speaking*. Cambridge: Cambridge University Press.

Baykal, A. 2007. 'Surviving the post-Soviet transition: changing family and community relations in urban Uzbekistan'. Unpublished PhD, Boston University.

Borovkov, A.K. 1952. *Tadjiksko-uzbekskoe dvujazychie i vzaimotnoshenija uzbekskogo i tadjikskogo jazykov* [Tadjik-Uzbek bilingualism and interrelations between Uzbek and Tadjik languages], vol. 4. Moscow: Ucheniye Zapiski Instituta Vostokovedeniya.

Bourdieu, P. 1977 [1972]. *Outline of a theory of practice*. Cambridge: Cambridge University Press.

Bromley, Y. 1973. *Etnos i etnografiya* [Etnos and ethnography]. Moscow: Nauka.

Bromley, Y. 1983. *Ocherki teorii etnosa* [Outline of ethnos theory]. Moscow: Nauka.

Brubaker, R. 2014. 'Beyond ethnicity', *Ethnic and Racial Studies* 37 (5), 804–808.

Brubaker, R. and F. Cooper 2000. 'Beyond "Identity"', *Theory and Society*, 29 (1), 1–47.

Candea, Matei. 2010. 'Anonymous introductions: identity and belonging in Corsica', *Journal of the Royal Anthropological Institute*, 16 (1), 119–137.

Candea, Matei. 2014. ' "There is Something": Charlie Galibert's Corsica', *Anthropological Quarterly*, 87 (2), 525–540.

Coleman, J.S. 1990. *Foundations of Social Theory*. Cambridge, MA: Belknap Press.

Donahoe, B., Eidson, J., Feyissa, D., Fuest, V., Hoehne, M., Nieswand, B., Schlee, G. and Zenker, O. 2009. 'The formation and mobilisation of collective identities in situations of conflict and integration', Working Paper No. 116, Max Planck Institute for Social Anthropology, Halle Saale.

Dudwick, N. and DeSoto, H.G. 2000. 'Introduction', in H.G. DeSoto and N. Dudwick (eds), *Fieldwork Dilemmas: Anthropologists in Post-Socialist States*. Madison, WI: University of Wisconsin Press, pp. 100–118.

Eriksen, T.H. 1995. *Small Places, Large Issues: An Introduction to Social and Cultural Anthropology*. London: Pluto.

Finke, P. 2006. Variations on Uzbek identity: concepts, constraints and local configurations. Habilitation thesis, Leipzig University, Leipzig.

Geertz, C. 1963. 'The integrative revolution: primordial sentiments and civil politics in the new states', in C. Geertz (ed.), *Old Societies and New States: The Quest for Modernity in Asia and Africa*. New York: Free Press, pp. 107–113.

Geschiere, P. 1997. *The Modernity of Witchcraft: Politics and the Occult in Postcolonial Africa/Sorcellerie et politique en Afrique: la viande des autres*. Charlottesville: University Press of Virginia.

Geschiere, P. 2004. 'Ecology, belonging and xenophobia: the 1994 Forest Law in Cameroon and the issue of "community" ', in H. Englund (ed.), *Rights and the Politics of Recognition in Africa*. London: Zed Books, pp. 237–259.

Guibernau, Montserrat 2004. 'Anthony D. Smith on nations and national identity: a critical assessment', *Nations and Nationalism* 10 (1–2), 125–141.

Guibernau, Montserrat. 2013a. *Nationalisms: The Nation-state and Nationalism in the Twentieth Century*. Hoboken, NJ: John Wiley & Sons.

Guibernau, Montserrat. 2013b. *The Identity of Nations*. Hoboken, NJ: John Wiley & Sons.

Gumilev, L.N. 1989. *Etnogenez i biosfera Zemli* [Ethnogenesis and biosphere of the Earth]. Leningrad: Izdatel'stvo Institut DI-DIK.

Gumilev, L.N. 1994. *Konets i vnov' nachalo.* [The end and again the beginning], Moscow: Publishing Institute DI-DIK.
Gumperz, J.J. 1997 [1982]. *Language and Social Identity.* Cambridge: Cambridge University Press.
Gupta, A. and Ferguson, J. 1997. 'Discipline and practice: the field as site, method and location in anthropology', in A. Gupta and J. Ferguson (eds), *Anthropological Locations: Boundaries and Grounds of a Field Science.* Berkeley, CA: California University Press.
Handelman, D. 1977. 'The organisation of ethnicity', *Ethnic Groups.* 1, 187–200.
Hechter, M. and Kanazawa, S. 1997. 'Sociological rational choice theory', *Annual Review of Sociology,* 23, 191–214.
Hilgers, I. (2006) 'The regulation and control of religious pluralism in Uzbekistan', in C.M. Hann et al. (eds), *The Postsocialist Religious Question: Faith and Power in Central Asia and East-Central Europe.* Berlin: Lit Verlag.
Humphrey, C. and R. Mandel 2002. 'The market in everyday life: ethnographies of postsocialism', in R. Mandel and C. Humphrey (eds), *Markets and Moralities: Ethnographies of Postsocialism.* Oxford: Berg, pp. 1–16.
Huntington, Samuel P. 2004. *Who are We? The Challenges to America's National Identity.* New York: Simon and Schuster.
Hymes, D. 1962. 'The ethnography of speaking', in T. Gladwin and W.C. Sturtevant (eds) *Anthropology and Human Behavior.* Washington, DC: Anthropological Society of Washington, pp. 13–53. (Reprinted in Fishman, J.A. 1968, *Readings in the Sociology of Language.* The Hague: Mouton, pp. 99–138.)
Hymes, D. 1964. 'Introduction: toward ethnographies of communication', *American Anthropologist,* 66, 6, 1–34.
Ismailbekova, A. 2012. 'The native son and blood ties: kinship and poetics of patronage in rural Kyrgyzstan', unpublished dissertation for PhD, Halle Saale
Jackson, A. 1987. *Anthropology at Home.* London: Tavistock.
Jackson, Stephen. 2006. 'Sons of which soil? The language and politics of autochthony in Eastern D.R. Congo', *African Studies Review,* 49 (2), 95–123.
Jenkins, R. 1996. *Social Identity.* London: Routledge.
Jenkins, R. 1997. *Rethinking Ethnicity: Arguments and Explorations.* London, Thousand Oaks, CA and New Delhi: Sage.
Jenkins, R. 2001. 'Ethnicity: anthropological aspects'. In J.N. Smelser and B.P. Baltes (eds), *International Encyclopedia of the Social and Behavioural Sciences,* vol. 7. Amsterdam: Elsevier, pp. 4824–4828.
Kandiyoti, D. 1998. 'Rural livelihoods and social networks in Uzbekistan: perspectives from Andijan', *Central Asian Survey,* 17 (4), 561–578.
Kandiyoti, D. 1999. 'Poverty in transition: an ethnographic critique of household surveys in post-Soviet Central Asia', *Development and Change,* 30, 499–524.
Kandiyoti, D. 2002. 'How far do analyses of postsocialism travel? The case of Central Asia', in C. Hann (ed.), *Postsocialism: Ideals, Ideologies and Practices in Eurasia.* London: Routledge, pp. 238–257.
Kehl-Bodrogi, K. 2006. '"Who owns the shrine?" Competing meanings and authorities at a pilgrimage site in Khorezm', *Central Asian Survey,* 25 (3), 235–250.
Kuehnast, K. 2000. 'Ethnographic encounters in post-Soviet Kyrgyzstan: dilemmas of gender, poverty, and the Cold War', in H.G. DeSoto and N. Dudwick (eds), *Fieldwork Dilemmas: Anthropologists in Postsocialist States.* Madison, WI: University of Wisconsin Press, pp. 100–118.

20 Prologue

Kurzman, C. 1999. 'Uzbekistan: the invention of nationalism in an invented nation', *Critique*, 15, 77–98.
Lubin, N. 1981. 'Assimilation and retention of ethnic identity in Uzbekistan', *Asian Affairs*, 12, 277–285.
McBrien, J. 2007. 'Brazilian TV & Muslimness in Kyrgyzstan', *ISIM Review*, Spring, 16–17.
Mascarenhas-Keyes, S. 1987. 'The native anthropologist: constraints and strategies in research', in A. Jackson (ed.), *Anthropology at Home*. London: Tavistock, pp. 180–195.
Mickiewicz, E. 1988. *Split Signals: Television and Politics in the Soviet Union*. Oxford: Oxford University Press.
Mitchell, J.C. 1969. 'The concept and use of social networks', in J.C. Mitchell (ed.), *Social Networks in Urban Situations: Analyses of Personal Relationships in Central African Towns*. Manchester: Manchester University Press, pp. 1–50.
Nyamnjoh, F.B. 2005. *Africa's Media, Democracy, and the Politics of Belonging*. London: Zed Books.
Nyamnjoh, F.B. 2007. *Insiders and Outsiders: Citizenship and Xenophobia in Contemporary Southern Africa*. London and New York: Zed Books.
Rasanayagam, J. 2003. *Market, State and Community in Uzbekistan: Reworking the Concept of the Informal Economy*. Halle/Saale: Max Planck Institute for Social Anthropology.
Reeves, M. 2007. 'Border work: an ethnography of the state and its limits in the Fergana Valley', unpublished PhD, Trinity College University of Cambridge.
Schlee, G. 2002. *Imagined Differences: Hatred and the Construction of Identity*. Münster: Lit.
Schlee, G. 2008. *How Enemies are Made: Towards a Theory of Ethnic and Religious Conflicts*. New York: Bergahn Books.
Shirokogorov, S.M. 2002. *Etnograficheskie issledovaniya. Kniga vtoraya* [Ethnographical studies: second book]. Etnos.
Smith, A.D. 1983. 'Nationalism and classical social theory', *The British Journal of Sociology*, 34 (1), 19–38.
Trevisani, T. 2007. 'After the Kolkhoz: rural elites in competition', *Central Asian Survey*, 26 (1), 85–104.
Trevisani, T. 2009. 'The reshaping of inequality in Uzbekistan: reforms, land, and rural incomes', in M. Spoor (ed.), *The Political Economy of Rural Livelihoods in Transition Economies: Land, Peasants and Rural Poverty in Transition*. London: Routledge, pp. 123–137.
Turaeva, R. 2008. 'The cultural baggage of Khorezmian identity: traditional forms singing and dancing in Khorezm and in Tashkent', *Central Asian Survey*, 27 (2), 143–153.
Turaeva, R. 2013, 'From rhetoric to identification: miscommunication in inter-ethnic contact', *Anthropology of Middle East*, 8 (2), 21–45.
Turaeva, R. 2014a, 'Linguistic and social contradictions within Uzbek national identity', in Birgit Schlyter (ed.), *Historiography and National-Building Among Turkic Populations*, Istanbul: Swedish Research Institute in Istanbul.
Turaeva, R. 2014b, 'Linguistic ambiguities of Uzbek and classification of Uzbek dialects', *Anthropos*, 110 (2): 463–476.
Weber, M. 1968. *Economy and Society*. New York: Bedminster Press.
Yakubovskiy, A.Y. 1941. *K Voprosy ob Etnogeneze Uzbekskogo Naroda* [To the question of ethnogenesis of Uzbek people]. Tashkent: UzFAN.
Yessenova, S. 2005. ' "Routes and roots" of Kazakh identity: urban migration in postsocialist Kazakhstan', *The Russian Review*, 64 (4), 661–679.

Part I
Uzbek identity

2 Making of Uzbek nationality

This chapter will touch upon the formation of nations and nationality policies of Russians in Central Asia. One of the main issues is the history of the formation of the Uzbek nation, which some argue was 'artificially' created by local elites with the help of the Russians at the end of the twentieth century.[1] Territorial boundaries and cultural collective consciousness in the territory of Central Asia was shaped as a result of great population movements, numerous conquests of the region and policies of rulers with heterogeneous ethnic and cultural backgrounds. More than 70 years of Russian/Soviet domination in the region did not pass without effect. These historical dynamics underlie the diversity of the linguistic background of Uzbeks, which is the main focus of this book. Kinship and family arrangements are closely connected to the state administration and political measures implemented in the region. The system during Soviet rule had direct implications for social life since it promoted modernity (*sovremenost'*[Ru]). In the post-Soviet period, the collapse of the welfare system led to the strengthening of kinship and family ties (Schatz 2004).

This chapter will outline some of the past social, political and economic developments in Central Asia, focusing on particular issues in certain periods. This will include an overview of past and present migratory processes, political and economic developments in the region, historical implications of the constitution of the society and social arrangements, its norms and values, including family and kinship ties, gender roles and relationships. Historicising and considering these issues retrospectively helps to trace the changes and developments that can shed light on the contents and dynamics of inter-ethnic relations analysed in this book.

An early history of the great population movements throughout Central Asia and beyond is important in order to see linguistic changes in the region and the basic tribal/ethnic/cultural content of the population, which is made up of Iranian sedentary and nomadic Turkic populations (Wurm 1954). This information allows one to smoothly contextualise the discourses, linguistic background of ambiguous mixture of language varieties and other references of Uzbek groups discussed in this book.

The period described in this chapter comprises the times from early history until the formation of three separate khanates, as well as the rule of diverse dynasties. This I consider as a prerequisite to understanding the processes of occupation by Russian and later Soviet interventions in the region, often named as 'Russian colonisation'. Russian political and socio-economic changes introduced in the region were influential and deserve considerable attention. These policies and transformations during the Tsarist and Soviet periods included massive resettlements of the populations throughout the Russian territory, which largely affected composition of population in Central Asia. Major policies of Russian and Soviet governments, namely *propiska* and welfare, will be approached retrospectively, considering their respective origin and meanings.

For my analysis of inter-ethnic relations, I look into different aspects of identity markers which my informants connected with the history of their place and peoples. I will have to situate those discursive imaginations of the past in their historical context by using various written sources. I am aware of the contested character of written sources on history. I have utilised as much of the existing sources as possible, including local (Central Asian), Russian and Western scholarly works in the field, in addition to my own local knowledge, having gone through ten years of schooling during the Soviet Union (1982–1991).

This chapter is chronologically ordered from early history to the current socio-economic and political situation in Uzbekistan. The periods are chosen on the basis of their importance to the related issues discussed in this book.

Early history: were there Uzbeks in the past?

Sedentary and nomadic populations AD 250–750

The region known under the name 'Central Asia' was part of several kingdoms, empires and khanates in the past. The term 'Central Asia' is arbitrary since the reference point in terms of geographical position or political entity is ambiguous.[2] The question is: central to what and/or for whom? I will use the term 'Central Asia' to refer to the territory which comprises present-day Uzbekistan, Turkmenistan, Kyrgyzstan, Kazakhstan and Tajikistan as well as Karakalpakstan (now an 'autonomous' Republic of Uzbekistan).

The earliest written sources on the region go back to the time before 700 BC. This book cannot cover the complete history of this region, which has already been done by others (Bartold 1965; Grousset 2002; Holzwarth 2005; Tolstov 1948). Peter Finke (2006) provides a very detailed and accurate account of the historical past of the region, particularly focusing on the developments which played a decisive role for the formation of nations/nationalism in Central Asia.

I will only briefly sketch some of the developments in the region starting with the period of great population movements. The first known nomadic invasion of the region was by Indo-Iranian nomads. These nomads mixed with the sedentary population in the second millennium BC until the Arabs destroyed their existing cultural and scientific wealth (Harmatta 1999: 19).[3] Other major movements of nomadic tribes and peoples came from present-day Mongolia and adjacent regions from the late first century BC up to the time of Chingiz Khan in the thirteenth century AD. The nomads spread south to China, south-west to western Central Asia and East Turkistan, west to the Volga, the Black Sea and even reached Italy and France. Among these nomadic tribes there were Hsiung-nu (also written as Xiongnu), the Huns, Alan tribes, Chionites, Kudarites and Hephtalites, Türks, Türgesh, Qarluqs, Uyghurs and Turkic tribal confederations (Litvinskiy and Zhang Guang-da 1999: 19, 28). The large-scale nomadic movements of Yüeh-chih[4] from north and north-east to south in Western Central Asia in the second half of the second century BC led to the formation of the first great Kushan Empire. At the same time and later, other greater and smaller empires, Caliphates and kingdoms were formed, including Parthian and Han, later Sassanian, Gupta, Sui and T'ang, as well as Arab caliphates. In the oasis states of Central Asia, these would include Tokharistan (Bactria), Margiana, Sogdiana, Khwarizm (also known as Chorasmia, presently Khorezm) and smaller kingdoms in the Tarim Basin such as Kucha and Khotan. These oasis states were known for their developed urban life and outstanding works of art. Sogdians were famous traders who travelled back and forth from Byzantium to China (Litvinskiy and Zhang Guang-da 1999: 24).

Among these empires and kingdoms, Khorezm deserves special mention since its history was very important to the region. It was here that an ancient state system developed that benefited from arts and science. The main local sources on the history of Khorezm are Al-Biruni, a Khorezmian encyclopaedist who lived from 973 to 1048, and al-Tabari, a Persian religious scholar who lived from 839 to 923 (Bulgakov and Nerazik 1999; Zabborov 1999). Bartold, however, argued that not all of the information found in the works of Al-Biruni is reliable (Bartold 1965: 545). Later, in the 1930s, Tolstov and other Russian researchers undertook several expeditions to Khorezm and Karakalpakstan to excavate and document the remnants of the ancient civilisation. The earliest known period of the history of Khorezm lasted from the late third century BC to the eighth century AD (Bulgakov and Nerazik 1999; Nerazik 1976).

The Khorezmian language belonged to the East Iranian group of languages of the Avestan branch alongside other languages such as Sogdian, Khotanese, Bactrian, and Old Ossetian. The remnants of these languages are Pashtun and Ossetic. Khorezmian was written in Aramaic script before the Arab conquest (712). The Khorezmians had their own calendar based on astronomical observations and seasonal celebrations. They practised Zoroastrianism together with local cults involving the belief in spirits. Elements of these ancient beliefs can be found in some of the rituals of modern Khorezmians until today. During the Arab conquest in 712, almost all of the manuscripts and other aspects of the cultural heritage were destroyed (Bulgakov and Nerazik 1999: 230).

Turkicisation of the region

The period of AD 750–1500 was known for the spread of Islam, first in Arabia, then later eastwards and northwards, covering much of Central Asia, south Siberia and the eastern regions of China (Bosworth 1999: 19). Westward migrations of Turkic nomadic tribes from Afghanistan through Iran to Anatolia had an impact on the process of Turkicisation of the regions, which mostly affected the Iranian populations, with their Iranian group of languages and beliefs. The most affected areas were Transoxania, Khorezm, most of the lands to the west including Azerbaijan, and parts of Fars and Anatolia. As a result, several Turkic empires developed. Among them were the sultanates of the Gaznavid rulers in eastern Afghanistan and northern India, the Oghuz principality in the middle and lower reaches of the Syrdarya in the Aral Sea region, and the empires of the Kypchaks, the Qarluqs and the Karakhanids.

In the tenth century, a Samanid state developed in Transoxania and later in Khurasan, Sistan, Tukharistan, Kabulistan, and eastern Fergana (Bosworth 1999: 1). Bukhara became the centre of this state. The Samanid dynasty was the last Iranian dynasty in the history of Central Asia (Finke 2006: 59). At the same time, the Seljuk dynasty emerged in the western areas near Khorezm. The Seljuks were a Turkic tribal confederation of mostly Oghuz groups. They later gave rise to the Ottoman Turks and Turks in Azerbaijan (ibid.: 61). They formed the Oghuz[5] principality, with its capital in Yangi-Kent. The Great Seljuk Empire was based in Iran.

Other Turkic tribes, including the Kimek, Kypchak and Pecheneg who were linguistically closely related, started to absorb the local Iranian nomads and Uralic groups (ibid.: 56). Kypchaks formed the Kypchak Empire, starting from the eleventh century with the collapse of the Oghuz and Kimek states. The Kypchak empire stretched from the Irtysh to the Volga and later controlled the southern Russian and Black Sea steppes and became known as Dasht-i Kypchak (in ancient Russian sources as *Polovetskoye Pole*) (Agajanov 1999: 73). Earlier Kypchaks were subject to Kimek Kaghans but became independent and established their power by the eleventh century, conquering Oghuz lands and establishing their borders with Khorezm (ibid.).

The thirteenth century was marked by Chingiz Khan's devastating invasion of the area and beyond. Chingiz Khan divided the conquered territory among his four sons. Jöchi, the first son of Chingiz Khan, died and his son Batu inherited most parts of Eastern Europe, west of Kypchaks' Volga and Khorezm (including the territory of the Golden Horde). Batu was renowned for his battles in Eastern Europe with his brother Shayban[6] (Jochi's son), especially in Hungary. His army consisted of Kypchaks, Bulgars and Oghuz, and that is why ethnically this Mongol army was largely Turkicised. In his state, Golden Horde Kypchak dialects were dominant although the official language remained Mongolian (Finke 2006: 64). Later, Toqtamish, a nephew of Urus from the line of Horde, the elder brother of Batu, would take over the Golden and White Hordes, and with the help of Tamerlane came to power (Grousset 2002: 408).

The second son of Chingiz Khan, Jagatai (Chagatay), occupied the steppes of the former Kara-Khitay Empire, including the Uyghur lands of Bukhara and Samarkand, Issiq Kul and Talas, as well as Kashgaria and Transoxania. In this territory the common Turkic language would come to be called Chagatay, a mixture of both Iranian and Turkic elements (Baskakov 1962, 1981; Finke 2006: 65). Tamerlane or Timur Lenk (the Lame) supported the development of the Chagatay language and established it as the official state language.

The third son, Ögödäi, inherited the territory of east and northeast Lake Balkhash and the Urungu. The last son, Tolui, 'was heir to the original patrimony comprising the region between the Tula, the upper Onon, and the upper Kerulen' (Grousset 2002: 255).

In the second half of the fourteenth century, power was shifting into the hands of the Turkic ruler Tamerlane, a member of the Barlas tribe (Manz 1999). Finke (2006: 67) argues that in this time 'a distinct Chagatay identity as a group developed [and was] the result of an already far advanced acculturation process, in which Islamic-Persian heritage was combined with a Turkic-Mongolian legacy'.

Formation of Uzbek khanates

There were various tribal groups and later confederations scattered all over Central Asia. Each of the tribes and local polities featured different patterns of social organisation. These patterns largely depended on the ruling dynasties, their cultural background, as well as the composition of their armies.

The brothers Shayban and Batu (Jochi's sons) had a large army consisting of Kypchaks, Bulghars, Oguzs and others. When the Shaybanids came to the region and established their political supremacy, there were tribal groups of Mongol and Turkic origin residing along the river oasis. In the second half of the fourteenth century, the eastern Kypchaks were called Özbegs as they served under the rule of a Chingizid called Özbeg Khan (Golden 1992: 330–332 cited in Finke 2006: 70). In the middle of the nineteenth century, the ruling dynasties emerged among Shaybanid Chingizid dynasties such as Ming, Manghit, and Qungirot. There were other numerous tribes and tribal confederations which were governed according to their residence and kinship rules. The kinship and residential units overlapped as Geiss (2003: 64) showed in his genealogical graphs. He located them in geographical units based on the residential proximity of patrilineal lineage groups. Geiss (ibid.: 56) defined residence groups as

> tribal economic communities based on mutual consent. The smallest residing unit was the *camp group*, which could include up to ten yurts. Close kinsmen like brothers, cousins and their families of one forefather group referred to form such groups [...] one or several camp group formed pastoral nomadic, pastoral semi-nomadic or even settled agricultural *tribal camps* or *villages* with temporal pastoral occupations of some of their members. A camp or village included up to fifty or sixty families and was guided or represented to the outside by a *headsman*. Several villages formed a *sub tribe* led sometimes by a *chieftain*, who was most likely a wealthy tribesman from the most numerous descent subgroups. [...] A *tribe* consisted of a number of sub-tribes which might be headed by a *tribal chief* and could include up to a few thousand households.

Traditional Islamic governance of Adat was enacted through locally authorised elders of the community. In Central Asia one can distinguish between

28 Uzbek identity

nomadic and sedentary ways of rule and socialisation. Governing structures and units of nomadic tribes in the fourteenth and fifteenth centuries included the following tribes or tribal confederations, some of which still can be found as tribal affiliations – for instance Kungrat, Kushchi and Durman in Khorezm; Tangut, Kungrat, Durman, Utadji (Utarchi), Kushchi, Nayman, Djat, Tubay, Hatan, Uyghur, Qarluq, Mangyt, Kurlagut, Yurchi and Kiyat. These were governed by the sultans of the house of Chingiz Khan. The head of all sultans was khan. Sedentary populations undertook agriculture, trade and craft work (Askarova 1993: 6).

During this time the Shaybanids came to power and ruled over Transoxania. They were the descendants of Shayban, Jochi's son. They ruled in Bukhara from 1598 and were replaced by the Janids or Astarkhanids, who were also of Jochid origin before the Manghit dynasty took over in Bukhara in 1785 (Finke 2006: 71). At that time Qongrats replaced the last Chingizid rulers in Khorezm and established a separate khanate with Khiva as its centre. Later, around 1710, a Shaybanid Shah Rukh founded an independent Uzbek Khanate of Qoqand, with Qoqand as its capital.

In the khanates, the main distinction was made between sedentary and nomadic populations. There were also ethnonyms used for different peoples such as Kazak, Kyrgyz, Turkmen, Uzbek, and Tadjik. Finke (ibid.: 75) argues that they were not as important as 'regional denominators like *Bukharalik* or *Ferganalik*, which typically included all ethnic groups'. The conflict between sedentary and nomadic populations in the khanates led to economic decline in the eighteenth century (Golden 1992: 334–335 cited in Finke 2006: 73). The peasant economy was based on growing grain, vegetables and fruit; cattle were kept, but usually by rich households. Pastoral nomads extensively used the vast steppes of the Dasht-I Kypchak and Mongolia, and migrated to seasonal pastures. The nomads were organised along kinship lines (Finke 2006: 73; Khazanov 1984).[7]

Geiss (2003) argues that applying kinship and clanship terms in the social and political organisation of the peoples in Central Asia prior to Russian conquest is not particularly helpful. He proposed a classification of units according to their commitment and particularities inherent to place and tribal arrangement. He cites examples of Kazak, Karakalpak and Kyrgyz nomadic tribes as exogamic units and/or serving as a military unit for the khan's army. These units might also serve as a community for the maintenance of peace and conflict prevention. Tribal units can also be defined as a community of law. For example, certain tribes or tribal groups can be responsible for the provision of customary law, as well as the prevention and resolution of conflicts (Geiss 2001, 2003: 28–40). Whereas among sedentary residential communities tribal belonging was not so important, they were rather divided according to their professional belonging. For example, as professions were passed on through generations, a kinship group was called by the name of its profession which is still the case in Khorezm; for example, *Qandchi* (sweets-makers), *Arqanchi* (rope-makers) and *Öli-yuvuvchi* (dead body washers – the lowest caste). In present-day Khorezm some of these names serve as the names of kinship groups, especially in rural areas.

It is widely accepted that the modern Uzbek nation consists of three 'layers', namely the 'non-tribally organised populations, in their majority former Iranian-speakers who had assimilated; descendants of the earlier tribes who had settled in the region prior to the Uzbek conquest; and a third layer that arrived during or in the aftermath of the Shaybanid rule and was largely Qipchaq speaking' (Finke 2006: 74 citing Karmysheva 1976; see also Baldauf 1991, 1993; Ilkhamov 2004; Shaniyazov 1978; Zhdanko 1978).

From tribes to nations

Russian occupation of Central Asia

In this section I will touch upon an important period of nation formation in Central Asia and how Central Asian nations come about. I will also briefly discuss Russians' attempts to create an overarching Soviet identity which involved ideological and social projects of forming a sense of collective belonging cutting across more than 15 nationalities. Later in this section I will further consider Soviet efforts of creating a *Homo Sovietikus*, which was the overarching Soviet identity.

Russia used the term 'Turkestan' to delineate the territory of Central Asia. 'Turkestan' as a term was earlier used by the Arian population of Central Asia to refer to the northern steppe occupied by nomads of Turkic origin, and later by Arab geographers in the ninth century to mark the territory between Mavaraunakhr and China. Turkestan is translated as 'a land of Turks'. The term was interpreted more widely during the times of the Seljuks, including some parts of Mavaraunakhr called Turkestan (Semyonov-Tyan-Shansky, 1913: 285). The territory referred to as 'Turkestan' by the Russians extended from the Caspian Sea in the west to China in the east, and bordered Russia to the north and Persia and Afghanistan to the south (ibid.: 1; Holdsworth 1959; Zarubin 1925). Although Russian plans to occupy Central Asia started in 1839, the conquests were not successful until the 1860s, after the end of the Crimean war in 1856. The major cities in the region were occupied: Aulie-Ata, Turkestan and Chimkent in 1864; Tashkent city in 1865, Khodzhent in 1866, Ura-Tube, Dzhizak and Yangi-Kurgan in 1868; famously, the Samarkand and Khiva campaign began slowly in 1873 (Vaidayanath 1967: 30) and later in 1881 Russian forces massacred Turkmen tribes in Gōk-Tepe, an event which is still remembered in the region. The occupied lands were governed by a military governor of each central city, but as the conquered territories grew, so did the need for administrative reorganisation. A decree was issued to form a new Governor-Generalship of Turkestan by the recommendations of the Giers Commission on 11 July 1867. In the late nineteenth century the territorial formation of Turkestan was completed with the incorporation of Semirechenskaya *oblast'*[Ru] and Zakaspiskaya *oblast'*. The administrative division of the final Russian Turkestan was then formed into five *oblasts*: Semirechinskiy, Syrdaryinskiy, Ferganskiy, Samarkandskiy and Zakaspiyskiy. The Bukhara and Khiva khanates were under the administration

30 Uzbek identity

of the general governor of Turkestan (Becker 1968, Holdsworth 1959). In 1900, Russian Turkestan comprised 1,731,090 km^2 (*versts*^{Ru}) in addition to Bukhara and Khiva at 238,000 km^2 (Semyonov-Tyan-Shansky 1913: 343). The population of Turkestan in 1897 was 5,280,983 people, to which Russians and Kozaks added almost one million in the following 12 years (Vaidayanath 1967: 33); for a basic overview over the territory, the population and also today's national divisions within former Turkestan, see Figures 2.1 and 2.2.

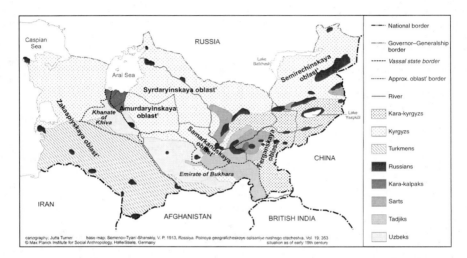

Figure 2.1 Borders of Turkestan and its ethnic composition at the time of the Russian conquest (source: adapted from Semyonov-Tyan-Shansky 1913).

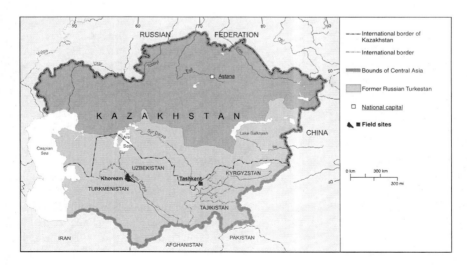

Figure 2.2 Today's Central Asia and former Turkestan borders.

Russia under the Tsar's rule advanced the policies of economic development and political loyalty (Abdurakhimova 2002). This was undertaken through the resettlement of as many Russians as possible to occupied Central Asia. Russian *poseleniya* (settlements) started to appear (Vaidayanath 1967: 39) in Turkestan with the beginning of Russian occupation (see Figure 2.2).

National delimitation under Soviet rule: from tribes to nations

After the 1917 revolution in Russia and assassination of all members of the family of Tsar Nicolay II, the Bolsheviks led by Lenin expanded their territorial power, forming the Soviet Union in December 1922. Following the October revolution, the Bolsheviks appeared in Turkestan in late 1917 to early 1918. They refused the participation of native intelligentsia (*Ulema*), in which Islamic scholars played a leading role, in the Tashkent Soviet (Central Governing Entity of Turkestan).[8] In reaction, the native intelligentsia formed its own autonomous government in Kokand. Turkestan was granted territorial autonomy at the Fourth Extraordinary Regional Muslim Congress (where peoples of Turkestan were given a chance for self-determination) and as a result there were two parallel powers and governments were established, one the Tashkent Soviet, and the other in Kokand, where the power of the latter was limited to Fergana Valley (Soucek 2000: 214) This arrangement, however, did not last long. The autonomous government in Kokand was dismantled by the Tashkent Soviet in February 1918 (Vaidyanath 1967: 83). The fall of the Kokand government did not stop the native elite resisting the Bolsheviks and, after 1922, Soviet government. Those opposed to Soviet rule finally established the *Basmachi* movement, which was a local guerrilla movement advocating 'jihad' against the unbelievers and invaders (ibid.: 83). The most significant result of the fifth congress was the formation of the People's Commissariat for Nationality Affairs (*Turkomnats*).[9] Uzbeks, Tadjiks, Turkmens, Kazaks, Tatars, Ukrainians, Jews and Armenians established themselves as separate national sections in this Commissariat (Vaidayanath 1967: 92).

At the Turkestan Central Executive Committee, Kazak and the Uzbek languages were proclaimed as official languages of the Turkestan Republic in addition to Russian. At this committee pan-Turkic and pan-Islamic ideas and sentiments were pronounced by a group led by one of the 'Jadidists', Ryskulov, and others who had made several attempts to promote the formation of a Communist Party of Turkic People renaming Turkistan as the Turkic Republic which would unite not only the Turkic peoples in Central Asia, but also other Turkic peoples beyond the Soviet Union.[10] The proposals from Ryskulov's group to form a separate Communist party were viewed as a threat. They opposed the principle of a single and Central Communist Party which ideally would unite members all over the Soviet Union and be unchallenged by any opposition. In order to have better control of the region, a Turkestan Commission was appointed by the central government, composed of Eliyeva (chairman), Frunze, Kuibyshev and others, arriving in Turkestan in 1919. This Commission issued a special decree, expressing the necessity of the administrative reorganisation of Turkestan in accordance with the ethnographic and economic conditions (Vaidayanath 1967: 106). Ruskulov's book about Islamic and Turkic union was refuted by the Bolsheviks. This contributed to anti-Soviet revolts by natives who were fought by the troops of the Turkestan Commission. The *Basmachi* movement extended to the Bukhara emirate and Khiva Khanate. These two 'states' suffered from internal feuding, and in Khiva there was a continuous struggle against Turkmen attacks. The Bolsheviks intervened and supported conflict resolution in both khanates. The Bolsheviks finally occupied and renamed both khanates as the Bukhara People's Soviet Republic and Khiva People's Soviet Republic.

The economic and social development in Central Asia was slow; much of the industrial enterprises created by Tsarist rule came to a standstill during early Soviet rule. The Bolsheviks concluded that Central Asian cultural and economic backwardness needed to be addressed. In order to combat the problem, the following measures were prescribed by the Bolsheviks:

(a) 'to organise (non-party) clubs and other educational institutions for popular enlightenment in the local language'; (b) 'to extend the network of educational establishments of all grades in the local languages'; (c) 'to draw in the more or less loyal national teachers'.

(Ibid.: 139)

After the establishment of the People's Commissariat for Nationality Affairs, national divisions were given the opportunity to transform into a national Republic within the Soviet Union. However, this was very complicated and difficult in the case of Central Asia because of its linguistically and culturally heterogeneous nature. National Delimitation Programs proved to be a very slow and long process in Central Asia by comparison to other Republics of the Soviet Union. Different proposals had been received by the Central Government about possible divisions within Turkestan; for instance, Fergana delegates arrived at the XIII Congress of Soviets of Turkestan Republic to demand autonomy from Turkestan. The delegation from Khorezm also demanded sovereignty. In order to solve national problems which perceivably were hindering the economic and political development of the region, the discussions on the national delimitation program started as early as March 1924 (ibid.: 167). National theories of the Soviets were based on the nation theories of Stalin, in turn derived from Marx. Stalin summarised the principles of national characteristics on four basic criteria, namely a community with its language, its territory, economic life and its similar psychological make-up (Vaidayanath 1967: 254). Preparatory work for the national delimitation programme was undertaken by the Turkestan Commissariat led by Frunze and Kuybyshev. In order to make up the plan of national delimitation, the Central Territorial Commission was established which would be assisted by the Statistical and Economic Commissions. Besides these Commissions, there were Uzbek, Turkmen, Kazak, Kyrgyz and Tadjik National Bureaus which were formed for the establishment of the new Republics. After long discussions, consideration and reconsideration of various proposals from various national and other groups in Turkestan, including government representatives of Bukhara and Khorezm and others, the following Republics appeared: the Uzbek Autonomous Soviet Socialist Republic (ASSR) with a territory of 167,500 km^2 and a population of 3,963,285 (48.7 per cent of the population of Turkestan); the Tadjik ASSR with a territory of 145,800 km^2 and a population of 739,503 (9.1 per cent of the population of Turkestan); the Turkmen ASSR with 443,500 km^2 and 855,114 inhabitants (10.5 per cent of the population of Turkestan); the Kazak ASSR with 685,900 km^2 and 1,468,724 inhabitants (18 per cent of the population of Turkestan); the Kyrgyz Autonomous *Oblast'* with 190,700 km^2 and 714,648 inhabitants (8.8 per cent of the population of Turkestan); and the Karakalpak Autonomous *Oblast'*. The Bukhara Republic was split between the Uzbek ASSR, the Tadjik ASSR and the Turkmen SSR, while more than 50 per cent of its territory was part of the Uzbek ASSR. Also, the Khorezm Republic was split, with half of it located in the Uzbek ASSR, and the rest divided between the Turkmen ASSR and the Karakalpak Autonomous *Oblast'* (ibid.: 196).

Much as in other colonial territories (e.g. Africa), the creation of nations in Central Asia by local elites with the support of the Soviets was an arbitrary and contested process and led to outcomes that still influence the relations of peoples and states in the region in the twenty-first century. I agree with many authors who recognise that it was not undertaken solely by the Soviets on the principle of 'divide and rule', but was rather an active process where local elites played a decisive role (Finke 2006; Hirsch 2000). It was also a seminal moment for the development of a *united* national self-consciousness of the many different tribes who constituted the complex cultural mosaic of the region. This multiplicity and diversity of the Uzbek 'national collectivity' (*natsionalniy kollektiv*[Ru]), to use a phrase by Polivanov (1933: 5), is principle concern in this book.

Creating *Homo Sovietikus*

From nations to the nation

Soviet policy envisaged a Soviet nation of young *kadry* (workforce), a so-called *Homo Sovietikus*, in an effort to eradicate traditional kinships reminiscent of national or ethnic identities which might disrupt the process of Sovietisation and modernisation. For these to become true it was necessary to create infrastructure (government, roads, schools, etc.) and an ideological backbone which would hold all that. The 'Marxist-Leninist ideology' introduced various mottos for lifestyle, media, education, and morality. Atheism was promoted throughout the Soviet Union, followed by strict prohibitions of religious traditions concerning marriage, death and funeral and other life events (Kappeler 1989). These changes were meant to be implemented within the framework of the project of Soviet nation and state building. However, it did not necessarily mean that the project was successful. The institutionalisation of ethnicity by the Soviet state has been discussed by many scholars, who argue that this project had various agendas beyond its explicit programmes, containing complex ideologies and strategies (Hann 1998, 2002a, 2002b, 2002c; Hann *et al.* 2002; Hirsch 2002, 2005; Humphrey 2002; Suny 2000; Suny and Martin 2001; Tishkov 1997).

There is a growing amount of literature on the nationality questions during Soviet rule (Abazov 1999; Akiner 1996; Allworth 1973, 1990, 1999; Beissinger 1998; Critchlow 1977, 1991; Clem 1977; Heuer 1997). In his seminal contribution to the studies of nationalities and national questions during Soviet rule and after its collapse, Francine Hirsch (2005) outlined the views expressed on the national questions in different periods during the Cold War and after the end of Soviet hegemony. Hirsch (ibid.) argues that Western scholarship on the Soviet Union has been mostly influenced by existing theoretical frameworks and related concepts. Comparative methods of 'analogy' have been applied to explain and theorise Soviet society by following 'a "top-down approach" [which] gave limited attention to the complex nature of local-level interests and conflicts' (ibid.: 2). Hirsch (ibid.) argues that it is misleading to look at the nationality question during Soviet rule as an 'affirmative action', 'nation making', or 'nation breaking'. She argues that far more complex policies were involved in Soviet socialist state building, through economic unification and development. She called this Soviet policy a 'state sponsored evolutionism' that 'placed all of the peoples of the former Russian Empire on an imagined evolutionary trajectory of development and made policy recommendations accordingly' (Hirsch 2000: 208). Suny and Martin (2001: 4) stated that in the mid-1970s the central focus of the research was the Soviet foreign economic policy, while area and nationality studies 'were peripheral, both geographically and intellectually'.

Creating a viable and vital 'Uzbek nation' was not a goal of the Soviet Union. Rather, a 'Soviet nation' ideology undermined authentic traditions of social life and traditional models of social security, and consequently did not leave any space for the struggles over resources or ethnic strife. Hirsch (2000) also argued that the Belarusian and Uzbek nations were examples of 'nation-making "from above"'. Local differences in Soviet Republics that existed during Soviet rule and persisted after its collapse have not been given the necessary attention when looking at post-Soviet national identities. In the rest of this chapter I will show how in practice the process of creating a Soviet nation looked in terms of establishment of the right environment, infrastructure and ideology building. I will touch upon the creation of what I call the one-city-centralisation system as a method of centralised governance; the welfare system which aimed at eradication of other traditional belonging systems such as kinship and local ethnicity; collectivisation as another ideology to unite culturally different groups under one larger collective with similar goals; and finally population relocations throughout the Soviet Union, which also contributed to the diversification of peoples.

Institutional basis of **Homo Sovietikus:** *capital city centralisation system*

The excessive centralisation of the administrative and political system of the Soviet state created a single direction of resource allocation from top to bottom,

Making of Uzbek nationality 35

from Moscow to Republic through its capital cities where the main government bodies were located, authorised to redistribute further down to *oblast*'s[Ru] and *rayons*[Ru].[11] Yet the strategic enterprises were governed directly from Moscow, which is the cornerstone of the capital city centralisation system policy (Lane and Ross 1995: 339). Some regions even had *Moskovskoye obespecheniye*[Ru] (Moscow provision), which was considered very privileged. The products from *Moskovskoye obespechniye*, be they food products or cloth, were always of the best quality. The one-city-centralisation system was about centring decision-making processes within government entities in Moscow and denying the autonomy of local representatives of the central government in the Republics. All important political and economic decisions were made by the government in Moscow.

Central Asia remained the main supplier of raw materials for agricultural and industrial production, including cotton, gold, gas and oil. After the Central Asian states gained their independence, the powerful centre of decision making simply transposed to the subsequent capital cities of the new independent states, and the policy of one-city-centralisation remained unchanged.

The Soviet government was quite successful in building itself as 'a total welfare state' (Madison 1968: xi). The Social Welfare System was the biggest, if not the main part, of implementing Soviet ideologies and the creation of Soviet society. In accordance with the principles founded by Lenin and the Bolsheviks 'on their way from socialism to communism', the social welfare system included such benefits as:

> (1) Family and child welfare services, including services for delinquent youngsters; (2) income maintenance programs, that is, programs that furnish monetary grants and assistance in kind either on a discretionary or nondiscretionary basis; (3) vocational rehabilitation and services for the aged. [...] Other social services in the areas of health, education, recreation, labour protection, housing, etc.
>
> (Madison 1968: xix)

The welfare system was based on the principles developed by Makarenko, a leading figure in the application of psychological concepts to the social life of the Soviet people. These theories emerged in 1936 and advanced over the course of the next 20 years of Soviet rule (Madison 1968: 28, 29). These theories were of strategic importance in the making of a Soviet man and the basis of Soviet social welfare practices. It was believed that by creating a positive social and economic environment, people could be changed for the benefit of communal goals and achieving communism.

> It was more or less assumed that once a socialist society came into being to intervene not only in directing such activities as industrialisation and collectivisation, but also in the shaping of 'Soviet Man' [*Homo Sovietikus*]: making sure that his motives, consciousness, and behaviour were appropriate

to the new socialist society. This entailed developing methods that would prevent or change undesirable behaviour.

(Ibid.: 33)

The Social Welfare System applied the following methods while implementing its programmes:

(1) an integrated casework-group work method that addresses itself simultaneously to the collective (*kolletiv*) and the individual, (2) community participation (*obshchestvennost'*), defined as the effort of every individual on behalf of the total community, and (3) work therapy (*trud*).

(Ibid.: 33–34)

Soviet scholars 'argued that the residual concept [of social welfare], which they associated with the detested means test and humiliation of charity was appropriate only for a capitalist society' (ibid.: 34). In contrast, Soviet social welfare was strictly institutionalised.

The major achievements of welfare policies during the early Soviet rule was the empowering of women's[12] status both in the family and in society through introducing family and child welfare policies in 1917 until late 1955, together with educational training and other programmes. Especially in Central Asia, the largest advancements had been made by unveiling women, making them literate, and training them to enter the labour market.[13] These policies were meant to constitute a decisive break with the old system of family relations and to create a Soviet family. The two parallel developments of urbanisation and industrialisation which were implemented throughout the Soviet Union influenced the family patterns and lifestyles of most Soviet citizens. These processes were coupled with the development of the infrastructure at the same time; building roads, gas pipelines as well as '*elektrifikatsiya vsey strany*'[Ru,14] (electrification of the whole country), which successfully reached remote rural areas.

Another major policy implemented within the framework of social welfare was the social security of Soviet citizens (*gosudarstvennoye sotsialnoye strakhovaniye*[Ru]/state social insurance), which covered:

(1) *all* risks – death, disability, sickness, old age, pregnancy and childbirth, and unemployment; (2) coverage of *everyone* working for hire and members of his family; (3) benefits equal *total* earnings, financed entirely by employers and government; and (4) administration of all forms of social insurance by unified organs of a *territorial* type, in which the insured exercise complete control.

(Ibid.: 50)

The institutional corpus of social welfare services in the Soviet Union consisted of four state entities: the Ministries of Welfare, Education and Health together with the All-Union Central Committee of Trade Unions which evolved in the 1930s (ibid.: 79). Trade unions provided benefits for those who were in the labour force, including working pensioners and those temporarily disabled by illness or forced to pause because of pregnancy and maternity. They also supported those who were disabled due to work injuries. Membership in trade unions was compulsory and the membership fee was 1 per cent of salary. The tasks of any trade union included financial support of sick leave, annual visits to sanatoriums, and cultural and social organisation of leisure time. Besides, trade unions had funds for holidays, organised holiday and travels (*putyovki*^{Ru}, plural), children's summer camps, various kinds of awards, housing provisions,[15] construction of sport facilities and promotion of sport activities, and various passes and subsidies. Besides financial provisions for workers, trade unions were also responsible for the moral and social improvements among their members through various incentive programmes, including prizes and other additional benefits for hard-working and disciplined employees. A healthy lifestyle was promoted, and the Ministries of Welfare were responsible for those outside the labour force, including the retired, disabled and unemployed.

A similar and major role was played by volunteer associations, promoting welfare arrangements on the local level. Community involvement and volunteer work were highly regarded as a result of the Soviet ideology of community and mutual help. Volunteer associations were publicly recognised and promoted by the mass media. The media were, of course, strictly controlled and served the socialist and communist ideologies. Volunteer labour was often used (and abused) in order to minimise state expenditure and revenues.

Although the Soviet state welfare system was ideally designed to eradicate poverty and improve the lives of Soviet citizens, in practice it could not fully achieve its goals. However, the system of social welfare did realise impressive achievements, considering the scale of its territory and size of its population.

Ideological basis of Homo Sovietikus: *kollektivizatsiya*^{Ru}, *(collectivisation)*

The social welfare system of Soviet government aimed not only to socially secure its citizens, but also to penetrate and influence their private lives. This was done through the principle '*odin za vseh vse za odnogo*' ('one for all and all for one', meaning: 'an individual stands for a collective and a collective for an individual'). Collective values were promoted at the expense of individual interests. State institutions of social welfare and other state organisations with the mass support of Soviet citizens were actively involved in this process of collectivisation.

Unlike labour unions in the West, trade unions were governmental organisations, principally serving state ideals. Aiming to dominate the working spirit and productivity of its members, it also worked to influence their opinions on political and socio-economic issues. A trade union's budget was directly dependent on the income of the enterprise it was part of. That was why not all trade unions had equal amount of benefits, although the kinds were almost identical.

While employees were part of trade unions, the youth were incorporated into the system of youth organisations. The system was organised in terms of age and integrated into the school system. There were three stages to pass through during the ten years of secondary education; becoming *Oktyabryata*^{Ru}, *Pioner*^{Ru} and *Komsomol*^{Ru}. This was the path for becoming a real communist. From the first grade in primary school until the third grade (end of primary school), schoolchildren would enter membership of *Oktyabryata* depending on their progress in school. There were general eligibility criteria for membership of all three organisations, entailing good academic performance, social behaviour and learning the oath by heart. There were three possible dates during each academic year (1 September to 25 May) to enter into the membership of all three organisations which were a day before 12 April (Day of the Cosmonauts, a public holiday), Lenin's birthday (22 April, a working day), Victory Day (Second World War victory on 9 May, a public holiday). Becoming *Oktybryata* would be recognised by a pin in the form of a red star with Lenin's picture as a small boy; *Pioner* wore a tie from a small red triangular silk fabric tied on the neck against a white shirt. Discrepancies in dates of membership could prove uncomfortable for late achievers, or those who had even one bad grade, marked only as 'satisfactory'. The system of passing these 'very important' three phases of school life was implemented in order to implant the values and ideas of Communism into the growing Soviet person. Becoming a *Komsomol* was the most challenging task. Only *Pioners* were eligible to become *Komsomol*. This organisation resembled the Communist Party and was meant to prepare future members of the Communist Party, and was the only way to prepare oneself for a future career. Besides these organisations were sports societies which were organised under the auspices of the State Committee for Physical Culture and Sports. The cultural life of Soviet citizens was also structured in such a way that every village had its own cultural centre where cinema, theatre and concerts could be performed.[16]

Internationalisation strategies: population movements

Population movements were one of the prominent characteristics of the early years of Soviet rule. There were several types of population movement during the Soviet Union. Most of the movements were administered by state policies and by force. These policies had different contexts and justifications (Conquest 1991 [1970]; Polian 2004)

According to Polian's (2004) distinction of forced migration in the USSR there were several criteria for 'resettling', deporting or 'voluntarily' compelling migration (see Figure 2.3 for an outline of population movements in Central Asia in Soviet times). One criterion concerned social status: so-called Kozaks, noblemen, were expelled between 1919 and 1935. Second, border territories were cleansed of some groups for security reasons. Nomadic populations were sedentarised. Further reasons for repression and deportation were based on the grounds of religion or political belonging. Also, prisoners of war were deported. The indications for so-called voluntary migration concerned the resettlement of

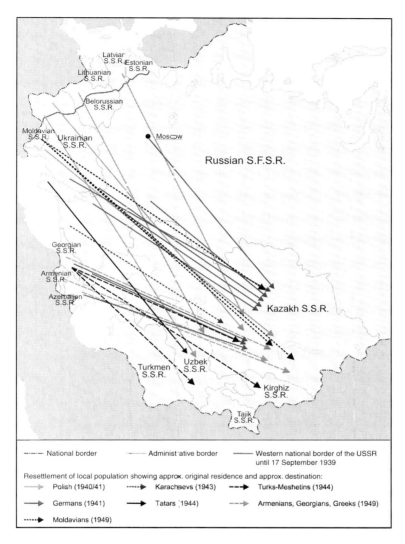

Figure 2.3 Population movements during Soviet rule: to Central Asia.

population from densely populated to deserted territories, from mountains to flat lands, or evacuation from regions of 'conflict' (Giese 1982, 1983).

Maksheyev, Obruchev and Zolotaryov, alongside other Russian statisticians, outlined that patterns of population resettlement during the Soviet Union followed the logic of what can be called a 'geography of disloyalty'. Among the disloyal populations were Jews, Germans, Caucasians, Central Asians, etc. (Kappeler 1993; Polian 2004). 'Loyal' populations were defined as such if they comprised not less than 50 percent of Russians among them. These categorisations of conquered peoples led to various policies of resettlement, and the movement of millions of people within the Soviet Union. Parts of these movements were 'planned and organised resettlements' (Polian 2004: 57). In order to balance the proportion of indigenous and 'disloyal' populations, exact statistics on crimes were produced. Its side-effect was that past cases of murder are now well-documented (Martin 1998; Rummel 1990). These policies were implemented in tandem with collectivisation and industrial reforms throughout the country. Particularly the sedentarisation policies directed towards the nomadic populations of Central Asia proved disastrous (Giese 1982, 1983). Many nomads lost up to 90 per cent of their cattle, leading to starvation and deaths among these groups. It is estimated that in the early 1930s one to two million nomads died in the wake of these policies.

Resettled people sometimes tried to resist, but had to face harsh government reactions. Polian (ibid.: 80) quotes a complaint written by members of the Red Army directed to *Narkom*[Ru] (*Narodniy Kommitet*/National Committee) on Military and Naval Affairs:

> we wanted several times to deregister, but they [government officials] do not deregister us. They [government officials] say that we are now local inhabitants, but we do not want that. We decided to go, and took our registered documents; they arrested us, took all of our documents and said that we could not go anywhere. We replied that we will not live here. They arrested us and say that they will file a court order against us.

Another major resettlement campaign concerned the deportation of Koreans from *Dalniy Vostok*[Ru] (Far East). Tens of thousands were deported from *Dalniy Vostok*, mainly to Central Asia and the Caucasus. Around 95,526 Koreans were resettled to Kazakhstan; about 76,525 Koreans came to Uzbekistan; others were distributed to other regions. The conditions of resettlement, including travel and adjustment to new locations, were extremely harsh, leading to many deaths. The process of resettlement of Koreans continued into the post-Second World War period. This led to the creation of new *posyolok*s ('living areas' or 'villages') in the host country (ibid.: 90–92).

In sum, all of these policies of resettlement, migration and deportation deeply affected the Central Asian region. After Turkestan had been divided into Uzbek, Tadjik, Kyrgyz and Kazakh Soviet Republics, this region suffered severely from the planned resettlement policies of collectivisation. As mentioned, nomadic people were forced to become sedentarised and join *kolkhoz*es (*kollektivniye hozyaystva*; collective farms). Industrialisation and modernisation projects involved *osvoyeniye*[Ru] *zemel'*[Ru] (land reclamation), and mass resettlements into industrial areas provided a workforce.

Central Asian countries were reorganised as the main suppliers of agricultural products, especially cotton. This led to a high proportion of rural vs urban population, and led to the so-called 'Central Asian problem', which refers to the great imbalance between the two population groups. Many scholars argued that the low level of rural out-migration was due to the absence of differentials between rural and urban wages, and the relatively low living costs in rural areas, the higher income from private plots and the better housing spaces to accommodate large families (Anderson and Silver 1989; Craumer 1992; Kaiser 1992; Polian 2004; Tishkov et al. 2005). Some also argued that low educational levels and vocational training in rural areas was a decisive factor in their immobile character (Patnaik 1995).

There was also a common consensus on the 'immobile character of the Central Asian population' that had to do with the traditional set up of extended families living in close proximity to one another. I share this view on the basis of my local knowledge and field observations, but argue that this pattern has been challenged since the collapse of the Soviet government.

Most of the resettlement policies faced failure in one form or another, be it the fact that many resettled people fled or died in transit, or were simply unable to adapt.

Notes

1 See special issue devoted to this debate edited by Abashin (2006) and also Kurzman (1999), Lubin (1981) and the earlier works on this (Yakubovskiy 1941).
2 See Bregel (1996) for a discussion of the terminological confusion and various uses of different terms for the region.
3 Considerable research is done on the history of nomadic populations of Central Asia (in a geographical meaning of the term which also includes Afghanistan); see Wolfgang Holzwarth (2005), Khazanov (1978, 1990, 1992), as well as Khazanov and Wink (2001).
4 Yüeh-chih (also written Yuezhi in Golden 1992) were called so in Chinese sources, and also known as Tocharians (Harmatta 1999).
5 The Oguz tribes had a strong influence on the formation of the Khorezmian population and its language.
6 Many scholars argue that the Shaybany dynasty provided the basis for unification of various tribes under the name 'Uzbek'; further details in this direction will be outlined later in this chapter.
7 Research undertaken on pre-Soviet Central Asia and its social organisation is full of confusion regarding kinship terminology. Soviet scholars studying family and kinship relations in Central Asia before the Tsarist times used the terms *plemya*, *rod* and *obshina* to describe kinship and tribal units. Paul Geiss (2003: 66) cites Hudson (1938), who used the terms 'tribe, gentes and subdivisions'; Kracer (1963) used the terms 'clan, lineages'; Benigsen and Wimbush (1985) used the terms 'tribe, clan and subclannish divisions', and Geiss (2003) uses the term 'tribal commitment' to describe the units of social organisation. Geiss (ibid.) stated that the confusion of kinship terms stemmed from the confusion in anthropological literature itself. However, to my mind this confusion derives from the lack of literature and scholarly research done on that period on Central Asia. The information about the social organisation in the pre-Soviet past is found in notes of geographers, travellers and short-term visitors in the region, as well as other sources such as correspondence, and documents and texts. None of them had really set on to conduct a systematic study on family and kinship.
8 The term *Ulema* refers to the community of all Muslims. Here it is used for a much more regional congregation. It indicates that Islamic religion played an important role

42 Uzbek identity

in Central Asia at that time. In fact, Islam had spread there already from the eighth century onward, and towns like Bukhara along the Silk Road were renowned centres of Islamic learning throughout much of the (European) Middle Ages and until the early twentieth century.
9 *TurKomNats*, an abbreviation from *Turkestanskiy Komitet po Nastsonalnym Voprosam* (Turkestan Committee on Nationality Questions).
10 The fact that pan-Turkic and pan-Islamic activists could, at least temporarily, cooperate with those interested in establishing a Turkic communist party hints at the particular character of Central Asian Islam. Central Asian Muslims have been exposed to various waves of conquest and rule by Mongols, Timurides, Russians and others. Moreover, since the Silk Road traversed the territory, local Muslims have for centuries been exposed to peaceful foreign and non-Islamic influences through trade. To survive (politically and economically) opportunistic arrangements had to be found.
11 There are numerous books and articles devoted to the studies of the structure of the Soviet government and its systems of governing, written by both Russian and Western scholars (Borisov *et al.* 1988; Pospielovsky 1987; Gleason 1986, 1989, 1991, 1993; Hazard 1980; Shelley 1990). See Gorlin (1985) on the power of Soviet industrial ministries in the 1980s (Sterheimer 1980; Taubman 1973).
12 Kandiyoti (1987) argues that the emancipatory movements do not always positively affect the rights of women in various Muslim societies. She brings examples from Soviet past practices as well as other countries.
13 Literacy rates were raised from 3 per cent to 99 per cent in a short period of time.
14 The phrase is taken from a famous flyer during the Soviet Union I remember seeing all over the place in Uzbekistan and Turkmenistan.
15 In order to obtain accommodation one had to queue for it. The waiting period could take from few to many years. Good connections in the upper levels of state government could help to move up the queue more quickly, which would make the waiting time for ordinary people longer.
16 This derives from my own experiences of taking part in cotton-picking campaigns in villages; we were either put into these cultural centres to sleep or in the sport halls of the schools, and once in the facilities of the kindergarten which was vacated for us in the late 1990s after the collapse of the Soviet Union.

References

Abashin, S.N. 2006. 'Invitation to discussion', *Anthropology & Archeology of Eurasia*, 44 (4), 7–9.
Abazov, R. 1999. 'Central Asia's conflicting legacy and ethnic policies: revisiting a crisis zone of the former USSR', *Nationalism and Ethnic Politics*, 5 (2), 62–90.
Abdurakhimova, N.A. 2002. 'The colonial system of power in Turkistan', *International Journal of Middle East Studies*, 34, 239–262.
Agajanov, S.G. 1999. *The States of the Oghuz, the Kimek and the Kipchak: History of Civilizations of Central Asia. The Age of Achievement: A.D.750 to the End of the Fifteenth Century: The Historical and Economic Setting*, vol. 4 Delhi: Motilal Banarsidass Publishers Private Limited.
Akiner, S. 1996. 'Islam, the state and ethnicity in Central Asia in historical perspective', *Religion, State and Society*, 24, 91–132.
Allworth, E. 1973. *The Nationality Question in Soviet Central Asia*. New York: Praeger.
Allworth, E. 1990. *The Modern Uzbeks: From the 14th Century to the Present; A Cultural History*. Stanford, CA: Hoover Institution Press.
Allworth, E. 1999 (ed.) *Central Asia, 130 Years of Russian Dominance: A Historical Overview*, 3rd edn. Durham, NC: Duke University Press.

Anderson, B. and Silver, B. 1989. 'Demographic sources of the changing ethnic composition of the Soviet Union.' *Population and Development Review*, 15: 609–656.
Askarova, A. 1993. *Istoriya Narodov Uzbekistana* [History of peoples of Uzbekistan], vol. 2. Tashkent: FAN.
Baldauf, I. 1991. 'Some thoughts on the making of the Uzbek nation', *Cahiers du Monde Russe et Soviétique*, 32 (1), 79–96.
Baldauf, I. 1993. *Schriftreform und Schriftwechsel bei den Mulsimischen Russland und Sowjettürken (1850–1937)*. Budapest: Akadémiai Kiadó.
Bartold, V.V. 1965. *Khorezm (Chorasmia). Sochineniya*. Vol. 3. Moscow: Izdatelstvo Vostochnoy Literatury.
Baskakov, N. 1962. *Vvedeniye v izucheniye tyurkskikh yazykov* [Introduction to the study of Turkic languages]. Moscow: Gos.Izdatelstvo Vostochnaya Shkola.
Baskakov, N. 1981. *A'tayskaya semya yazykov i yeyo izucheniye* [Altaic family of languages and its study]. Moscow: Nauka.
Becker, S. 1968. *Russia's Protectorates in Central Asia: Bukhara and Khiva, 1865–1924.* Cambridge, MA: Harvard University Press.
Beissinger, M.B. 1998. 'Nationalist violence and the state: political authority and contentious repertoires in the former USSR', *Comparative Politics*, 30 (4), 401–422.
Borisov, Yu. *et al.* 1988. *Politicheskaya sistema kontsa 20–30h godov. O Staline I stalinisme: istoriki sporyat. Trinadtsat' besed.* [Political system of the end of 20–30s. About Stalin and Stalinism: historians argue. Thirteen conversations]. Moscow: Politizdat.
Bosworth, C. 1999. 'Introduction', in M. Asimov and C. Bosworth (eds), *History of Civilisations of Central Asia Volume IV: The Age of Achievement: A.D.750 to the End of the Fifteenth Century. Part I. The Historical, Social and Economic Setting.* Delhi: Motilal Banarsidass Publishers Private Ltd.
Bregel. Y. 1996. *Notes on the study of Central Asia.* Research Institute for Inner Asian Studies, Indiana University.
Bulgakov, P.G. and Nerazik, E.E. 1999. 'Khwarizm: history of civilisations of Central Asia', in B.A. Litvinsky (ed.). *III The Crossroads of Civilisations: A.D.250 to 750.* Delhi: Motilal Banarsidass Publishers, pp. 207–231.
Clem, R.S. 1977. 'Recent demographic trends among Soviet nationalities and their implications', in G.W. Simmonds (ed.), *Nationalism in the USSR & Eastern Europe in the Era of Brezhnev & Kosygin.* Papers and Proceedings of the Symposium Held at University of Detroit on 3–4 October 1975. Detroit: Detroit University Press, pp. 37–43.
Conquest, R. 1991 [1970]. *The Great Terror: A Reassessment.* New York: Oxford University Press.
Craumer, E.R. 1992. 'Agricultural change, labour supply and rural out-migration in Soviet Central Asia', in R.A. Lewis (ed.), *Geographic Perspectives on Soviet Central Asia.* London: Routledge, pp. 132–175.
Critchlow, J. 1977. 'Nationalism in Uzbekistan in the Brezhnev era', in G.W. Simmonds (ed.), *Nationalism in the USSR & Eastern Europe in the Era of Brezhnev & Kosygin.* Papers and Proceedings of the Symposium Held at University of Detroit on 3–4 October 1975. Detroit: Detroit University Press, pp. 306–321.
Critchlow, J. 1991. *Nationalism in Uzbekistan: A Soviet Republic's Road to Sovereignty.* Boulder, CO: Westview Press.
Finke, P. 2006. Variations on Uzbek identity: concepts, constraints and local configurations. Habilitation thesis, Leipzig University, Leipzig.
Geiss, P.G. 2001. 'Mahallah and kinship relations: a study on residential communal

commitment structures in Central Asia of the 19th century', *Central Asian Survey*, 20 (1), 97–106.
Geiss, P.G. 2003. *Pre-Tsarist and Tsarist Central Asia: Communal Commitment and Political Order in Change*. London: Routledge.
Giese, E. 1982. 'Seßhaftmachung der Nomaden in der Sowjetunion', in F. Scholz and J. Janzen (eds), *Nomadismus: Ein Entwicklungsproblem?* Berlin: Reimer, pp. 219–230.
Giese, E. 1983. 'Nomaden in Kasachstan: Ihre Seßhaftwerdung und Einordnung in das Kolchos- und Sowchossystem', *Geographische Rundschau*, 35 (11), 575–589.
Gleason, G. 1986. 'Sharaf Rashidov and the dilemmas of national leadership', *Central Asian Survey*, 5 (3/4), 133–160.
Gleason, G. 1989. 'The political elite in the Muslim Republics of Soviet Central Asia: the dual-criterion of power', *Journal Institute of Muslim Minority Affairs*, 10 (1), 246–263.
Gleason, G. 1991. 'Fealty and loyalty: informal authority structures in Soviet Asia', *Soviet Studies*, 43 (4), 613–628.
Gleason, G. 1993. 'Central Asia: land reform and the ethnic factor', *RFE/RL Research Report*, 2 (3), 28–33.
Golden, P.B. 1992. *An Introduction to the History of the Turkic Peoples: Ethnogenesis and State Formation in Medieval and Early Modern Eurasia and the Middle East*. Wiesbaden: Harrassowitz.
Gorlin, A.C. 1985. 'The power of Soviet industrial ministries in the 1980s', *Soviet Studies*, 37, 353–370.
Grousset, R. 2002 (1970). *The Empire of the Steppes: A History of Central Asia*. New Brunswick, NJ: Rutgers University Press.
Hann, C. 1998. 'Foreword', in S. Bridger and F. Pine (eds), *Surviving Post-socialism: Local Strategies and Regional Responses in Eastern Europe and the Former Soviet Union*. London: Routledge, pp. x–xiv.
Hann, C. 2002a. 'Postsozialismus: Transformationsprozesse in Europa und Asien aus ethnologischer Perspektive', paper presented in November 2000 at 'Actually-existing Postsocialism' in Halle.
Hann, C. (ed.), 2002b. *Postsocialism: Ideals, Ideologies and Practices in Eurasia*. London: Routledge.
Hann, C. 2002c. 'Farewell to the socialist "other"', in C. Hann (ed.), *Postsocialism. Ideas, Ideologies and Practices in Eurasia*. London: Routledge, pp. 1–11.
Hann, C., Humphrey, C. and Verdery, K. 2002. 'Introduction: postsocialism as a topic of anthropological investigation', in C. Hann (ed.), *Postsocialism: Ideals, Ideologies and Practices in Eurasia*. London: Routledge, pp 1–28.
Harmatta, J. (ed.), 1999. *History of Civilisations of Central Asia*. Delhi: Motilal Banarsidass Publishers.
Hazard, J.N. 1980. *The Soviet System of Government*. Chicago, IL: University of Chicago Press.
Heuer, B. 1997. '"Nationaler Aufbruch" in Uzbekistan: Perspektiven für Frauen – Perspektiven von Frauen', in T. Eggeling, W. van Meurs, H. Sundhausen (eds), *Umbruch zur "Moderne"? Studien zur Politik und Kultur in den osteuropäischen Transformationsländern*. Frankfurt/Main: Peter Lang, pp. 133–163.
Hirsch, F. 2000. 'Toward an empire of nations: border-making and the formation of Soviet national identities', *Russian Review*, 59 (2), 201–226.
Hirsch, F. 2002. 'Race without the practice of racial politics', *Slavic Review*, 61 (1), 30–43.
Hirsch, F. 2005. *Empire of Nations: Ethnographic Knowledge and the Making of the Soviet Union*. New York: Cornell University Press.

Holdsworth, M. 1959. *Turkestan in the Nineteenth Century: A Brief History of the Khanates of Bukhara, Kokand, and Khiva.* Oxfurt: St. Antony's College Soviet Affairs Study Group.

Holzwarth, W. 2005. 'Relations between Uzbek Central Asia, the Great Steppe and Iran, 1700–1750', in Stefan Leder and Bernhard Streck (eds), *Shifts and Drifts in Nomad–Sedentary Relations* Wiesbaden: Reichert, pp. 179–216.

Humphrey, C. 2002. *The Unmaking of Soviet Life: Everyday Economies After Socialism.* Ithaca, NY: Cornell University Press.

Ilkhamov, A. 2004. 'Archaeology of Uzbek identity', *Central Asian Survey*, 23 (3–4), 289–326.

Kaiser, R.J. 1992. 'Nations and homelands in Soviet Central Asia', in R.A. Lewis (ed.), *Geographic Perspectives on Soviet Central Asia.* London: Routledge, pp. 280–311.

Kandiyoti, D. 1987. 'Emancipated but unliberated? Reflections on the Turkish case', *Feminist Studies*, 13, 317–338.

Kappeler, A. 1989. 'Die zaristische Politik gegenüber den Muslimen des Russischen Reiches', in A. Kappeler *et al.* (eds), *Die Muslime in der Sowjetunion und in Jugoslawien: Identität-Politik-Widerstand.* Köln: Markus Verlag, pp. 117–129.

Kappeler, A. 1993. *Russland als Vielvölkerreich. Entstehung – Geschichte – Zerfall.* München: C.H. Beck.

Khazanov, A.M. 1978. 'Characteristic features of nomadic communities in the Eurasian steppes', in W. Weissleder (ed.), *The Nomadic Alternative: Modes and Models of Interaction in the African–Asian Deserts and Steppes.* The Hague: Mouton.

Khazanov, A.M. 1984 *Nomads and the Outside World.* Cambridge: Cambridge University Press.

Khazanov, A.M. 1990 'Ecological limitations of nomadism in the Eurasian steppes and their social and cultural implications', *Asian and Africa Studies*, 24, 1–15.

Khazanov, A.M. 1992 'Nomads and oases in Central Asia', in J.A. Hall and I.C. Jarvie (eds), *Transition to Modernity.* Cambridge: Cambridge University Press, pp. 69–89.

Khazanov, A.M. and A. Wink (eds), 2001. *Nomads in the Sedentary World.* Richmond: Curzon Press.

Kurzman, C. 1999. 'Uzbekistan: the invention of nationalism in an invented nation', *Critique*, 15, 77–98.

Lane, D. and Ross, C. 1995. 'The CPSU ruling elite 1981–1991: commonalities and divisions', *Communist and Post-Communist Studies*, 28 (3), 339–360.

Litvinskiy, B.A. and Zhang Guang-da 1999. *The Crossroads of Civilisations: A.D. 250 to 750. History of Civilisations of Central Asia*, vol. 3. Delhi: Motilal Banarsidass Publishers.

Lubin, N. 1981. 'Assimilation and retention of ethnic identity in Uzbekistan.' *Asian Affairs*, 12, 277–285.

Madison, B.Q. 1968. *Social Welfare in the Soviet Union.* Stanford, CA: Stanford University Press.

Manz, B.F. 1999. *The Rise and Rule of Tamerlane.* Cambridge: Cambridge University Press.

Martin, T. 1998. 'The origins of Soviet ethnic cleansing.' *The Journal of Modern History*, 70 (4): 813–861.

Nerazik, E.E. (1976). 'Rural dwellings in the Khorezm (1st–14th centuries)', in *Annals of the Khorezm Archaeological-Ethnographic Expedition of the USSR Academy of Sciences*, vol. 9. Moscow: Nauka

Patnaik, A. 1995. 'Agriculture and rural out-migration in Central Asia, 1960–91', *Europe–Asia Studies*, 47 (1), 147–169.

Polian, P. 2004. *Against their Will: The History and Geography of Forced Migrations in the USSR*. Budapest: Central European University Press.

Polivanov, E.D. 1933. *Uzbekskaya Dialektologiya i Uzbekskiy Literaturniy Yazyk (K sovremennoy stadii uzbekskogo yazykovogo stroitelstva)* [Uzbek dialectology and Uzbek literary language (Modern stage of building the Uzbek language)]. Tashkent: Oqituvchi.

Pospielovsky, D. 1987. *History of Soviet Atheism in Theory and Practice, and the Believer.* 3 vols. New York: St. Martin's Press, Inc.

Rummel, R.J. 1990. *Lethal Politics: Soviet Genocide and Mass Murder Since 1917.* New Brunswick, NJ: Transaction.

Schatz, Edward. 2004. 'Modern clan politics: the power of blood.' In *Kazakhstan and beyond*. Seattle, WA: University of Washington Press

Semyonov-Tyan-Shansky, V.P. 1913. *Rossiya: Polnoye geograficheskoye opisaniye nashego otechestva (Russia: Complete Geographical Description of our Motherland), XIX.* St Petersburg: Izdanie A.F. Devriena.

Shaniyazov, K. 1978. 'Early elements in the ethnogenesis of the Uzbeks', in W. Weissleder (ed.), *The Nomadic Alternative: Modes and Models of Interaction in the African-Asian Deserts and Steppes*. The Hague: Mouton, pp. 147–155.

Shelley, L.I. 1990. 'Policing Soviet society: the evolution of state control', *Law & Social Inquiry*, 15, 479–520.

Soucek, Svat, 2000. *A History of Inner Asia*. Cambridge: Cambridge University Press.

Sterheimer, S. 1980. 'Administration for development: the emerging bureaucratic elite, 1920–1930', in W. Pintner and D. Rowney (eds), *Russian Officialdom: The Bureaucratization of Russian Society from the Seventeenth to the the Twentieth Century*, London: Macmillan, pp. 343–345.

Suny, R.G. 2000. 'Nationalities in the Russian Empire', *The Russian Review*, 59, 487–492.

Suny, R.G. and Martin, T.D. 2001. *A State of Nations: Empire and Nation-Making in the Age of Lenin and Stalin.* Oxford: Oxford University Press.

Taubman, W. 1973. *Governing Soviet Cities: Bureaucratic Politics and Urban Development.* New York: Praeger Publishers.

Tishkov, V.A. 1997. 'The culture of ethnic violence: the Osh conflict', in V.A. Tishkov (ed.), *Ethnicity, Nationalism and Conflict in and After the Soviet Union: The Mind Aflame*. London: Sage Publications, pp. 135–154.

Tishkov, V.A., Zayinchkovskaya, Z. and Vitkovskaya, G. 2005. 'Migration in the countries of the former Soviet Union', paper prepared for the Policy Analysis and Research Program of the Global Commission on International Migration.

Tolstov, S.P. 1948. *Drevniy Khorezm, Opyt istoriko-arkheologisheskogo issledovaniia* [Ancient Khorezm, Experience of Historic Archeological Study]. Moscow: Izdaniye MGU.

Vaidyanath, R. 1967. "Nationalities in the Russian Empire"', *The Russian Review*, 59: 487–492.

Wurm, S. 1954. *Turkic People of the USSR: Their Historical Background, Their Languages and the Development of Soviet Linguistic Policy.* Oxford: Central Asian Research Center in association with St. Anthony's College Soviet Affairs Study Group.

Yakubovskiy, A.Y. 1941. *K Voprosy ob Etnogeneze Uzbekskogo Naroda* [To the question of ethnogenesis of Uzbek people]. Tashkent: UzFAN.

Zabborov, I. 1999. *Buyuk Horazmsohlar davlati (Kadimij tarih sahifalari)* [Great State of Khorezmshahs (Ancient historical pages)]. Tashkent: Shark.

Zarubin, I.I. 1925. 'Spisok Narodnostey Turkestanskogo Kraya' [The list of nationalities in Turkestan]. *Trudy Komissii po izucheniyu plemennogo sostava naselenia Rossii i sopredelnykh stran*, 9.

Zhdanko, T.A. 1978. 'Ethnic communities with survivals of clan and tribal structure in Central Asia and Kazakhstan in the nineteenth and early twentieth centuries'. In W. Weissleder (ed.), *The Nomadic Alternative: Modes and Models of Interaction in the African–Asian Deserts and Steppes*. The Hague: Mouton, pp. 179–188.

3 *De jure* boundary among Uzbeks; de facto *propiska*

Yol azobi gŏr azobi
[The pain of the road is like the pain of the grave]

(An Uzbek proverb)

I have outlined the historical trajectory of nation formation processes during Soviet rule; I will now turn to the current situation of Uzbek nation formation and collective identification among Uzbeks in Tashkent. I have so far told the story about the making of Uzbek identity; in the rest of the book I will detail real challenges to the same identity. These challenges primarily constitute state policies of restricting mobility of populations, which create *de jure* boundaries among Uzbeks, dividing them into Tashkentis (*tashkentskiy*) vs others (*oblastniye*). Furthermore, these boundaries take ethnic/cultural tones on the ground as a result of further grouping and divisions among Uzbeks (five main groups).[1] In other words, *propiska* de facto provides a political field on the ground on which identity politics evolve.

In this chapter I will detail migrants' experiences of travelling and settling in the capital city of Tashkent. I will do this in two parts. First, I will try to engage the reader in the story of a long journey, an impression of travel, albeit within the same country, yet an experience similar to illegal international travel over longer distances. Second, I will present a subsequent phase of the migration process, namely arriving and settling in the big city, and the challenges of accommodation and local registration. As the title of this part suggests, I will address the personal dynamics of migration, setting the background and shaping of identification processes in the everyday interaction of migrants in Tashkent.

Mobility implies change, flexibility, new contacts and adaptation to a new environment. In a wider sense, these all relate to individual experience of the Other, shaping attitudes and behaviour. These experiences include confronting the state in all its forms and structures, as well as challenges connected with relocation in a new environment. Choice of collective identity in this context entails decisions on with whom a newly arrived migrant is willing to identify, as other options may have also opened up in this new place far from home.

In order to explain the motivations and lived experiences of migrants in Uzbekistan, I will devote considerable space to the state registration policy called *propiska*. This policy of limiting rights of the citizens within the territory of their own country makes the patterns of internal migration resemble those of international migration. These are illegal migration, inter-ethnic relations and migrant networks. When studying regions such as Uzbekistan or other post-Soviet countries in general, I argue that this simplistic dichotomy between internal vs international migration can be misleading. Furthermore, I argue that national border crossing or other geographic indicators cannot be the sole indicators of that dichotomy. Rather, I believe it is crucial to consider the patterns of migration processes, focusing migration research on the experiences of migrants themselves, instead of taking existing typology as a given.

Social developments in post-Soviet countries have taken a somewhat different pattern and character, where few Western models are necessarily applicable for analytic scrutiny of the migration processes. Talking about the extraordinary idiosyncrasies of Bolshevik rule, Conquest (1991: 3) noted that 'some of them hardly credible to foreign minds derive from a specific tradition'. Particularly, such policies as *propiska* can only be compared to similar policies in post-socialist countries, such as, for instance, the *Hukou* system in China (Chan 1999). Also in China, internal migrants have to overcome a host of bureaucratic and legal hurdles when moving within national borders.

This kind of policy restricting mobility of the population in general entailed outcomes and developments that had already been shaped and crystallised by the end of the Soviet Union. After the collapse of the Soviet Union, state policies of registration (*propiska*) became even more restrictive, which led to the formation of migration patterns where international and internal markers merged, in other words, now migrants must deal with a state culture that sees internal migration as inherently suspect, just as it views international migration. Regulation of population mobility opened up a space for state authorities to exercise further hegemony, creating severe insecurities for migrants travelling and settling in Tashkent.

The chapter contains a brief detour into the historical trajectory of the development of state regulation of the mobility of the population in general, as well as a short description of the migratory behaviour of Uzbeks. This introductory section explains the meaning and purpose of *propiska*, which is otherwise not easily understood and is a complex system in itself. I devoted much space in this book to explaining this policy, since *propiska* not only draws *de jure* boundaries among Uzbeks, but also provides a political field for collective identification on the ground. These processes of identity politics among Uzbek groups are the main plot of the story I am telling in this book. Furthermore, I delve into the stories of migrants regarding their preparations for the journey, including the setting up of strategic contacts beforehand. I will then follow the long journey from Khorezm to Tashkent, which ends with residential arrangements in the city. Furthermore, the chapter will indulge in the ethnography of the *propiska* office. On arrival, this is a priority for all migrants, since they are deemed illegal after being in the city for more than three days. I will also draw upon the experiences of those who have been unable to secure their *propiska*s, and thus live as illegal residents in Tashkent.

Propiska policies: historical trajectory

Propiska[2] has attracted the attention of a few scholars studying the Soviet period of government control (Hojdestrand 2003; Matthews 1993). *Propiska*[Ru] as an institution developed during the early period of Soviet rule.[3]

In the Soviet Union, *propiska* and the internal passport regime[4] were legitimised as strategies to ensure and control the 'proper' intermixing of the population. The official aim was thus an internationalisation and Sovietisation of the population of the Soviet Union. During the Soviet period, as far as I can recall from my parents, the *propiska* regulations in Uzbekistan (and possibly elsewhere in the USSR) were not as restrictive as they are today. *Propiska* was a matter of administrative necessity. There were no restrictions on registering at a new place of residence. People travelled and lived where they wished; much as my parents did (they came from Turkmenistan to Uzbekistan, lived in Tashkent and moved later to Urgench, Khorezm). However, some limits were imposed on the major cities in order to control the balance of the population, but there were still options for those who strongly intended to live in those 'closed cities', as Buckley (1995) called them. There were special decrees issued for capital cities and generally big cities which restricted the incoming movements.

A decree was issued especially for Moscow on 27 April 1972 which made entry to the capital more difficult (Matthews 1993: 32). During Brezhnev's rule, 'anti-parasite' campaigns were conducted in February 1970. In their course, local militias were allowed by law to enter any house or flat and check passports. Five years later, in 1975, further definitions and decrees concerning 'parasites' were established in regulations which remained unpublished (ibid.: 32). The secrecy of administrative regulations is still practised and upheld in Uzbekistan.

After the Soviet Union collapsed, independent Uzbekistan retained the registration policies of *propiska*. The Uzbek state strengthened the institutional structure of *propiska*, endowing the police and government forces with comprehensive rights of control in public and entry into private homes. Thanks to internal regulations to 'improve a [proper] registration of citizens of the Republic of Uzbekistan',[5] it became almost impossible to obtain *propiska*, especially after 1999 when 'terrorist' bombings took place in the centre of Tashkent. These restrictions on the mobility of Uzbek citizens within the territory of their own country have made most migrants at least 'half legal', if not illegal.

Without a *propiska* document, a citizen is deprived of his civil and social rights, including rights to employment, property ownership, health care, or secondary schooling. This is, in Kabeer's (2005: 18) words, a 'brutal denial of rights to the majority of citizens' by the state that challenges the notion of citizenship and political/national belonging.

The development of registration policies form Soviet to post-Soviet Uzbekistan can be described as a 'post-Soviet *propiska* paradox'. *Propiska* initially served the strategies of the Soviet government to ensure and control the 'proper' intermixing of the local populations. This was part of the above-mentioned Soviet nation-building policy (*Homo Sovietikus*). After the collapse of the Soviet Union the continuation and reconsideration of *propiska* regulations in Uzbekistan led to internal divisions within the Uzbek nation. Hindered and oppressed by state control and restrictions of movement, individuals had to rely increasingly on kinship and ethnic networks in order to find opportunities to move and resettle safely (but informally) within Uzbekistan. These dynamics are described in detail in several chapters of this book. The *propiska* paradox therefore concerns the creation of alternative spaces for social and economic security, people drawing on collective identities along ethnic lines, in conscious circumvention of state regulations and the ideology of nationalism and unity (promoted first by the Soviets, and currently by the Uzbek government).

Migration after the Soviet Union

Since Uzbekistan gained its independence in 1991, the mobility of the population has been increasing (Aman 2000; Hanks 2000). Official statistics covering the years 1996–2003 show that an annual average of 200,000 people migrate in Uzbekistan both internally and internationally. Real numbers of migrants are much higher. The last assessment indicated that 500,000 to 800,000 people worked abroad (before 2005). It was estimated that remittances sent to Uzbekistan from abroad constitute 8 percent of the Uzbek GDP. The worsening economic conditions after the collapse of the Soviet Union left Uzbeks with no choice but to become mobile and seek better income.

The potential migrants are mainly young people from the age of 17 (the age when they finish high school and up). People who are older than 55 years do not usually move out for work or permanent residence. Especially at that age, individuals start to enter the respectable age where they usually have several *kelin*s (daughters-in-law) in the house to serve them full-time, and the families are financially supported by the sons of the house (Turaeva 2012a, 2014a). If one asks them if they would like to live somewhere other than their village, they usually answer 'we are already old. Where could we go at this age? What could we do, let the youth now do that.' Only in rare cases are parents relocated by their children to a new place of residence. Thus, an average potential migrant is usually aged 18–50.

The difficulty of gaining 'legal' residency status through *propiska* and a subsequent failure of proper registration leads to the invalidity of official statistical information on population movement, both external and internal. As a result, the necessity of two types of statistics arises 'to count *de jure* and de facto population' (Dominique 2002: 807). Thus, there are no reliable statistics on internal and international migration from which to derive quantitative data concerning general migration.

International migration is also restricted. In order to leave the country, an Uzbek citizen needs to obtain an exit visa issued by the visa department of a regional police office. The visa is valid for a maximum of two years. Obtaining an exit visa is not an easy task and involves intense and unpleasant interrogations by the security services. After two years, the exit visa must be renewed.

52   Uzbek identity

After the expiry of the exit visa, Uzbek citizens are not legally permitted to travel outside of Uzbekistan in their country of current residence, but are obliged to return to Uzbekistan to renew their exit visa. For the past two years (2002–2003), Uzbek consulates abroad have stopped renewing exit visas for Uzbek citizens residing outside of the country.

There are two distinctions of abroad which are '*blijniy zarubej*^{Ru}' (near-abroad) and '*dalniy zarybej*' (far-abroad) countries. These categories were used during the Soviet Union and continue to be used after its collapse. Countries of near-abroad comprise the former Soviet Republics; the rest of the world refers to the far-abroad (Pearsall and Hanks 1998). An exit visa is not necessary for travel to the countries of the CIS (Commonwealth of Independent States). Thus, those people who go to Russia, Kazakhstan, and Kyrgyzstan are not required to possess exit visas from Uzbekistan. This also means that the exact number of people who migrate to these countries for work does not appear in the official statistics. The numbers of undocumented migrants is very high due to the socio-economic and political situation in the country.

Migration from Khorezm to Tashkent

Ways of migrating

Depending on their reason for travel, migrants can be divided into several groups: students, business travellers, resettlers and seasonal workers. Each year, students usually go in July to apply for a university or college. If the parents of the applicant have no contacts in Tashkent to provide accommodation and guidance, then those applicants join other applicant-friends with contacts in Tashkent. After finishing high school, young people know beforehand who is going to apply where. The application documents must be submitted in person during the fixed annual application period. Application deadlines and test dates are the same for all of the universities throughout Uzbekistan. This restricts the applicants' choice to only one university at a time (one can apply only once per year). In the case of failure, the applicants can only apply to professional training schools which have deadlines later than university admissions in order to accept failed university applicants. Thus, July and August are very busy, with applicants coming from all over Uzbekistan to Tashkent since most of the universities are concentrated in Tashkent. Additionally, though, and after a large students' strike in Tashkent, almost all of the universities have been forced to open *filials*^{Ru} (daughter institutions) in almost all regional centres of Uzbekistan. As part of the agreement to prepare for the admission to university, some students are accompanied by their private tutors. The private tutor business itself has grown into a very lucrative one, and is even institutionalised by business-minded professionals, mostly university teachers. Since then, students in high schools have changed their priorities from finishing school to successfully enrolling into private courses offered by either school teachers or university teachers. Here, they prepare for the relevant one of three subjects needed to pass the university admission tests. In this way, students usually have two or three private tutors. When this takes the form of a private school, it offers all of the required subjects, which are limited in number. The competition among tutors in this business has grown very high, and tutorial services have extended to offering teaching until the very last day before the university test, 31 July. This sometimes requires travelling to Tashkent, and teachers or students may offer free accommodation in Tashkent for the period leading up to the tests. Students are required to travel to Tashkent in order to submit their applications personally and register from the end of June until the end of July. The test day for all universities is 1 August.

If a group of students decide to go together, they agree upon the date once they have established where they can stay in Tashkent. If the place of origin is a village, there is always at least one contact person who lives in Tashkent, or travels there frequently to sell rice or other commodities. After that person is contacted they may agree to the students staying in his flat in Tashkent. Below is the story of a student (Guliston), 19, whose trip to Tashkent was organised through her father. She went to Tashkent after finishing her school at the age of 17. She is from a rural area of Khorezm, and her family lives on a small trade, growing rice and vegetables.

> I came to Tashkent to apply for Agricultural Economy as everybody did. My father has a friend whose daughter [Nodira] is studying in Tashkent but she is in her third year of the Medical Institute (*TashMI*). She stays together with two other girls from Khorezm in the apartment of her father's friend's flat who is a trader and also from our village. So together with two girls from our village who also wanted to apply to the same faculty we travelled in a bus to Tashkent in early July.
>
> (Guliston, 19, 25 January 2006, Tashkent)

Below is another story of a student (Pulat) who came in a group from his village with his tutor to Tashkent. He is 29 years old, working as a dentist in two different private clinics. He has come to Tashkent as a student, and stayed there after his graduation.

> I had been preparing to enter the university with a private tutor on chemistry and biology as I wanted to enter dentistry department of the medical institute. I used to go to a gymnasium in another village [like a boarding-type school, but not compulsory: only if the student lives far from the school's location]. I came together with ten other boys with my teacher who was preparing us for university admissions. It is a tradition that usually a teacher brings his students to Tashkent. Usually a teacher teaches to prepare for university exams on a private basis. Therefore, he brings them to Tashkent and teaches them in Tashkent after the documents are submitted till the end of July. There are about 15–20 days in between to wait until the test takes place in August first.
>
> Once when we were living in the flat with my brother and another relative of mine who was also studying in Tashkent, my brother's teacher

called from Gurlen [a district in Khorezm region] and asked if he can come for few days with his students. He came with six students, we were living in a two room flat, and I could not find any space to sleep. I was happy I did not see them during the day as I came home late only to sleep. Then I asked my brother not to let his teacher bring his students next time since he was doing business. It is not about being a good host. Hospitality and business do not go together. They are two different things. In our village there are three teachers who bring their students to Tashkent.

I lived with the uncle [MB], Bahodir aka, of Komil who came with me at the very beginning when I first arrived to Tashkent.

(Pulat, 29, 3 February 2006, Tashkent)

As was stated by Pulat in his judgement of their village teacher (his brother's high school teacher in math), often the contacts are abused for the sake of profit. In this case Pulat measures the politeness in respect to his brother's teacher, and the limits of it – namely financial benefits for the requester [the teacher] at the expense of the host's limited accommodation capacities in Tashkent. This kind of abuse of contacts in Tashkent by their co-villagers is not promising in the long term, as the relationship is not reciprocal. Those who have long-term interests in maintaining a reliable contact in Tashkent must ensure that they maintain reciprocity by offering something in return.[6]

As the examples above show, there is a particular way of coming to Tashkent as a student or private tutor involved in the business of the preparation for university admission. As shown above, the main concern before coming to Tashkent is the vitally important issue of securing cheap or free accommodation. Those who have their own accommodation gain much symbolic capital in the eyes of their kin groups and co-villagers back 'home'. On the other hand, they often complain that their flat or house becomes a *gostinitsa*[Ru] (hotel) for free.

In my view, their often negative views can be balanced by the fact that this symbolic capital is used by the families, kin or even friends of the hosting family while the host in Tashkent must cope with the never-ending guests. It was even often pronounced as the main reason for their unwillingness for contact with too many people 'at home'. The most practised avoidance strategy was to find good reasons to limit visits when back in Khorezm, even when one had been invited as a guest of honour. However, even if a migrant visiting home finds a good reason not to meet others, people still visit them with presents. Resettlers other than students and teachers act in much the same way. Nevertheless, their concerns are not only in securing initial accommodation, but, more important, *propiska* in Tashkent.

Several guest visits are made to those who have contact persons in Tashkent. Presents are delivered to please the host in exchange for information or further support in the city. The process of making future contacts in Tashkent can sometimes take place several months or weeks before actual departure. Even daughters may be strategically given or taken to a family who has contacts in Tashkent. In the section below I present a case illustrating this strategic marriage, as well as the other ways of securing contact before travelling.

Securing contacts in Khorezm for Tashkent (a case study)

Nazira, 55, and Batir, 57, have five grown-up children – three daughters and two sons – and live in a small village in Khorezm. The three daughters are 'married out' and each have several children themselves (*balali bop ketgan*). Their elder son is married and has two children, and lives together with his parents. Nazira and Batir are both retired (*veteran truda*[Ru])[7] and receive pensions. Their elder son works on their fields (they have a land plot of 12 *sotok* (1,200 m^2) where they grow rice and vegetables) together with his wife. The 'only income we have is from our land' explains Nazira.[8] Her youngest son finished school two years ago and then was a second-year student in Urgench in the Physical Training Faculty. Nazira gathered her relatives for *Kengyash* (elder's meeting) to advise on the marriage of her son, where they decided to ask for the youngest daughter of Shuhrat and Almagul. Before they went to the house of Shuhrat and Almagul, Nazira inquired around who might know more about this family, as well as their daughter's age. She also talked to her son about the girl (Gulnora) and showed him her picture in order to confirm his agreement to marriage. His answer was the answer of a 'proper obedient son', saying, '[y]ou know these things better than I do as you lived most of your lives. If you will find the girl good then I will be of the same opinion.'

Almagul and Shuhrat have two daughters (Altinay and Gulnora) and two sons (Eshmat and Orazmat). One of their youngest sons was a student in Tashkent (one of my key informants). Almagul's uncle's son (MBS), Gafur, has lived in Tashkent for more than 30 years. He is *domla* (a university teacher) in a 'very prestigious' university and owns several flats in the city. His three sons also live in Tashkent and the entire family is in the rice trade business. Gafur owns a big house in the same village as his eldest son, who takes care of the land plots of the entire family. In Tashkent, his three other sons sell the rice sent by the eldest son from Khorezm.

Two years after marriage Altinay's (Almagul's first daughter) husband became 'very rich', meaning he bought a 'new' car and renovated the house of his parents where he lived together with his family since he started to bring rice to Tashkent for sale. Nazira, as any other co-villager of Almagul's, knows very well about their family and her kin, particularly the famous Gafur, whom everyone knows in the village, since he celebrates all of the lifecycle events of his entire family, together with all of its kinship members. Nazira gathered several respected elderly women in the village and her sister in the early evening before the sunset to go to the house of Almagul. The *sovchi* women's group arrived unannounced at the house of the family where the girl was about to be asked for marriage. The sudden and spontaneous arrival of the women's group at the house where there are unmarried girls is considered a good sign – namely '*sovchi* came for' one of the daughters in the house. Nazira's fellows in her *sovchi* group praised her son, highlighting his education, future plans, financial status, etc. During our interviews Nazira, of course, did not mention the real reasons behind the marriage plan of her youngest son (Murat). I was only told about how she organised the marriage of Murat and about what he was doing then. After the marriage, the newly married couple is invited by relatives from both sides and presents are given to the bride when she visits a relative of her in-laws and the groom is given presents when he visits his in-laws (*Qudala*). Murat was invited by his wife's relatives (Gafur *akam*) in Tashkent. They both went to Tashkent and were met with full respect and he was offered an opportunity to engage in the rice trade if he had access to rice in Khorezm. He later became 'very successful' (in three years) and bought a two-room flat in Tashkent in Chilanzar district. His wife remained with his parents to help with the household and children of the other *kelin*[9] in the house, since she (the other *kelin*) had to work in their plot for growing rice and other things. Gulnora took care of her little daughter as well as the other two children in the house (of her *avsin*[Kh] or HBW).

Establishing these contacts before departure is not a very easy task and particularly is not very accessible to young women due to their low social status both in their families and in their communities. The only way for them to go to Tashkent is marriage, which is welcomed by their kin and friends living in Tashkent. Migrants living there consider the girls 'at home' more decent than those who have grown up in the city. That is why it is very rare that, independent of marriage, young women successfully make it alone to Tashkent. I will present one of those rare examples of having successfully achieved 'establishment' in Tashkent as a rice trader. Zuhra, a rice trader in Tashkent, is a young woman of 29, has two children and is divorced.

> I came to Tashkent two years ago. Before I came here I was living in my parents' house in my village. I got married when I finished my school at 17. When I was 21 I had given birth to my second child and got sick, I had inflammation and complications afterwards. The place where I went for marriage (*meni tushgan yerim*) was not very well off. They were not happy that I could not work in the fields any more, and I was staying at home with children, doing all the housework, cooking and looking after the home cattle. In the village it was important to have as much labour as possible to be able to work in the field, as most of the living comes from the field. I went to live at my parents' place after 6 years of living together with my in-laws.
>
> In my parents' house I was a burden with my two children and I decided to go to Tashkent to make some money. My brother sometimes takes rice to sell to Tashkent during the season which my family grows at home. Our *daiyi* [MB] have initially helped my brother to get his business going. I asked him if he would help me to get to Tashkent to work, and he agreed. He took me with him and introduced me to the sellers in the bazaar in Tashkent.... It was also difficult to get registration. I did not have registration during the first five months and had constant problems with the police. Gradually I made contacts and found ways to get my *propiska* [*propiskamni togirladim*/fixed my *propiska*]. I asked my uncle [MB] to help me with my *propiska*.

(Zuhra, 29, 12 May 2006, Tashkent)

Figure 3.1 Preparing rice for the sale in the bazaar: Khorezmian rice traders in Tashkent, 2005.

She decided to go to Tashkent to escape the social pressure and make earnings for herself and her children. She divorced her husband since neither her in-law family nor her husband could afford her and her children anymore, due to her health problems. In the case of the divorced woman outlined above, she usually would not be encouraged to leave the home village to work. Instead, she would be expected to find another husband and remarry. Only if this would be impossible and after considerable time has passed would she be supported to travel, find a job and become self-sufficient. In that case, family ties or friendship and acquaintances are employed to gain information, and establish 'useful' contacts. In the case above the sister used her brother to support her, since he was involved in the rice trade in Tashkent.

In this section I have illustrated strategies of establishing contacts in Khorezm before travelling to Tashkent. These strategies were represented by two case studies, namely strategic marriage and kinship ties There are many more aspects of strategic marriage planning which I will discuss in more detail later in this book. Before I continue with the next section on travelling, I would like to demonstrate one example from an intermarriage pattern taken from a larger kinship diagram. Most of these group members reside in Tashkent, though originally come from one of the districts in Khorezm. Later in this book I will talk more about this kinship group and their social organisation.

Journey from a region to the capital

In the following I will present a thick description of a long journey from Urgench to Tashkent, drawn largely from my own travelling experiences (both in the times I was a migrant myself, and also during my field research). It can be taken as a typical experience of travelling by bus in the summer time. Travelling by bus in the winter is even worse, considering the severe weather conditions, and more dangerous as icy roads are only covered by sand or salt in the cities but not on the highways in between. When the roads are icy, travellers prefer taking the train to Tashkent instead of risking their lives by bus – that is, if they are lucky and train tickets are not sold out.

The transport preference is also decided on the basis of how quickly passengers would like to arrive, since passport control on the way in a big bus takes quite a long time.

> We took a bus from Urgench in early July ... at the check points we did not have any trouble with passing *postdan* [check point] as soldiers [at the check points] know the application period for the university entrance. They usually check if you have application documents at hand. It was really hot and the bus was more than full, I really do not like travelling by bus and all these check points. Until they will check all the passports and the luggage it takes at least one hour on each post. That is why I prefer taking *hunday* [a small van] because it is not only few hours quicker but also there are only 12 people to check the passports from.
>
> (Pulat, 29, 3 February 2006, Tashkent)

Bus ride Urgench–Tashkent

It is a hot Saturday afternoon in early July. The temperature in the shade shows 45 °C. The sun burns the skin within the first 5–10 minutes. Streets are not as busy as usual; some taxis disappear down narrow streets. One typical point of departure is the central bus station where 'state' buses, usually Mercedes Benz, leave for various regions. At other smaller stations nearby private buses, small vans and taxis go to Tashkent.

There are five ways to get to Tashkent from Khorezm. By aeroplane it takes one hour and 20 minutes; by bus one travels around 18–20 hours; small vans take 2–3 hours less; by train one is 23–24 hours on the road, and by taxi it is 10–12 hours.

The cheapest way is to go by bus; a little more expensive is a van, and then comes the train, a taxi and finally the aeroplane as the most expensive way of travelling. Buses, vans and taxis take the same route. These three types of transportation are the most common. The route from Urgench to Tashkent is a little more than 1,000 km. The moment you start approaching the departure point, you are attacked by drivers' assistants or people advertising the vehicle. They start with the same question: 'Where are you going and how many of you are going?' You are literally pushed in the direction of the advertised vehicle.

Before setting out, the bus driver asks if anybody has problems with his/her passport. Passengers with 'problems' in their passports usually 'talk' (*gaplashadi/galishadi*) to a driver about it and ask if he can 'take them through' the check points (*postdan otiradi*). The journey starts with a driver asking some elderly man among passengers to make a blessing for the journey (*omin atibaradi*), which sounds like 'let our journey be without barriers, let us go and return in good health and safe, let our journey happen, Amen'.

The bus continues the journey until the first check point. It is full of smoke within the first three hours due to the men smoking in the back. It is around six or seven in the evening, and everybody wonders where the driver stops for dinner. The first check point is passed. The driver did not get out of the bus, but handed over several bills of 200 *soms* (less than US$1) to the officer who approached the driver's window and the latter gave the sign to a soldier to open the metal roadblock. The bus passed the check point. Another two hours passed and the most notorious check points lie ahead under the name of *Sary May* and *Bukhara post*, known to be the most severe check points where people usually get into trouble. These are considerably bigger than other check points and have many more soldiers and officers standing outside in front of their three-storied building along the highway, as well as inside the building. The check point is in the middle of nowhere in the desert.

The bus stops at the *Sary May* check point and two officers enter the bus. Everybody has their passports at hand. Passengers are prepared to show their passports at any time at check points. Some want to complain, but do not dare to do so openly. Any complications will prolong the journey. Some passengers are asked to get off the bus and follow the officer. Others are asked to open their luggage. The driver usually announces that the bus is approaching the check point and asks the passengers to prepare their passports. I will relate here some stories of those who were asked to get off the bus.

A young man who transports TV sets and other electronics
I bring different technical home appliances from Urgench; it is cheaper there because they bring them from Tashauz [Turkmenistan]. Usually I transport from three to five pieces each time that is why I do not put them into the truck and just simply take them with me in the bus. I have a friend who has a little shop where he can help me to sell them. I do not stay long in Tashkent only for a couple of days. Often I bring the appliances on the basis of orders. When I return back from Tashkent I buy things that are more expensive in Khorezm so that I use the money paid for the appliances. It is not so bad but the only problem on the way when passing check points. I always get into trouble with the police in the check points although I do not have so many things with me. In most of the cases I will have to pay them off, but I cannot pay if they ask too much. Usually I ask passengers to tell the police that one item is theirs so that not all items are in my name. It works often, but if officers want to get money nothing helps and no reasons can be given. Usually when you're asked to get off the bus, you're asked

about the luggage you have. They ask for which purposes I am bringing several items. I answer that they are presents, but that does not always work.

Passengers who have trouble on the check points usually get away with bribery. There are two types of passengers, the first who regularly travels, and the other who is new to doing business or dealing with check points. The new traveller has the most trouble in passing through them. Those who had to transport things in the buses pay off or negotiate the fee to pay with the officers at the check points:

> On the way coming to Tashkent I didn't have problems with my passport but I had problems together with my brother as we had two sacks of rice with us transporting in the bus to Tashkent.
> (Zuhra, 29, 12 May 2006, Tashkent)

Those who have problems with passports have major trouble if their passports have expired and they had not replaced them on time, whether they had a permanent *propiska* stamp or not. It is also a serious problem if someone has travelled outside the country and has several visas on his/her passport (it was my passport), then one is usually checked, together with one's luggage, and interrogated by several officers, which takes a long time. It is best to be very polite and show no signs of anger – as polite as possible. Passengers and drivers try not to make an always-trouble-seeking officer angry or irritated otherwise 'he will find problems if he wants' so one should watch one's tone and intonation when asked questions by a checking officer. If one or two passengers are asked to get off the bus, the remaining passengers and especially the drivers worry over how long it might take, or if there will be the usual dilemma of leaving the passenger at the check point and continuing the journey without him/her.

Finally, the bus arrives at the dinner place. The most prominent place to have dinner is *Kalta Korgon*. On all of the outskirts of small settlements, the chains of cafés are situated along the highway. Waiters, usually young teenagers or boys of around 18–19, stand along the street beckoning passing vehicles towards their cafés. Most of the cafés along the highway are small, about 20–30 m^2 in all, and have one to several tables outside. The chains of cafés stretch along the highway for about 1–2 km. Usually small vehicles like cars or vans stop in these small cafés, as buses prefer bigger dining halls to stop to eat. Intensive traffic, mostly from Tashkent to other cities of Uzbekistan, has created favourable conditions for the growth of the small catering businesses in the settlements and towns situated along the highways to Tashkent. It has also prompted competition among the businesses, which led to an increase in the quality of food and service. Shuttle traders also found their niche within the chain of food cafés.

I have travelled from Khorezm to Tashkent and back since 1999 on a regular basis, at least twice each year. It is amazing how highway cafés, at least, have changed from small one-room cafés to huge, two-level, modern dining halls. The most prominent café where many and most vehicles stop to have an evening meal is crowded from 9 to 11 p.m., with around 250–300 people at once. There is a parking space before one goes into the café, and around there small stands form a mini-market in the open air, where shuttle traders sell snacks and sweets, souvenirs and fruits. Each stand has a small bulb to light the products which young women and men sell, sometimes with their children. They have good sales at the café as an average of four or five buses, as well as small vehicles, stop to have an evening meal.

After the bus stops everybody runs to the toilet, which is behind the building of the café. Most of them are outside, around 20–25 m from the building. Usually, people who travel alone find themselves some company to pass the hour of the meal stop at this big, crowded and noisy place. Women try to get company to go to the toilet, as it requires a few minutes walking in the dark behind the building, where empty fields stretch into nowhere.

The toilets are usually without running water and seldom cleaned. Back from the toilet, there is a tub from a pipe arranged into the ground, or there is a barrel filled with cold water, and a metal stick at the bottom of the vessel which can be lifted, where some water spills out to wash the hands. There is neither towel nor soap, so all must have a handkerchief to dry their hands, which can be very unpleasant outside in a cold winter.

Now entering a huge café hall which has seating space both in and outside, one can see *shashlyk* (Uzbek national dish with grilled meat) smoke coming from the right side where there are two big *tandirs* (Uzbek traditional oven made out of clay) located, and customers and waiters queuing for *somsa* (baked dough with meat filling) there. The garden is filled with plastic tables and chairs where people are eating traditional Uzbek food. On the left-hand side there is a kitchen where crowds of people without a proper queue are trying to get something to eat. Some people do not trust waiters and some are not willing to pay waiters and rather get into the crowd in front of the window where the food is sold. The menu is nicely printed and hung on the wall and does not have to be changed as only a few dishes from the traditional menu are on offer. The drivers get free food at any café as a bonus for stopping there and bringing customers. They can order as much as they want and whatever they want from the menu. The whole meal-eating ceremony lasts about one hour. Passengers who finish the meals quickly loiter at the shuttle traders' stand lights and wait until others come, as the bus is locked by drivers and will be open when everybody has returned from the café.

Men usually have spirits with their meals. This is usually vodka, which can be detected from the lingering smell of vodka in the salon of the bus after 'dinner'. After a long period of enduring heavy cigarette smoke, the smell of vodka is added and becomes unbearable, especially when the tired feet of heavy men are freed from the sometimes incorrectly sized or uncomfortable shoes. There are still 13–14 hours left to reach Tashkent – if the bus does not break down on the way.

Arrival

If this is their first time in Tashkent, newcomers from Khorezm are usually met at the bus station by their relatives, friends or acquaintances. Their first and initial destination for staying at least one month is the place (flat, house or dormitory) of those relatives, friends or acquaintances. Pulat (29) continued his story of his first arrival as a student to Tashkent to prepare for his entrance exam to the medical university to become a dentist.

> Komil's family helped a lot, Bahodir *aka* [a kinship term used for showing respect for particular age][10] strictly made us sleep at ten in the evening and would wake us up at 4 in the morning, read and prepare for the test until 11 or 12 in the afternoon and then we went running and swimming in the canal Ankhor and came back to eat and then again continued preparing. We only paid for our food and nothing else.
>
> So two boys and me were admitted to the university successfully and we moved to the hostel. There we found another three Khorezmian guys but they were third and fourth year students. So we found one 'section' for us which was two rooms with two beds in one room and three in the other one. It is really difficult to find a room in a hostel, there are no empty rooms so that everybody could live together.[11]
>
> However gradually (*asta-sekin*) we made arrangements so that we were all Khorezmians living on the same floor.
>
> After that in three years my brother came with another relative of ours, they stayed with me in my hostel, and prepared to enter the university. I had very good contacts and it was not a problem to bring my brother or anybody else to my room. After they entered university they decided to move out to rent a flat so I had to join them. We rented a flat from our friends but we have changed so many flats as the owners were not nice or *uchastkoviy*s [policemen of the neighbourhood] gave us a hard time.
>
> (Pulat, 29, 3 February 2006, Tashkent)

Zuhra, 29, a young divorced woman rice trader briefly described her accommodation arrangements when she first arrived in Tashkent together with her brother:

> We stayed in the flat of our uncle [FB] with his wife and four children. I started to sell part of my brother's rice and partly selling others' rice. My children stayed at home with my parents.
>
> (Zuhra, 29, 12 May 2006, Tashkent)

Student girls continued to tell about their initial stay in Tashkent to prepare for the entrance exam on 1 August:

> We were met by Nodira in the Hippodrome. She took us to her flat [two-room flat] in Chilanzar. We had brought bread, vegetables, oil and rice with

us. From time to time our parents sent us meat, rice and bread from home in the bus with some passengers, and then we met the bus with food in the Hippodrome. So we didn't have to worry about food, and the only thing we had to pay was transport which is very expensive in Tashkent. The flat payment we all shared. After the test [1 August for all university admissions] we stayed and waited for *mandat* [admission decisions announcement, usually 13–14 August]. We were successful but one of my friends failed and went back to the village to prepare for the next year with her *repetitor* [private tutor]. In September, I and my friend moved to the students' *obshejitye*[Ru] [hostel]. We shared one room for the first two years and then moved to our shared flat with other three girls from our village, also students from different faculties in our university.

(Guliston, 19, 25 January 2006, Tashkent)

These, then, are some fragments of migrants' and students' stories about their first arrival to Tashkent and their initial arrangements for accommodation. In all of these cases, including all of my other informants and their stories of first coming to Tashkent, they confirm that they stayed with their relatives, parents' friends, friends and acquaintances. At the beginning of their stay, migrants and newcomers need initial assistance and support from their families. Food products including vegetables, rice, bread and even sometimes meat (usually in the winter) are sent by families (usually parents) of migrants. Students often receive these food products and money from home during their entire study time in Tashkent.[12] Others who came to Tashkent to make money (*ozgina pul ishlaik dab galivadik*[Kh]/came hoping to make a bit of money) and if possible to stay and live in Tashkent, depend on the support of their families until they start earning and sending some remittances home (which is rare, as life in Tashkent is demanding). The main aim after having 'established' oneself to a certain degree is to get permanently settled, which is very valuable capital in itself for the relatives back at home for its symbolic nature above any monetary considerations. This capital brings social recognition and status to the family members back at 'home' (*oy yandakila*[Kh]/those back at home) in Khorezm, and even more to the migrant himself. This capital can be used for extracting some services, high-value presents during lifecycle events (e.g. bringing musicians; drinks – a very expensive part of the event; animals – usually sheep), employment in Khorezm, and other favours in return for initial support in Tashkent. A look at the accommodation options and regions in Tashkent is helpful to draw a picture of residential arrangements, which are often arranged along kinship and ethnic lines.

Residential arrangements

Residential arrangements is an important topic in the discussion of identity politics. Physical boundaries are an important aspect in making differences and designation of social status in general. Each region of Tashkent city has its own prestige and difference according to the residential pattern, as well as its economic, demographic or political function. Chilanzar, Akmal Ikromov, and Sergeli are notorious for being places of residence for '*priezjiye/oblast'niye*'[13] (newcomers), since the biggest bazaars are located in these regions.[14]

Other locations in Tashkent are relatively prestigious and reflect the higher level of social status of people residing there. Subsequently, the security situation in these regions differs from those mentioned above. The higher class of Tashkent lives mostly in the central part of the city, where Western European-style stores, supermarkets, restaurants and clubs are situated; accordingly rent and flat prices are usually higher in that region. A middle-class group lives in Shayhantaur and Yunusabad regions, which are also considered as relatively central. Lower middle classes are usually newcomers and live near big markets (bazaars), predominantly Chilanzar, Akmal Ikromov, and Hamza regions.

Poor people live in the mostly industrial region where plants and factories are generally situated in the suburban parts of the city. The houses are shabby, and water and sewage facilities have either not been set up or not maintained.

The distinction is subjective, but more or less approximate and not necessarily defined. I have incorporated the distinction here because it was cross-checked with many informants and by comparing the prices of accommodation of different regions of Tashkent from local newspapers.

As employment with state organisations is formally constrained by regulations provisioned by *propiska*, as well as very low salaries, migrants from other regions of Uzbekistan have to occupy the economic niches that do not require local registration (*propiska*). Only in this way can they earn more than an average state salary, which is not higher than US$50, even for a high-ranking university teacher.

Khorezmians who have moved to Tashkent reside in different regions of the city according to their proximity to their kin members. They can be divided into groups by occupation and family networks. I have separated them out by the intensity of connections among them. The division was by occupation and mostly by family networks. Khorezmians' first priority to be included in the group is belonging to the kinship group. If this is not the case, their second preference will be given to friends from the same village or town; the last preference is for members of the same ethnic group. Therefore, the Khorezmians I have studied were mostly part of family networks, besides being rice traders or construction workers.

Most of the rice traders were resident within walking distance from the bazaar, where they sold their rice brought from Khorezm. Most of the rice traders come from Gurlen district of Khorezm region, and most of them are females aged 20 and above. The average age is 27–30. Most of the rice traders, who live near the bazaar and trade rice there, are interconnected if they do not have other relatives or families living in Tashkent.

Another family network has located itself in the neighbourhood, which is the poor region I mentioned above. This group originally comes from the same region and village in Khorezm region. Many members of the families work as doctors in the same medical clinic of Tashkent.

Among these family networks the older families came to Tashkent first as students in the 1970s. Subsequently, they stayed to work and 'established' themselves with the help of their richer relatives, after getting married. Establishing oneself in Tashkent means to obtain *propiska* first, and then to find a permanent job or get into business and subsequently buy a flat.

Renting a flat has a negative connotation within Uzbeks and Khorezmians due to their strong sense of locality. When one is at home, it goes without saying that a person has 'his own' place to live in Khorezm. It has a negative connotation to live in an apartment house in Khorezm unless he or she is coming from another region. Living in apartment houses or flats is considered to be characteristic of the Russian population (*orisladin*[Kh]/like Russians). Young couples who are living in apartment houses are defined as those who have run away from their jobs to serve their parents, and failed to respect them. Another category of people living in apartment house flats are young couples, usually the first children in the family, as the last child is supposed to stay at the parents' house. Others are provided with the flat because of lack of space at home, and are promised support from parents to build them a house.

There are other options to arrange accommodation after or before arrival in Tashkent. A good example may be the case of a relatively large and well-connected network of Khorezmians whom I happened to study. They comfortably located themselves in one of the prestigious regions of the city. Almost all of the families that have come to that neighbourhood have been brought by their family members or friends who already live there. For this particular neighbourhood, a woman (Sayora) maintaining the network is a person to contact if help is needed to find a place in the neighbourhood.[15] As she once put it:

> If you want to move to Tashkent or want to bring your family just let me know how much you can spend for your accommodation and I will do my best to build you a nice small but beautiful house. It is better than to live in small flats without your own garden.

She even showed me her catalogue with interior and exterior designs for houses. Most Khorezmians in this neighbourhood are 5–15 minutes' walking distance from each other.

'*Propiska* is the first thing to do and organise before coming to Tashkent; otherwise you cannot come and live here'[16]

Who needs propiska?

Before I go into in the ethnography of the *propiska* office and its clients, it is necessary to say a few words about the nature of *propiska*, and who needs it. Earlier in this chapter, I briefly outlined the historical development of the *propiska* policy during Soviet rule, and after its collapse.

Those who are not very much 'exposed' to state authorities, such as traders who travel back and forth to Khorezm, usually working in private houses, private firms, etc. do not find it necessary to obtain *propiska*. But those who are 'exposed' or 'act' or are 'visible' in the spheres where they are required to present the documents, such as traders with their granted space in selling stands in the bazaars, employees in state institutions or students, have to get their *propiska*.

There are two types of *propiska*s available for the citizens of Uzbekistan: short-term and permanent. The short-term *propiska* (*vremennaya propiska*) is usually applied for by most of the migrants in Tashkent since the permanent *propiska* (*postoyannaya propiska*) is by now unofficially closed for the city of Tashkent. The short-term *propiska* is issued for three to six months (in 2014 the term was shortened and one now needs to renew it every three months). It is almost impossible to obtain permanent propiska and the informal fees for it are much too high (several thousand US dollars), whereas short-term *propiska* is possible to obtain in a short period of time, such as one week, depending on whether one has all documents at hand. The conditions for obtaining a short-term propiska are also difficult, requiring a long list of documents including the official agreement of the flat owner and proof of the reason to reside in Tashkent (e.g. employer's request).

Propiska[17] remains the biggest problem that a person faces when deciding to move to Tashkent, particularly after 1999, when Tashkent was shaken by explosions in the city centre and the government tried to restrict any mobility both internally (*propiska* system) and internationally (exit visas). Officially the Constitution of Uzbekistan grants free mobility within the territory of Uzbekistan. Article 28 of the Constitution of Uzbekistan says 'Any citizen of the Republic of Uzbekistan shall have the right to freedom of movement in the territory of the Republic, as well as free entry to and exit from it, *except in events specified by law*' (emphasis mine).

Propiska *office*

In the following, I will present a thick description of the *propiska* office in order to give the reader an approximate idea drawn from my own impressions. *The Propiska*/registration office is situated in the area known as a residence location of migrants. The office is integrated into a regional police station. Getting off the bus, one has to pass a small trading spot to reach the office. The small trading spot looks like an open mini-bazaar, where one can buy food products such as bread, milk and vegetables sold at very small stands. The spot is located at the end corner of a living quarter of Soviet-style apartment houses, surrounded by the green of tall and ancient trees, and one has to pass a group of drunken men of different ages who hang around an alcohol-selling mini-shop which sells vodka in small amounts out of bottles (*v razlivnuyu*[Ru]). Once past all these selling points, apartment buildings appear on both sides of the road. On the left-hand side, right after the selling spot, there is an apartment house where a flat on the ground floor has been made into an office, and the big placard in front of the entrance advertises services written in Russian '*passportniye uslugi: oformleniye dokumentov na vremenuyu propisky, zapolneniye anket dlya vyezdnyh viz, raspechatka i kopii*' (passport services: preparation of documents for short-term *propiska*, filling out of application forms for exit visas, printing and copy services). This service centre is hardly to be passed without notice by anyone who is going to the passport office in the police department. After one apartment building there is a single-storey, long building with wooden double doors, and a sign that says in Uzbek, written in Cyrillic, 'Regional Department of Republican Department of Internal Affairs', which means a local police department responsible for the given district of Tashkent. When one enters, there is a long, dark corridor with numerous rooms on both sides. The doors have signs indicating names of persons and room numbers. There is a door in the middle of the corridor which has a big room with several chairs and a small quadrangle opening on the wall to another room where a young female receptionist sends applicants to the appropriate rooms. Working hours are general for the whole building, but the persons inside have obviously different schedules that are not found in the signs indicated on each door. The last door at the end of the long, dark corridor is always locked, which is a toilet (for staff only and which has rarely running water). The 'Visa Department' is located on the right side at the end of the corridor, the entrance of which is a small door leading to a small hallway and two small adjacent rooms. The so-called 'waiting room' is actually an entrance floor from another corridor where two persons can just about fit. The room of the secretary of the 'department' is much like a kind of broom cupboard. Adjacent to this is the office of the 'department' head who sits in a relatively more spacious environment.

 The 'department boss is a tall but heavy man (Halmurat) in his late forties, wearing a green uniform. He sits on a very large, black leather mobile chair next to a long, yellow, polished table covered with small papers, folders and a very 'fancy' desk organiser. On the left-hand side there is a kind of exhibition corner where enlarged portraits of two small girls (his daughters), work-related brochures and other small articles have piled up. To the side is a high cupboard, almost empty, with only a few basic necessities for making coffee or tea. There is also a very comfortable armchair in the right-hand corner, in addition to normal chairs placed directly in front of the table of the 'boss'. On the wall in the centre, behind the chair of the boss, there is a portrait of Islam Karimov (the current president of Uzbekistan).[18] In the left corner of the room there is a small TV which is always on when Halmurat is in the office, with the volume down, so one can only see the pictures moving, without sound. He puts the volume up if there are no visitors, but this is very rare. On the left-hand side of the big table there is a clumsy and old multi-channel phone that is connected to each room in the building but does not have access to the outside telephone network. There is a separate modern-type black phone which also says the number of the incoming caller very loudly. Next to that, there is the latest model of Motorola mobile phone that rings non-stop, together with the landline phone, creating a cacophony of different ringtones: one played on the mobile phone (depending on who calls) plus the number boomed out by the black landline telephone. The landline telephone is usually left unanswered, while each call on the mobile phone is picked up.

It is amazing to observe Halmurat's style of working with two telephone receivers in each hand, talking to a visitor, and at the same time signing documents that are brought by a secretary from time to time. The waiting room is always full of people who hover at the door, regardless of the boss' presence or absence. The main thing is that the working hours are written on the door plank, whereas others do not have such a sign.

I have known Halmurat since 2002. I first met him in Tashkent. My colleague introduced me to him to obtain my own *propiska* when I first arrived to Tashkent to work as a teacher at a local university in 2002. He helped me a lot with organising my short-term registration/*propiska* every six months during two years of my stay in Tashkent before I left for Germany. When I came back to do my fieldwork in Tashkent, I again contacted him to organise my registration and exit visa. We had known each other for three years when I came to do my fieldwork. We had lunch together once when I arrived. I told him about my present work and research. He made his career as a police officer after he served in the army as a lieutenant, following graduation from his university. A university degree gives any graduate a lieutenant degree if he goes on to military service or gains employment within the security structures in Uzbekistan.

Halmurat helps to obtain *propiska*s, and also serves as a good contact if somebody is in trouble with the police. He is well-connected and able to solve any legal problems. According to the visitors, the type of their requests and their regional background, they can be divided into the following categories. The first one is complete 'strangers' (*begonalar*) as Halmurat put it, who addresses Halmurat according to his 'official' position and direct capacity in the police station connected to passports and other papers. These clients usually reside officially in the district for which the police station is responsible.[19] His indirect duties also include supervision of the local registration of residents of the district, although done by the *passport stol* (translated from Russian 'passport table', meaning an office responsible for issuing passports and registration stamps of all kinds put in the passports). Usually clients who had complaints about *passport stol* would come to him with requests that included waiving the fines taken for failure to renew a passport after its expiration date.[20] Once an old woman came in with a passport in her hands, together with some papers and large old notebook (obviously *domovoy*/from Russian literary a 'home-book', where a list of registered persons in the house are authorised by stamps and names). She broke into tears, saying 'I am on a pension right now and my husband died a long time ago. This is my son's passport, he is unemployed and we all live on my only pension. I was told to pay a fine.' Halmurat immediately took the small paper that was meant to be signed to waive the fine, and signed it without even letting her finish her dramatic monologue.

The second type of client is usually an applicant for exit visas, usually 'businessmen' and not necessarily residents of the region, who travel very often for trade and other reasons. In other words, these are clients who 'have money' (*pulli-la*^{Kh}/those with money); these are the most wanted clients, especially those who need their exit visas very urgently, in the shortest time possible. Halmurat's task in these cases is to make sure application documents reach the right department on time, without gathering dust alongside other application documents (which have obviously not paid their special fees for speeding up the process) and who must wait longer to be sent to the right department. Furthermore, he also makes sure he has a contact who will ensure the decision is made as quickly as possible.

The next main types of clients are people coming from other regions with various requests relating to their passport, usually for short-term *propiska*. It is common knowledge that when one is caught in the street by the Tashkent police for lacking a *propiska* stamp, it is always useful to claim that one has newly arrived there, and no later than three days ago. The police sometimes uselessly request to see tickets, but the usual transportation operates without them and fees are paid to drivers in cash since everybody in Uzbekistan tries to avoid taxes. Now I have given a rough idea about the types of clients coming to Halmurat, I will shed some light on their needs and conversations with him.

Clients of the propiska office

People came to Halmurat with various requests and different problems. Most of them did not know Halmurat personally and were referring to some people who Halmurat was supposed to know and Halmurat often would not recollect these names. Some would not bother to name anyone and just say, 'I have heard about you a lot and I came here to ask you for a favour if it is possible.' It is always helpful to know someone whose name can be mentioned in order get things done smoothly.

Following, I will relate some of the stories during my visits to the *propiska* office. A man of about 30, dressed in sport trousers, sneakers and white shirt, and dark from the sun, looked a bit nervous and worried when he entered the office. He came in and said his uncle's name, which obviously sounded familiar to Halmurat, and after Halmurat approved the name of his uncle he (Halmurat) asked what help was needed. The man told him the following story after closing the door.

> I came to Tashkent with my friends a month ago to do some business together. We made contacts at home with a TV shop and came to Tashkent to find cheaper versions of tape recorders, telephones and one or two TV sets. We were not going to stay long here [in Tashkent] as we made debts at home and interest rates are high if we do not hurry up. That was the reason we did not come to you to make our *propiska*. In the metro we were caught by a police officer in the Chilanzar station and he kept our passports because we did not have our *propiska* stamp in it. Without our passports we cannot travel back home and we cannot pay the money which is asked by these police guys there so we are here if you know them and could help us.

70 Uzbek identity

Halmurat looked at them and said that they should have told the police that they had just arrived in Tashkent and the police had no rights to take their passports if they could not prove that they had been in Tashkent longer than three days. The man said that he did not know this rule. Halmurat asked the date; place and names of the police officers, but the man did not know the last name of the police officer as the latter had not identified himself at all. He said that he even did not let him go and wanted to bring him to the police station but he escaped. Halmurat said that he should not have fled, and it would be difficult to get his passport back but he would try.

On another occasion a tall and heavy woman of about 55 entered the room. She wore a large golden chain on her neck and golden earrings, as well as three golden rings on fingers of each hand and had several golden teeth which sparkled in the daylight. She had a nice small scarf on her head but dressed in a modern style in a black top and a black, long skirt. She was holding two passports in her hands. She spoke Halmurat's dialect:

> Hello, how are you and how are your family and your children? Is everybody in good health and everything fine at home? Did not you recognise me? I am a wife of Bekmurad and also in-law relative of Sadikov's. I have met lately with Sadikov's family and they send you very warm greetings. And this is a very small (*kichgina*) present [hands in a plastic bag and at the same time looks in my direction thinking or hesitating over whether it is alright to do so in my presence. She had been waiting outside and was not taking her turn to enter for a long time, obviously waiting for me to leave the office. But after seeing that I was talking to Halmurat as if he was my uncle or close relative, she finally entered after twice being asked to do so by Halmurat] I have a small request if you could do me a favour, my son and his wife moved here to live with us now and we have a house here [in Tashkent]. My son goes back and forth and does business so he did not find time to do these things himself so I have to deal with these passport issues. My passport was handled last year by my husband as you know. He is back home now for about several months as we are organizing a *sunnat toy* [circumcision party] for our grandson soon. We will of course inform you about the dates. If you could offer us a bit of help with these passport issues we would be very grateful. We will not remain in debt to you, of course, you know us.

The woman's style of speech needs a little clarification here. Her lengthy preamble and concern for Halmurat and his family was full of strategy, and peppered with performance and irony. First, the traditional manner of personal query of one of the regions is by custom rather brief as I will show in the linguistic part of this book (Chapter 4). Instead, she undertakes a long Tashkenti way of personal query. Nonetheless, she is very much in favour of strategically using her ethnic identity – an irony in itself. The gift in a plastic bag as a 'small' (*kichgina*) present of congratulation is not only a present from her family but part of the payment for his services. The rest of the payment is the strategic contact she casually mentions (Sadikov) and diplomatically sends his regards to Halmurat. Of course, using the name of Sadikov will entail further maintenance of 'good' relations with that family who seem obviously very important to Halmurat. Inviting Halmurat to her 'big event' is also an opportunity for Halmurat to be where he can update his social contacts, meet others and be treated as an honourable guest who might expect very good and expensive presents from the host.

Later, Halmurat asked her if she had all documents ready for *propiska* and she said she did not have any idea what she needed as her own passport had been handled by her husband previously and that this was her first time dealing with these issues on her own. Halmurat told her to go to the service centre next door and said that the girls (*bizani qizla*, our girls) knew what documents they needed, and what forms must be completed before applying for *propiska*. He said those girls at the service centre would take care of all the necessary documents. When they were ready they would even bring them to him so she need not worry about it. He promised he would do his best to get the *propiska* as soon as he had prepared the documents at hand and would let her know when they were ready to pick up. The woman was very happy and left the office thanking Halmurat and sending greetings to his family, as well as saying 'please be our guest whenever you will find time. We are always glad to receive you as our honourable guest.' Halmurat just smiled and picked up his ever-ringing mobile phone and wrote the names, date of birth and passport numbers on small sheets of paper that were ready on the table. That was one of the normal telephone requests which can only be afforded without a personal visit to his office when one is connected to an official with a higher position in the government, or other close friends and relatives of Halmurat. People did not stop entering his office, and everybody had his or her own story to tell, and had been referred by various people to Halmurat.

In our conversations Halmurat was not very happy about some clients, and said that people had become greedier and no longer even greeted him if they did not need him anymore. He said:

> Our people changed lately. They use you, and when their business is finished with you, they do not want to know you anymore. Today people do not invite you for lunch because they want to have lunch with you. What I hate about people inviting me for food is they trick you. They invite you for food almost forcibly, and follow you until you go to eat with them. After the food is finished, only then do they tell you what they want from you, taking the food as payment for the service they want. I consider it is very low this kind of behaviour of our *own* people.

The complaints of Halmurat about 'his own people' (from his region) concern those people who use all kinds of means to make his services as cheap as possible. Other ways to get the service for 'free' is mentioning the name of a person to whom Halmurat would owe something or somebody from whom Halmurat would not be able to refuse any request. Consequently, the person whose name was used to request a favour from Halmurat would automatically owe something to Halmurat. Eventually what happens is that people are caught in a continuous state of 'owing something to somebody' which interconnects different people within various types of dependencies.[21] The favours go either paid or unpaid, often creating negative attitudes, as for example was expressed by Halmurat.

What if one fails to secure *propiska*? I asked my informants. In the following I will present those who could not manage or found it too expensive to obtain *propiska* in Tashkent. These migrants without registration are considered to be illegal. Below I will detail the experiences of what it means to be an illegal resident in Tashkent.

Difficulties in being illegal residents

In this section I will bring up the issues related to being an illegal resident in Tashkent. This involves various experiences of illegal migrants in Tashkent. In the section below I will focus on the interaction of migrants with state officials. It demonstrates the process in which a person confronts the significant reduction of expectations of a citizen in Uzbekistan. It will also touch upon the processes of everyday face-to-face interaction of ordinary people with the representatives of government institutions, notably the police. Another side of the same coin will be implied throughout the book, namely the particular attitudes and identification used while interacting with different people from various cultural backgrounds. In other words, the following experiences of migrants in Tashkent create certain attitudes about with whom to identify oneself as a group; namely to 'join' a Khorezmian community in Tashkent or not. This will be discussed later in the book.

Labour markets (mardikor bozor)

In the following I will bring up examples of ways of starting life without *propiska*. Below is the story of a young man who came from a village not far from Tashkent. He is 19 years old, the youngest child in a family of eight, and his parents are retired.

> I came to Tashkent to find jobs to see life and learn how to live. Of course the main reason for coming to Tashkent is *tirikchilik*.[22] I finished nine years of secondary school in my village. I have two brothers and three sisters. I am the youngest in the family and all my brothers and sisters are married and live separately. I have two *kennoim* [wives of his brothers] living with my parents. Both of my brothers are in Russia [*Rossiyada*]. They were sending money and we were living on the money they sent to us. But lately they had some difficulties and had to pay for something so we are in great need and I am the only one to 'find money' [*pul topish*]. So I came to Tashkent for *mardikorchilik* [manual labourer]. I joined other men from our

village and we are jointly renting a one-room flat where another three men who are friends of our village men are also working as *mardikors*. We all stand in Yunusobod but it is not a very good one. That stand was agreed with the boss who controls the stand. My friends knew of and agreed on a reasonable payment for it. We have often trouble with police as they catch us and ask for our *propiska*. The fine is too much for us and we often have to run away when the police come. If we are lucky and hired for not only one day's work but several days we can get our food in the house of the employer. Otherwise we have to stand on the point until we are not hired without lunch break. We cook in the evenings together. We do not make our *propiska* as it is very expensive and time consuming and it is not worth it, we would rather go home in the worst case. We try not to be caught by the police and stay always alert. It is difficult at the very beginning, when you are new to Tashkent and do not know the rules of how not to be caught by police. For example, it is better not to take the metro, not to carry big bags, dress properly, and when caught by police, know what to say and pretend that you have only come to visit your friends for not more than three days. During holidays we all go home because it is not possible to hide anymore as they raid all the houses and it becomes impossible to walk on the streets, as everyone will be asked for the passport and *propiska*. They [policemen] recognise us [those who came to work to Tashkent from other regions] immediately and at first glance [*bir qaragannan darrov*].

Mardikors comprise the most significant segment of the population of migrants who work and live illegally in Tashkent. *Mardikor* has become a popular profession and is ranked as the lowest and the last work one can ever do in Uzbekistan. *Mardikor* 'bazaars' have increased in number. One can easily locate them. They usually look like a small gathering of men of working age, standing mainly at the road so that cars can stop. In those 'spots', whenever a car stops all of the standing group of men or women run towards the car, almost breaking the windows and try to get an offer, competing against each other in the crowd. I was in a taxi with my male assistant as I anticipated this crowd of *mardikors* and was unsure of my ability to deal with them. Our taxi approached the 'spot' and like a wave of thunder, suddenly the small crowd of men standing not far from the road became bigger than it looked from the distance, and I was a bit shocked by the loud offers pronounced at the same time by all the men, each of whom tried to get their face into the small window of our car. My assistant knew how to react, opened his door, grabbed the hand of a randomly chosen *mardikor* and pulled him into the car without saying a word. We moved on. The reason was that our aim was not really to hire a *mardikor* for work. We were more interested to talk to some of them and pay their fee for the spent time. Therefore we did not care so much about negotiating the price, or choosing the fittest among them as is usually done by approaching clients of this business. The 'hiring' process is done as quickly as possible, since police always have their eyes on those spots and raids them. Whenever the police appear in those

74 Uzbek identity

Figure 3.2 Male *mardikor* bazaar, 2006.

spots the standing *mardikor*s quickly run in different directions away from the police, who always try to catch them. Thus I had a chance to talk to only two of them; one male and one female *mardikor*, which is why I cannot shed much light on this business in Tashkent, but limit myself to bringing their stories as examples of illegal migrants.

I heard similar stories from people who come from different regions of Uzbekistan, including Khorezmians who are primarily recognised by their language. This, they try to conceal if they do not want to be detected, especially those who do not have *propiska* and so illegally reside in Tashkent.

Trouble with the police

I studied two teams of construction workers in my fieldwork. Two of them were organised under the auspices of a family and business network, and another one was led by a headman who himself had a contract with a client. The headman assembled his team by going back to his home village. A headman is responsible for everything from the organisation of the work to its administration. One of the stories told by a headman follows.

> When one walks in the streets one should be always alert not to be caught by police like a rabbit in the wood. I was walking with four of my men [here in Tashkent] and two policemen approached us in the street, of course

requesting our passports. I asked why they [policemen] only asked us for our passports and they [policemen] answered that we looked 'suspicious', so they had to stop us and check our documents. The policemen took all of our passports and asked us to follow them to the police station.[23] I refused and proposed to the policemen to check our bags and passports right there on the street without taking us to the police station. I said to the policemen that the four men were my friends and had only arrived today. I asked the policemen to only take my passport and return the others as I was the one who lives in Tashkent and I told them that my friends were visiting me and had no intention to stay in Tashkent longer than three days.[24] The policemen did not even bother to listen to what I was saying and the boys got lost and scared because it was their first day in Tashkent and – imagine – they had never been outside of their village before. Finally I had to tell them the truth. I said that we were not doing anything wrong in the city but came to work and earn money to feed our families at home. But the police replied, saying that if we work hard by using our tools for earning money, then they also work hard using their pens for earning their living. We had to follow them to the police station as they started to use force. At the police station the boys were forced to write a statement [*obyasnitelnaya*[Ru]] which was dictated by the policemen and it said: 'we, [full name], confirm that we were approached by policemen. After they showed us their IDs they asked for our passports but we lied by saying that we do not have them with us. We apologise for that. We were hired by [my full name] based on an oral agreement where he was supposed to take us out of the country to work in Kazakhstan.'

The above accident described by Husan is one of the frequent events one can observe more often in the metro in Tashkent and less in the streets. Metaphorical irony used by both policemen and the headman needs to be clarified here. The pen is compared to a heavy tool of a construction worker as a tool for earning one's living i.e. police can write reports, fines for punishing people and this tool can be used not only to earn their official salaries but also the bribes paid for not writing those. Police usually ask for passports without first introducing themselves, despite the fact that this is prescribed by law. Usually people do not ask policemen to introduce themselves and show their (policemen's) IDs, but even if they do so, the policemen take it as a threat and become angry with them. However there is a possibility that the police might believe that the person asking for his ID either has contacts that could get him (the policeman) into trouble or knows his rights and knows how to officially make a complaint about him (policeman). A person could try it but if he has no luck there is a risk that in case the police realises that neither of the above are true or will assume so then the policeman may become angry and cause more trouble than they would have caused, had they not been asked for their (policemen's) ID. The situation is like the Prisoner's Dilemma.

Husan and his team were on their way to Kazakhstan where they had an agreement to build a private house. Husan said that those statements signed by

76 *Uzbek identity*

four 'scared' and 'lost' men would mean several years of imprisonment[25] for him. After I asked if policemen had the right to detain people without proof and officially approved orders, Husan answered that they did and that it was written in the regulations (codex) that they could detain anybody 'suspicious' to them (policemen) from three hours up to three days without any official orders.

I responded that if a person knows his rights then the police cannot do anything to them, even in Uzbekistan. He replied that now 'the power is in their [the police's] hands [*hukumat*[26] *hozir ularning kolinda*], they can do whatever they want and the only thing they want is money'. I asked him what would happen if a person had no money. He answered that he would have to find money if he did not want to have problems all the time. I asked if he (Husan) had left the police station by saying 'go ahead and file charges to the court'. He said that that would not have worked; if the case were passed on to the court then it would be very difficult to get out of there and 'in a regional police station [*ROVD*] they beat you up in any case'. I tried to suggest ways that he could have gotten rid of the police, but he came up with answers like 'that does not work, they do not care and they aim to get money and they do everything to get it'. The story ended with Husan paying the equivalent of US$45 as a bribe, which the policemen said was a fine for breaking the law. I asked if they were given receipts but they were not. In this context Husan used the word *öldja* (booty/prey) and asked 'Didn't you know that they go out to hunt?' This metaphor of the police as a hunter and ordinary people as prey is not ironic or amusing. Husan depicts a central aspect of the relationship of migrants in Tashkent with the authorities. Encounters can sometimes be even more dramatic. The state institutions abuse their power on a regular basis. Husan said that he and his team were used to this kind of behaviour; once they had even been arrested in their own flat just before sitting down to have their evening meal. The police usually accused them of living without *propiska*. If they had *propiska*, then they were accused of bringing girls and organising orgies or of being involved in activities that are against the law. They never let them go until they paid bribes. According to Husan, these conversations always start with a policeman asking what he and his people do and why they were in Tashkent. Husan said that the money used for the bribe after they were stopped in the street was a serious financial problem for him and his team. The money paid was the only money they had left for buying necessary construction materials for their work. Husan sounded very angry about it and indicated that he showed his anger to the police at the end and said that he told them that what they do is not correct because they are poor men trying to make their ends meet and that the God is above all and he is the only judge to every human being.

Chistka[Ru], *comb out, deportation*

Settling down in Tashkent is one of the most important phases in any migrant's life in Tashkent, as I have shown above. I have also shown how crucial it is to obtain *propiska* upon arrival in Tashkent as well as describing the situation where illegal migrants cope with their illegal status in Tashkent. If one does not have enough useful contacts in these matters, for example, contacts in the *propiska* office, it is a difficult problem. In order to obtain *propiska* according to the local regulations one has to provide proof of residence in Tashkent, which can be either *hodataystvo*[Ru27] or by marriage to a person who has a Tashkent *propiska*. After the reason (proof) for staying in Tashkent is secured, one subsequently needs documents for accommodation, namely an agreement from an owner of an apartment or house where one stays, which is in turn a very tricky undertaking. It is highly inadvisable to let someone register in your house or flat, because any registered person has legal rights to claim part of the accommodation. Without knowing the person, an owner cannot agree with registering a stranger into his or her own flat or house. Hence, there are two ways to solve this problem: either you find a person who can trust you or who has his own flat or house, or you have a relative who owns a flat or house in Tashkent. If the subject is a student, they register in a hostel without any problem, even if they live somewhere else in a shared flat. Consequently, many Khorezmians end up with 'overcrowded' flats both on paper and in reality. Epstein (1969) offers similar observations for African cities, where unregistered inhabitants of overcrowded flats, called 'loafers', wait until the police 'comb them out'. This 'combing out' or 'cleaning' is called *chistka*[Ru] in Uzbekistan.

What might happen to illegal residents of Tashkent who have no *propiska* stamp in their passports? The 'loafers' will be 'combed out' or Tashkent police will conduct '*chistka*[Ru]' and 'deport' them to their homes. The deportation process is usually implemented in the following way: in a period starting around three months before a national holiday the police carefully register the residents of each household, including 'formal' (registered) and 'physical' or informal inhabitants, by asking neighbours and in close cooperation with the *mahalla*[28] committee. In fact, each *mahalla* committee building has an '*uchastkoviy milisa*', meaning the police offices are located within the building. After the lists have been completed and compared with the previous lists, the police implement the deportation process on their assigned territories, which they call the '*chistka*' of people in the *mahalla* with only a short-term *propiska* or with no documentation at all. People are kindly asked to leave the city within three days' time; if they do not do so, they are taken to the *Ippodrom*[29] where buses go from Tashkent to the outlying regions of the country. This practice of asking people who have short-term *propiska* to leave their flats until the end of holiday celebrations is implemented with extreme rigour in the central part of Tashkent. This observation by state officials and the demand for constant compliance with other registration requirements leads internal migrants to live their lives in an almost perpetual state of 'immigration'. They must constantly be able to prove that they have permission to live where they do or face state sanctions.

Internal migration requirements are similar to registration requirements for foreigners. In order to comply with the law, internal migrants must provide proof of employment, recommendations from local authorities or some proof that they have close family living in the region they want to migrate to. Even if the migrant is able to comply with all local procedures and meet the requirements to receive a permanent *propiska*, the waiting period is between six months and two years (most of the applications are refused without indication of any reasons).

International migration within one country

The stories above present the context of travel and arrival of migrants in Tashkent. I have also presented the interactions and relationships that are enacted in the process of relocation. All of these show the importance of relations and knowledge when dealing with the severe environment surrounding mobility and migration.

The sheer scale of arrangements and contacts needed prior to departure indicate the difficulty of migration, even within the territory of one's own country. The very process of travel is a long and challenging one. The above stories illustrate the continuous negotiation with police and authorities over the right to travel, which in turn shapes their attitudes and behaviour. The manner of establishing contacts and maintaining relationships indicates their strategic character as a means to migrate. They also show how solidarity of kinsmen, friendship and regionalism play a critical role in making and maintaining these contacts. The travelling process presented in this chapter demonstrates all of the nuances and difficulties of internal migration, and highlights the similarities between domestic travel, and its counterpart across national boundaries.

Migration theories have been challenged recently by globalisation processes. 'Transnational' and 'global' have become key adjectives when describing political and socio-economic developments in the world. Migration is a very complicated phenomenon which has been studied from different perspectives (Brettel 2003; Cohen 1969; Glick-Schiller 1999; Glick-Schiller *et al.* 1992, 1995; Hischman and De Wind 1999; Kearney 1986; Massey 1999). Current theories on migration mostly explain the dynamics of the whole phenomenon by diverse criteria that measure the mobility, distance, space and quantity of migration flow (Hischman and De Wind 1999).

The major dichotomy in the typology of migration is internal and international, although some researchers have studied internal and international migration as a continuum (Ranis and Frei 1961 cited in Massey 1999). Most researchers assume that, because international migrants as opposed to internal migrants must cross a national border, they confront unique issues of legal, cultural and linguistic definition as aliens or foreigners. The issue of undocumented migration is usually studied as a topic in international migration studies. Similarly, questions of the social and cultural incorporation of migrants, including issues of citizenship, have primarily been addressed by scholars of international migration. When studies of transnational migration developed in the 1990s, the focus was again on transnationalism, with Glick-Schiller *et al.* (1992, 1995) distancing themselves from studies in internal migration.[30] Studies of internal migration have typically concentrated on urbanisation and issues of economic incorporation. Yet the experiences of migrants in Uzbekistan can be similarly understood in terms of the analytical concepts studied in international migration. These include simultaneous incorporation and the maintenance of identities within a social field that connects homeland to the new place of settlement.[31]

Migration in Uzbekistan can be *geographically* considered as internal migration, whereas those from rural areas or small towns tend to move to a big city. These internal migrants confront all of the above-mentioned issues usually faced by international migrants, starting from the very beginning of their journey.

After arrival in Tashkent, there are many more obstacles for migrants to face. Despite the fact that they have crossed no international border, and are legally citizens of Uzbekistan, they become legally and culturally foreigners at home. The migration dimensions and patterns in this case are far more complicated than internal migration. This becomes clear when one considers the obstacles consisting of the Tashkent *propiska* – the equivalent of re-obtaining citizenship – added to its trials, and the whole, untimely nature of the procedure. In other words, propiska draws *de jure* boundaries among Uzbeks and de facto leads to further divisions of Uzbeks into several groups. Even during settlement, migrants in the city must cope with the 'xenophobic' attitude of the host population, regular police checks and illegal status. As a result and counteraction, illegal systems emerge for the channelling and settling of migrants, and maintaining support in finding jobs. In this context, ethnicity and kinship ties are instrumentalised in order to survive in a new hostile environment.

Ethnographic material supports the theoretical discussion on the challenges of recent developments in migration patterns, where the patterns of international and internal migration merge. These developments, particularly within the post-Soviet countries undergoing a transition period, require a different approach to migration and ethnicity studies. Throughout the process of migration, starting from departure, moving on to travel, and finally arrival and settlement in the city, kinship and ethnicity plays a crucial role in overcoming difficulties.

Notes

1. I will come back to these divisions in a more detailed manner later in the book.
2. *Propiska* is a regulation involving the issuing of residence permits. Citizens of Uzbekistan have *propiska* automatically in their place of birth. If they move from there and stay in another place for more than three days, they are required to register there. For more detailed studies of *propiska* and internal passport policies in other Soviet countries, see Matthews (1993) and Buckley (1995).
3. See Turaeva (2012b) for a more detailed description of the history of the *propiska* system and how the meaning of this system changed throughout its history from pre-Soviet space to the current systems in post-Soviet space.
4. For a detailed retrospective account of the origin and development of Russian and Soviet passport regimes, see Mervyn (1993).
5. Phrasing from the brochure of internal regulations.
6. I will discuss reciprocity later in this book (Chapter 7) in a more detailed manner.
7. The title 'Veteran of Labour' (*veteran truda*[Ru]) was granted to individuals who have worked '*chestno i dobrosovestno*[Ru]' (honestly and conscientiously for more than 20 years), as it is written behind the medal.
8. Nazira, 55, 20 August 2006.

80 *Uzbek identity*

9 *Kelin* is a young woman who has a mother-in-law and does not have her own daughter-in-law. *Kelin* usually has a very low status in the families or even kinship networks. It can be seen from the labour distribution during bigger or smaller family and other social events, as well as their roles and influence in the decision-making processes of different importance. Often these circumstances make *kelin*s of different families within one or several kinship networks unite and do some things together, although it can be quite difficult if a *kelin* lives together with her parents-in-law.

10 *Aka* (brother) is an appellation used to show the age of the person addressed who is married but not yet an elder; *uka* (younger brother) demonstrates the relative youth of the addressee. *Ota* (father) in the meaning of an elder when used after a name as well as *sestra*[Ru] (sister), *apa* (elder sister) and *ana* (grandmother) perform a similar function for females, indicating age and status.

11 During our conversation, while he was telling about room arrangements in the hostel I interrupted the story, saying that I was sure that even though there were no free rooms there were at least free beds. He answered by saying that they did not need free beds but rooms in order to stay together in one room with his Khorezmian friends.

12 Students cannot technically work during their studies because university curriculums (standardised by the Ministry of Higher Education in Uzbekistan) are assigned in a way that lessons (lectures and seminars) in any university or faculty are scheduled for six days per week from 9 to 15:20 (4 *para*s–1 *para* is an hour and 20 minutes); often on Saturdays there are only three *para*s or two *para*s are scheduled. It is very rare that students miss entire semesters for working and even part-time jobs do not fit into this kind of tight schedule, where the time for preparation for the seminars is very small.

13 *Priezjiye* is a Russian word for 'a newcomer' and *oblast'niye* is also a Russian word taken from *oblast'*, which is region and *oblast'niye* is an adjective of region (regionals).

14 The evidence is anecdotal and has no reliable or available statistical data. The evidence is mostly derived from conversations with taxi drivers in Tashkent, observations in the region, in family and other events in the region, as well as from conversations with the residents.

15 I will present Sayora's biography later in Chapter 6 and talk in length about her networks later in Chapter 7.

16 This and similar statements were made in interviews about difficulties and incentives in leaving the home town or village.

17 For a detailed study of *propiska* and internal passport policies in other Soviet countries, see Buckley (1995).

18 Each and every state employer who has his own office has the portrait of the president up behind his seat, which is a tradition from Soviet times when the portrait of Lenin used to be used.

19 Uzbek citizens are obliged to obtain official permission to leave Uzbekistan no matter whether it is for tourist or business reasons. Exit visas are valid for only two years and are subject to renewal. One goes through the same procedure again for obtaining it next time. The minimum duration of the application process for exit visa is one month without an interview. Interviews are not a must and are subject to the decision of National Security Service officials (SNB is a local abbreviation from Russian '*Slujba Narodnoy Bezopasnosti*' which is equal to the FBI in the United States). The application forms consist of 15 questions and include the information about the purpose of the visit, destination country, one's personal autobiographic details and working history, which ends with the current employment place. The current employer is responsible for putting a stamp on the page with working history. In case one is unemployed the stamp on that page is put on by a neighbourhood chair (*mahalla rais*) and without this stamp the application form is not valid. In addition to the family members' details and contact information, the applicant should provide all the information about her parents and their legal and employment status. In the case of

children under 16 travelling together, details with photographs must also be submitted with the application forms. Children above 16 have to submit an application independently from their parents. After the application forms and other documents are completed in Halmurat's 'department' they are sent directly to the central office of the SNB where these documents are carefully screened. The decisions are taken by SNB officials whether to issue an exit visa or not. Rejection of this application is usually not provided with reasons or grounds. At the time of doing my fieldwork it was two years since the government issued an internal policy (not publicly announced) not to issue exit visas to young applicants of working age because the emigration rate had increased dramatically after independence. That made officials positions responsible for issuing exit visas very lucrative because of the high 'fees' paid 'under the table'.

20 Passports are issued when one reaches 16 years of age. Sometimes police departments make 'charity' actions by presenting new passports to school leavers who have poor family backgrounds or orphanages – usually on 25 May, when an official end of the school year in all primary and secondary schools which is always celebrated as '*ohirgi kongiroq*' (the last school ring), where schoolchildren with teachers and parents gather outside in an ordered square and where speeches are made and a musical programme prepared. Otherwise one has to pay for documents, photos and fees for issuing passports. Passports are subject to renewal every ten years. Passport holders who travel more than the number of pages in the passport allow will also be required to renew their document. When one has to obtain a new passport he has to reapply for any visa he had in his passport as the visas that have not expired in the old passport are not transferred to the new one. The only stamps that are transferred to the new passport are the registration stamps, although an applicant must provide additional proof of the registration documents that include documents for the house or apartment flat.

21 I will come back to this aspect of social relations of dependence in the example of several case studies analysing each dyadic relation later in this book.

22 *Tirikchilik* is a term used by almost all as a way of explaining what one does for a living as opposed to *hukumat ishinda, hizmatda*, which means in a state service or employed by the state. See Turaeva (2013a, 2014b) for a more detailed explanation of *tirikchilik* and theoretical implications of this phenomenon.

23 Being suspicious is a widely used reason for local police to stop people in the streets, the metro stations or make check-ups even at private homes. Police and officials of other force structures have used and misused the recent developments against Islamic terrorists and discourses around it as tools to detain and interrogate people.

24 According to regulations, people have a right to stay in a place without being registered for up to three days, which is also the rule for foreigners, who are also given three days to register upon arrival.

25 There is a law against trafficking people, which can result in several years of imprisonment.

26 *Hukumat* (from Arabic '*hukuma*'/justice) means government in Uzbek but is used in the meaning of power, an analogy to the people's understanding of power as the power of the state. It is understood that the power is in the state while the people remain powerless.

27 *Hodataystvo* is a Russian name of a legal document that is issued by an official employer (state registered organisation) requesting authorities to issue residence permits indicating the need for the applicant as a specialist.

28 A *mahalla* is a traditional neighbourhood of 2,000–3,000 people. Each *mahalla* has its *mahalla* committee. See Coudouel and Marnie (1998) on *mahallas* in Uzbekistan.

29 *Ippodrom* is a former race track where the biggest bazaar (usually for clothes) in Tashkent is located and where private buses, small vans and taxis gather to pick up passengers.

30 See also Brettell's (2003) edited volume which includes ethnographic essays on transnationalism, identity and ethnicity.

31 See Chapter 5 for a detailed discussion of connecting with 'home' and making of 'home'.

References

Aman, A. 2000. *Population Migration in Uzbekistan 1989–1998*. Tashkent: United Nations High Commissioner for Refugees.

Brettell, C. (ed.), 2003. *Anthropology and Migration: Essays on Transnationalism, Ethnicity, and Identity*. Walnut Creek, CA: Altamira Press.

Buckley, C. 1995. 'The myth of managed migration: migration control and market in the Soviet period', *Slavic Review*, 54 (4), 896–914.

Chan, K.W. 1999. 'Internal migration in China: a dualistic approach', in F.N. Pieke and H. Mallee (eds), *Internal and International Migration: Chinese Perspectives*. Richmond: Curzon.

Cohen, A. 1969. *Custom and Politics in Urban Africa: A Study of Hausa Migrants in Yoruba Towns*. London: Routledge and Kegan Paul.

Conquest, R. 1991 [1970]. *The Great Terror: A Reassessment*. New York: Oxford University Press.

Coudouel, A. and Marnie, S. 1998. *Targeting Social Assistance in a Transition Economy: The Mahallas in Uzbekistan*. Florence: UNICEF.

Dominique, A. 2002. 'Demography and politics in the first post Soviet censuses: mistrusted state, contested identities', *Population*, 57 (6), 801–827.

Epstein, A.L. 1969. 'The network and urban social organisation', in J.C. Mitchell (ed.), *Social Networks in Urban Situations: Analyses of Personal Relationships in Central African Towns*. Manchester: Manchester University Press, published for the Institute for Social Research University of Zambia.

Glick-Schiller, N. 1999. 'Transmigrants and nation-states: something old and something new in U.S. immigrant experience', in Charles Hirschman, Josh DeWind and Philip Kasinitz (eds), *Handbook of International Migration: The American Experience*. New York: Russell Sage, pp. 94–119.

Glick-Schiller, N., Basch, L. and Blanc-Szanton, C. (eds), 1992. *Towards a Transnational Perspective on Migration: Race, Class, Ethnicity, and Nationalism Reconsidered*. New York: New York Academy of Science.

Glick-Schiller, N., Basch, L. and Szanton-Blanc, C. 1995. 'From immigrant to transmigrant: theorizing transnational migration', *Anthropological Quarterly*, 68 (1), 48–63.

Hanks, R. 2000. 'Emerging spatial patterns of the demographies, labour force and FDI in Uzbekistan', *Central Asian Survey*, 19 (3/4), 351–366.

Hischman, C.P.K. and J. De Wind (eds), 1999. *The Handbook of International Migration: The American Experience*. New York: Russel Sage Foundation.

Hojdestrand, T. 2003. The Soviet-Russian production of homelessness: *propiska*, housing, privatisation. www.anthrobase.com/Txt/H/Hoejdestrand_T_01.htm.

Kabeer, N. 2005. 'The search for inclusive citizenship: meanings and expressions in an interconnected world', in N. Kabeer (ed.), *Inclusive Citizenship Meanings and Expression*. London: Zed Books, pp. 1–30.

Kearney, M. 1986. 'From the invisible hand to visible feet: anthropological studies of migration and development'. *Annual Review of Anthropology*, 15, 331–361.

Massey, D. 1999. 'Why does immigration occur? A theoretical synthesis', in P.K. Charles Hischman and J. De Wind (eds), *The Handbook of International Migration: The American Experience*. New York: Russel Sage Foundation, pp. 43–52.

Matthews, M. 1993. *The Passport Society: Controlling Movement in Russia and the USSR*. Boulder, CO: Westview Press.
Pearsall, Judy, and Hanks, Patrick (eds), 1998. *The New Oxford Dictionary of English*. Oxford: Clarendon Press.
Turaeva, R. 2012a. 'Kelins and bride schools in Uzbekistan'. Available online: http://cesmi.info/wp/?p=337.
Turaeva, R. 2012b. 'Propiska regime in post-Soviet space: regulating mobility and residence', Central Asian Studies Institute at American University of Central Asia. Available online www.auca.kg/en/casiwp.
Turaeva, R. 2013a. '*Post-Soviet uncertainties: micro-orders of Central Asian migrants in Russia*', *Inner Asia*, 15, 273–292.
Turaeva, R. 2014a. 'Linguistic and social contradictions within Uzbek national identity', in Birgit Schlyter (ed.), *Historiography and National-Building Among Turkic Populations*, Istanbul: Swedish Research Institute in Istanbul.
Turaeva, R. 2014a. 'Private Initiative, religious education, and family values: a case study of a brides' school in Tashkent', Uzbekistan Initiative Papers No. 7, February 2014, Central Asia Program at Elliot School of International Affairs and CIDOB Barcelona Center for International Affairs. Available online: http://uzbekistan-initiative.org/private-initiative-religious-education-and-family-values.
Turaeva, R. 2014b, 'Mobile entrepreneurs in post-Soviet Central Asia: micro-orders of tirikchilik', *Communist and Post-communist Studies*, 47 (1), 105–114.

Part II
Identification and communication

4 Linguistic means and rhetorical strategies in identification processes

In Uzbekistan, as probably anywhere else in the world, speakers are generally well aware of the sometimes subtle, sometimes salient differences between dialects. In the first place, differences between the Khorezmian dialect and literary Uzbek in Tashkent give rise to many jokes. One of these jokes told by a Khorezmian goes as follows:

> A father teaches his son how to speak the Tashkent dialect before he leaves to Tashkent. The father says: 'If you are ever asked "*Qatdansan?*"[1] (Where are you from? [in the Tashkent dialect]), you should say: "*Shyotdanman*".[2] ('From here' [in the Tashkent dialect]), and you will be fine'. When the son is in Tashkent, he is once asked by a Tashkenti: '*Qatdansan?*' [in the Tashkent dialect]. He answers the question, as he learned it from his father: '*Shyotdanman, shyotdanman*'. [in the Tashkent dialect]. But, as the answer was not so convincing, the interrogator asks again: '*Aniq shyotlimisan?*' (are you really from here? [in the Tashkent dialect]). Then the son says: '*Hava*' (yes [in Khorezmian, which in Uzbek means 'air']).[3]

The moral of this anecdote is that, even if you did your best to speak *tashkencha*[Kh]/*toshkencha*[T], it will be recognised at the end who you are and where you are from. Depending on who is telling the joke it can be interpreted differently.[4] If it is told by Khorezmians, then the underlying message is something like 'do not try to hide your own identity; be proud of it'. If it is told by non-Khorezmians then the message would be something like 'accept that you are not *Tashkenstkiy*[Ru] but a regional'.[5] The former tells 'a story of pride' of Khorezmian identity, the latter stresses the stigma of being a non-Tashkenti, which includes also other stereotypical discourses behind it.

Among Uzbeks in Tashkent, different groups are distinguished. The number of groups depends on who makes the distinctions. The categories and stereotypes make sense to those who ascribe and create them, not necessarily to the categorised or stereotyped persons or groups. Language is a very important marker in this categorisation. Jackson (1974: 59) defined any marker of identity, such as language, as 'a badge of identity', a metaphor adopted from Barth (1969), who referred to badges of identity as 'diacritica'. Linguistic differentiation at the intra-group level varies greatly, depending on who categories it.

The question arises why the language is so important in such a constellation where all the groups are supposed to speak 'one language' and belong to one nationality. How salient are the linguistic differences? Do they matter when marking those differences discussed above? The answers to these questions will be offered in the following analysis of the distinctions made on the basis of linguistic means.

The Khorezmian dialect is the most distinct dialect among other Uzbek dialects. When spoken at a certain speed and using certain lexical units that are not found in the literary Uzbek language and other Uzbek dialects, it becomes difficult for non-Khorezmians to understand the Khorezmian dialect. My informants argued that this has 'advantages' as well as 'disadvantages'. Some mentioned that speaking Khorezmian is 'comfortable' (*udobno*[Ru] or *qulay* in literary Uzbek and other dialects). Others stated that '*bir tomonlama yahshi hech kim tushunmidi*' (on the one hand it is good since nobody understands you).[6] The disadvantages, according to my own interpretation, include the fact that it is quite demanding for Khorezmians to learn literary Uzbek or even the Tashkent dialect since the phonological system of Khorezmian is quite different from that of literary Uzbek and other Uzbek dialects.[7]

Unlike the other Uzbek groups, Khorezmians have to learn at least *adabiycha* (literary Uzbek) if not the Tashkent dialect. Other Uzbeks do not necessarily have to learn literary Uzbek because their dialects are not linguistically very far from it. This linguistic barrier for Khorezmians creates a major incentive to stay within Khorezmian networks or communities. The speakers of other dialects find it amusing to learn Khorezmian or listen to it. They compare some words to literary Uzbek equivalents but with different meaning. Often they also make jokes about linguistic misunderstandings. As an advantage, Khorezmians are eager to make strategic use of the fact that they are not easily understood by non-Khorezmians.

This creates certain linguistic attitudes and certain linguistic behaviours that form a space for engaging in exclusion and inclusion practices. Later on in this chapter I will outline the main distinctions that are based on the use of language and rhetorical strategies in identification process. Language choice (choice of a language variety) and the way linguistic tools are employed serve as a background against which linguistic attitudes and communicative strategies are analysed. This helps to understand identification processes and politics of difference. In other words, language choice and its use are the basis of linguistic attitudes of speakers and partly predefine linguistic strategies during the identification process.

First, however, I will briefly present the working definitions of the most frequent concepts used throughout the chapter. It will also be useful to make some comments upon the linguistic strategies I employed myself while doing my field research that have, of course, certain implications on the data I produced.

The terms I frequently use are 'interlocutor', 'speaker', 'conversant' – as actors involved in the communication. I will develop working definitions of each term. This helps to make certain differences without mixing the meanings of each term. I will use the term 'speaker' as a more general term for a person who is able to communicate herself in a certain language or a dialect. It implies that a speaker has enough linguistic and communicative competence[8] in the language she is speaking. The term 'communicative competence' is borrowed from Hymes (1974, 2001) which he defines as knowledge about the existing speaking norms in a specific cultural context.

The term 'interlocutor' refers to a speaker who enters into at least a minimum of a linguistic contact with another interlocutor; it is not a necessary condition that the speech event (Hymes 1972) took place or not. According to Hymes (1972), a speech event is considered to have taken place when there was at least a minimum degree of shared knowledge and social values during communication. The term 'conversant' refers to a participant of a speech event (Hymes 1972).

Regarding the terms 'language' and 'dialect', it is well-known that they can be, and often are, defined and used in different ways. On the one hand, there are linguistic and scientific definitions of 'language' and 'dialect'. On the other hand there are definitions drawn from political reasoning. This is nicely reflected in the old linguistic saying: 'A language is a dialect with an army and a navy.'[9] The two kinds of definitions do often not coincide with the distinction between both. 'Political' definitions are closely connected with national ideologies and the formation of national identities (Laruelle 2008, 2010). They can differ significantly from the existing linguistic definitions and their ambiguities that are related to the field of historical linguistics and etymology of world languages and their varieties (Fishman, 1991; Fishman *et al.* 1968; Gumperz 2005; Haugen 1966; Woolard 1998). Thus, I will avoid entering this field of debate about the definition of a language and dialect. Instead, I will make use of the emic use of the terms. In general, I will use the official national version of established distinction between a language and a dialect. As a simple example, Khorezmians usually use *Khorazm dialekt*.[10] However, officially Khorezmian is one of the *dialects* of Uzbek.

Regarding my own language choices, I must clarify here the positions I took when conducting my fieldwork as a social anthropologist and a native at the same time. I spoke Khorezmian to Khorezmians and was accepted as a member of this group. I spoke the Tashkent dialect without accent to all non-Khorezmians, a fact which had, of course, certain implications according to the perceptions described in this chapter. In the case of non-Tashkentis my acceptance as a member of the group can always be disputed.[11] In the best case, I had the possibility to be viewed as a member of the desired group. My 'playing a Tashkent card' among Tashkentis worked most of the time. Among non-Tashkentis I did not make so much effort to prove it and acted the same way they – non-Tashkentis – themselves did. Non-Tashkentis are not always open about their place of origin and rather avoid lying about their origin by saying they live in Tashkent.

The Uzbek language and its dialects

Origin of Uzbek and classification of Uzbek dialects

The Uzbek language originates from a conglomeration of various languages of different language families of Turkic origin. Therefore, Uzbek dialects are difficult to classify. The heterogeneity and variety of dialects is explained by two major reasons: first, that the lands of the Central Asian oasis attracted Turkic tribes with different language backgrounds for agriculture; second, that those Turkic tribes that came to settle in the region had to struggle with the sedentary indigenous Iranian population and 'entered to some kind of ethnic amalgam' with them (Polivanov 1933: 4).[12]

In his account of origin and formation of Uzbek, Polivanov (1933) used the term 'Uzbek *Natskollektiv*[Ru]' instead of 'Uzbek nation' when referring to Uzbeks and subsequently to their 'common' language.[13] He argued that this language had been formed through the 'unification of linguistically different Turkic collectivities' (ibid.: 4). Polivanov (ibid.) called the process of formation of the Uzbek language '*gibridizatsiya*[Ru]', or the process of hybridisation of different languages of three genetically different families into one. He (ibid.: 4–5) called the further development of this language into a common national language '*uzbekizatsiya*[Ru]' or the process of 'Uzbekisation' (ibid.: 4–5).

It is also very important to note that there was a clear distinction between written and spoken languages.[14] There were surely influences between spoken and written languages, but due to low degrees of literacy between ordinary people, these mutual influences might have been very small. Consequently, literary languages were more preserved in the form of literary work. That is why it is not very helpful to define which language was spoken by whom and which language played what role in the formation of literary Uzbek. In fact, the above-described reality of this language situation is not far from today's situation of literary Uzbek and its dialects. There is a clear division of spoken and written language forms, and there is a considerable distance between literary Uzbek and its dialects.

How can these dialects be classified? Numerous proposals have been made by Russian and local scientists (Abdullaev 1960; Batmanov 1934; Gozi Olim 1936; Polivanov 1933; Reshetov 1946, 1966, 1978; Samoylovich 1922; Shoabdurahmanov 1962). They differ substantially in depth of analysis and in the linguistic variables on which the classification is based. But they all, at least, agree that there are three families of dialects, namely Oghuz, Kypchak and Chagatay. The main question concerns the distance between these three groups and how it contributes to the whole picture of linguistic differences between Uzbek speakers.

In this regard, the available linguistic literature, though surely important, is of somewhat limited value, because most of these studies reflect older stages (Henning 1956; Johanson 1998, 2002, 2005, 2008). Therefore, I will primarily take into consideration the differences that were pronounced by my informants and, of course, my own linguistic knowledge of Uzbek (I am a native speaker of both Kypchak and Oghuz groups of Khorezmian dialect, Tashkent city dialect and literary Uzbek). I will focus on the Khorezmian group of dialects (Oghuz group), since this is a dialect spoken by Khorezmians. There are two groups of dialects in Khorezm region – the Kypchak and the Oghuz groups of dialects.

Some dialects are closer to literary language and some are further, which makes some dialects the basis of literary Uzbek. According to Reshetov the three major groups of dialects can be compared to other languages; Reshetov concluded the following view of these dialects in reference to the languages that have more or less similarities with the Uzbek language (see Figure 4.1).

Figure 4.1 shows Uzbek dialect groups in oval forms, other related Turkic languages in squares and a non-Turkic (Iranian) language in broken lines. The block arrows in black indicate the mutual influence between dialect groups and the relevant language. The spatial proximity indicates the linguistic distance among the shown dialect groups and languages. N, S, W, E stands for the cardinal points. As shown, the geographical location of a given language is important to consider when looking at mutual influence and linguistic distance.

One can get a rough idea about similarities and differences between dialects when looking at Figure 4.1. I would additionally add more languages in to the figure in the 'Turkmen language' cell, such as the Azeri and Turkish languages.[15] Figure 4.1 also shows the implications for dialect distances between Uzbek dialects, where the Oghuz group of dialects (usually spoken in Khorezm region) is the most distant from all of the Uzbek dialects and literary Uzbek. Figure 4.2. shows current geographic distribution of the dialects within the territory of Uzbekistan where one could also trace the distance in terms of geographical location of the speakers

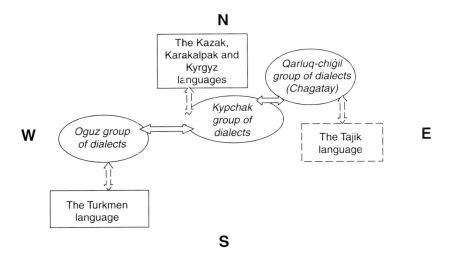

Figure 4.1 Spatial location of Uzbek dialect groups and other Turkic languages and their mutual influence.

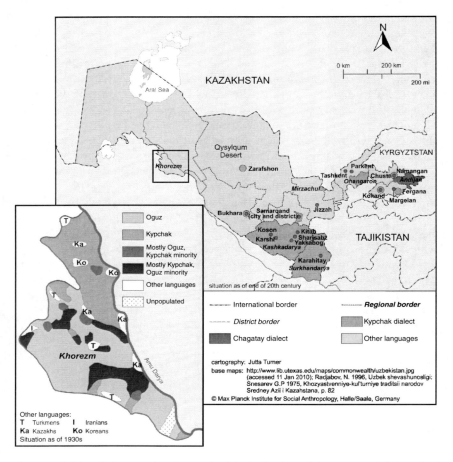

Figure 4.2 Linguistic map showing territorial distribution of the groups of dialects in the territory of Uzbekistan.

Status and role of the official Uzbek literary language in comparison with Uzbek dialects

Before I discuss linguistic attitudes of Uzbek speakers towards each other, I will briefly discuss a few questions of status and language prestige among Uzbeks. This is related to an official national status of literary Uzbek and its dialects in Uzbekistan. The main questions will be 'which language is used where, and what are the hierarchies of dialects?'.

After the collapse of the Soviet Union alongside the nation-building processes, new independent states had to reconsider the status of their national languages.[16] In post-Soviet Uzbekistan this implied that literary written Uzbek became the official language used in media, publications and in all official texts and publications. Before independence (1991) the written language was Russian. It was used as a *lingua franca* among people in Uzbekistan.[17] The use of Russian had been partly preventing people from making differences on the basis of one's language.

Literary Uzbek is used for all written texts, official speeches and in communications both official and unofficial, in the mass media and TV broadcasts. The spoken form of literary Uzbek (*adabiycha*) is used in everyday speech by different groups of Uzbeks as a kind of *lingua franca* in Tashkent today.[18] Everyday life interactions in Tashkent city comprise such spaces as bazaars or other trade facilities, *choyhonas* (tea houses), cafés and restaurants, private homes and neighbourhood facilities, streets, parks and other public spaces including state facilities of education, and other state institutions. Tashkent city is the largest city of Uzbekistan and has the highest concentration of populations with various ethnic and regional/cultural backgrounds. Tashkent is the centre where all existing dialects of Uzbek come into contact. Hierarchies in the context of everyday communication are different from those in the context of state language politics. Analytically it is necessary to distinguish between the status (from) above and the status (from) below. In transactions or interactions in the state domain and in the domain of official publicity, literary Uzbek has a high status as the official state language. In everyday life interactions, colloquial Uzbek or any Uzbek dialect can be important for the speakers themselves. The status of a local dialect is valued by its speakers as the language of their ancestors. This is particularly the case with Khorezmians. There are symbolic and partly pragmatic values attached to a dialect. In this regard, abstract 'high–low' definitions of language or dialect status do not make sense. Language status, both written and spoken, can be assessed and defined only within the boundaries of its actual usage and those definitions are limited to those boundaries.

Here I will leave aside the state level of language politics and turn to the hierarchies on the level of everyday communication or 'social field' to borrow Bourdieu's term (1999).[19] According to Bourdieu (1977), everyday practices and interactions become habitual through actions and behaviour. During interaction processes, various types of capital such as symbolic, cultural, economic or social capital, are continuously transformed by the actors. When considering communication behaviour of each agent (actor), Bourdieu (1999) describes an agent (actor) as having various types of capital and power depending on his linguistic capacity. Depending on the situation and the context, different issues are at stake and various capitals are employed. First, the hierarchies of power and social status matter in defining linguistic attitudes of speakers. To give an example, if a Khorezmian has found himself surrounded by predominantly Tashkentis, the hierarchy is different than in a mixed group setting or from the setting where a group consists of predominantly Khorezmians. When Tashkentis are the majority, the Tashkent dialect will usually be spoken. Non-Tashkenti members will try their best to speak it as well, if they master it enough. In this situation, the top of the hierarchy of dialects will be reserved for the Tashkent dialect. In a mixed group, everybody will be speaking his or her own dialect except Khorezmians, who will be trying to speak *adabiycha* to make themselves comprehensible to others as other dialects are not so far from literary Uzbek. Even if Tashkentis will be present in such a mixed group, their dialect will not be opted for. In a group dominated by Khorezmians, Khorezmian will be spoken. Usually, it is not easily learned by non-Khorezmians. This means that members of non-Khorezmian groups, including Tashkentis, will be marginalised due to the fact that Khorezmian is not easily comprehensible. In this context, the hierarchies change and different forms of linguistic and symbolic capital are employed by the interlocutors.

Social status plays an important role in defining power and agency of an interlocutor. If a person is a Khorezmian and is talking to another Khorezmian, then social status in the Khorezmian community will be important to take into account, as well as his economic situation. If a Khorezmian is talking to a non-Khorezmian, then hierarchy and status are defined differently in terms of the intention of the communication held between the two persons. The values and hierarchies, as well as the subjects at stake, will be different when communication takes place inside or outside the Khorezmian community in Tashkent. This difference implies that during conversations among themselves Khorezmians follow other kinds of values than when communicating with the Others.

Contexts of communication

Context 1 (a Khorezmian event)

The events organised in Tashkent are usually smaller lifecycle events. Mostly birthday parties, engagement ceremonies, *sumalak* preparations, holidays such as international women's day, Navruz and other smaller ceremonies related to childbirth are celebrated in Tashkent by Khorezmians. In the following I will describe an engagement party celebration in one of the houses of my Khorezmian informants.[20] The family who hosted the event was well-off and lived in a big house in Tashkent suburb region. The family head, Haydar, and his wife, Nadira, had three daughters and a son. Two daughters were married to Khorezmians, one daughter lived in Khorezm and the other daughter lived in Tashkent. Their son was also married and lived with his little son together with his wife in the house. The third and youngest daughter was getting married to a Khorezmian man whose parents were friends with her parents in Tashkent. So all three families – the family hosting the engagement party, the bridegroom's family and another family (all my informants) – were related to each other and were in the same network I studied in Tashkent.

The event started at around six o'clock in the evening. I came earlier and chatted with the youngest daughter of the family, who was getting married. Her name was Muqaddas. She was supposed not to show up very much to the guests, and especially to try to hide from members of her future in-laws. When the guests started to come I joined the group (hosts and their relatives) who were welcoming the guests. Greetings and small talk before taking the guests to the tables for the feast were conducted in Khorezmian only. The greetings were short, in Khorezmian style.

Linguistic means and rhetorical strategies 95

(H is for Host, G for Guest, Kh for Khorezmian, NKh for non-Khorezmian.)

1 H: *Salam, **nichiksiz**, yahshimisiz, yahshi **gal**dingmizmi?* [smiling]
(Hello/good evening [short version of greeting], how are you, are you well, have you come well? [in Khorezmian]).

2 G (KH): *Salom, Rahmat yahshi ozingiz yahshimisiz?* [smiling back and nodding].
(Hello [short version of greeting], Thanks I am fine, and are you yourself fine? [in Khorezmian]).

3 H: *Rahmat yahshi. Qani oting, oting.* [shows to the door going upstairs]
(Thanks fine. Let us go in the house, please come).

4 H: *Assalom, yahshimisiz, yahshi **kel**dingizmi?*
(Hello/good evening [compromised not short but not full version of greeting], are you well, have you come well? [in literary Uzbek]).

5 G (KH): *Assolomalekum* [short version of '*assolomu aleykum*'], *rahmat* ... [looks around, nods, puts the smile in her face]
(Hello/good evening, thanks [in the Tashkent dialect]).

6 H: *Ichkariga oting* [smiles, shows to the door]
(Go inside [please is missing] [in literary Uzbek]).

In the two short greeting dialogues the difference of greetings between Khorezmian and a non-Khorezmian is the length of greetings in other words in the Khorezmian style of greeting (*salam* instead of the full version *assalomu alleykum*) and full version in non-Khorezmian style (1, 2, 5). The short version, *assalom* instead of *assalomu alleykum* (in literary Uzbek) and *salom* (in Khorezmian), was used towards non-Khorezmians. The host omitted (lines 1, 4) the question 'how are you?' which she did not when addressing a Khorezmian guest which is in Khorezmian *nichiksiz*, and in literary Uzbek and other dialects it is a different word, *kandaysiz/kalaysiz*. In the first conversation, the Khorezmian dialect form of 'come' has been used: shift of voiced consonant to voiceless consonant at the beginning of the verb g > k *galdingizmi* > *keldirgizmi* and vowel change in the root of words a > e (lines 1, 4) *gal* > *kel*. The proposal to enter the house after the greeting is interesting to analyse. The repetition of the imperative verb *oting, oting* in Khorezmian will suggest politeness without inserting the Uzbek word *marhamat*/'please'.[21] In this context the intended '*polite* suggestion to enter the house' and missing *hush kelibsiz*/'welcome' before, on the side of a Khorezmian host might have been differently perceived by non-Khorezmian guests considering linguistic differences and styles of greeting.[22] In the exchanged greetings and small conversations above, both aspects of communication are important to note. The codes were used to differentiate the guests, such as the use of language varieties (different dialects) and linguistic tools through replacement of consonants and others. The use of these codes has certain purposes that are part of inclusionary or exclusionary practices interlocutors employed. Another, no less important, aspect in these dialogues is the 'perceived intent' that is part of the perception of the ways non-Khorezmians were greeted

96   *Identification and communication*

by Khorezmians. I assume that the intent of Khorezmians to *politely* welcome non-Khorezmian guests was not perceived as was intended. This is because of the semantic mismatch in the style of greeting by both sides. The existing stereotypes about the groups in this event are also at work during the process of perception of the spoken intent.

After the greeting, guests were taken to the big living room (size of a small sports hall). There was a big table for approximately 25 people, laden with all kinds of starters, salads, sweets and Khorezmian-style bread. The guests were sitting along the big table as they come by three or four on the empty chairs in a row. Therefore, the groups were sitting next to each other as they came together. If there was one person coming she would take the next free seat or join somebody she wanted to talk to. So the seats were randomly taken, but in a row. The non-Khorezmian guests were usually neighbours of the host family, so they came as a group and sat next to each other. They sat down and expected the usual long greeting ceremony. This involves the exchange of asking about each known or unknown member of one's family. Instead, rather a short version of it, adopted by Khorezmians, was performed by Khorezmians. Non-Khorezmians, following that, kept the greeting also short. So anybody who could reach the other one with a look or voice exchanged greetings or nodded. The music was on and people were talking all over so the greeting exchange was only symbolic nodding of the head. If persons were closer to each other they could ask how family members were. Khorezmians were speaking Khorezmian to Khorezmians. If a Khorezmian spoke to a non-Khorezmian, then she spoke not the Tashkent dialect but *adabiycha* with a heavy Khorezmian accent. The music was Khorezmian and singers sang in Khorezmian. Many Khorezmians at the table spoke Khorezmian even to non-Khorezmians, and when the latter could not understand the former would repeat the sentence in *adabiycha* with a Khorezmian accent. The language choice in this setting was predominantly Khorezmian since the majority of the guests were Khorezmians.

Below I present a part of the usual initial dialogue between those who did not know each other after they greeted each other. It is an average type of dialogue that can take place between strangers in any public gathering in Tashkent. In the following basic dialogue I will show the scale of linguistic barrier between Khorezmians and non-Khorezmians.

7   KH: *Siz nedansiz?*
    (Where are you from [in Khorezmian]?).
8   NKH: *uzr, tushunmadim nima dedingiz?*
    (Sorry, [I] didn't understand what you said [in the Tashkent dialect])
9   KH: *Siz kayerdansiz?*
    (Where are you from [in literary Uzbek]?).
10 NKH: *shotliman, biza shy mahallada tyramiza, Nadira opamni koshnilari bolamiz. Sizchi?*
    (From here [Tashkent], we live in this neighbourhood, we are neighbours of Nadira. And you? [in the Tashkent dialect]).

11 KH: *Haaaa. Man Khorazmnanman, beda yashimiz oilamiz bilan.*
    (Ah, ok. I am from Khorezm and we live here in Tashkent with our family. [In Khorezmian]).

The word *nedansiz* (where are you from) (line 7) used by a Khorezmian woman does not exist in literary Uzbek. Only the suffix and ending form *-dansiz* is understood as suffix *-dan* (from) and personal pronoun ending *-siz*/'you', in the respective form, are in literary Uzbek. The lexeme *ner*/'where' is Khorezmian only. The Khorezmian interlocutor in the above dialogue repeated a Khorezmian lexeme *ner* in literary Uzbek using the form *kayerdansiz* (line 9), whereas in the Tashkent dialect the ending and pronunciation would be a little different as *qatlisiz* whereas *qat* in the Tashkent dialect is a shortened version of *qayerda*/'where' (in literary Uzbek). A Khorezmian interlocutor switches (line 11) back to Khorezmian, further responding to her Tashkenti interlocutor by starting her response with a Khorezmian interjection *Haaaa*. This would be *hmm/ha* in both literary Uzbek and the Tashkent dialect. The ending *-nanman* of the word *Khorazmnanman* (line 11) is the genitive ending *-nan* that would be *-dan* in literary Uzbek and the Tashkent dialect plus first-person singular ending *-man*. The Khorezmian word *beda*/'here' has two different forms in literary Uzbek *by yerda* and in the Tashkent dialect *shotda* (lines 10, 11). The verb *yahshimiz* (line 11) is close to both literary Uzbek form yashay*miz* and the Tashkent dialect form *turamiza* (line 10). The phrase *oilamiz bilan*/'with our family' (line 11) is the same in literary Uzbek as well as in the Tashkent dialect. The sentence (line 11) did not require any translation from a Khorezmian as most of the sentence was understood by a Tashkenti interlocutor.

Another example of basic misunderstanding can be found in small introductory conversations, such as asking for one's name.

12 KH: *Adingiz kim?*
    (What is your name? [in Khorezmian]).
13 NKH: *Tushunmadim?*
    (I did not understand [in the Tashkent dialect, same in literary Uzbek]).
14 KH: **Ot***ingiz nima?*
    (What your is your name. [still in Khorezmian with only *nima* in literary Uzbek])
15 NKH: *Ismimni soravossizmi*
    (are you asking my name. [in the Tashkent dialect])
16 KH: *Kechirasiz, ismingiz nima?*
    (Sorry, what is your name? [in literary Uzbek])
17 NKH: *Zuhra, Siznikichi?*
    (Zuhra, and yours? [in the Tashkent dialect, the same in literary Uzbek]).
18 KH: *Sadokat*
    (Sadokat).
19 NKH: *Tanishganimnan hursanman*
    (I am glad to meet you [in the Tashkent dialect, the same in literary Uzbek]).

98 *Identification and communication*

20 KH: **Manam**.
(Me too [in the Khorezmian dialect]).

In the above dialogue a Khorezmian interlocutor used the word '*ad*' (line 12) in Khorezmian 'name', which she changed later into '*ot*' (line 14), automatically correcting herself which was still a wrong word. Alas, the word '*ot*' in literary Uzbek and the Tashkent dialect means 'noun' and name is '*ism*' which a Khorezmian interlocutor realised later and corrected herself (line 15). Another word a Khorezmian used in her question initially was the interrogative word '*kim*' (line 12) which is 'who', also the same in literary Uzbek and other dialects. Normally in literary Uzbek and other dialects, as well as in many other languages, one uses the interrogative 'what' in the question 'what is your name?' not 'who is your name?' as it is done by Khorezmians. This was immediately corrected by a Khorezmian interlocutor (line 14). The last answer also has bold script in order to show the difference in Khorezmian '*manam*' – one word with a vowel shift in the root phoneme and the reduction of two words into one word with omission of the first phoneme. This word in literary Uzbek and other dialects has a form of '*men ham*', 'me too'.

As shown in the above dialogue, consisting of only a couple of verbal exchanges, there was a misunderstanding of basic Khorezmian verbs by a non-Khorezmian interlocutor. The verbs that were not understood by non-Khorezmians were replaced by verb stems from literary Uzbek. Using Khorezmian towards non-Khorezmians is 'not a friendly tone' from Khorezmians' perspective, considering the fact that Khorezmian is not normally well understood by non-Khorezmians. Using the Khorezmian dialect in the presence of non-Khorezmians also serves as a more or less secret language to talk among Khorezmians. Trying to speak the Tashkent dialect is a more inclusive attitude expressed towards Tashkentis, but is negatively accepted by Khorezmians.

Context 2 (public spaces: bazaar)

Bazaars are the main shopping places for people in Central Asia. Although Soviet-style central department stores were replaced with supermarkets and other small stores after independence, the bazaars always were and still are the main – if not the only – shopping place for ordinary people. There are all kinds of people interacting with each other in bazaars. The Tashkent expression '*Bozorni korgan*' literally means 'a person who has seen bazaar' in other words 'a person who has seen many things in his life'. So bazaar is equated to life. It is very interesting to observe how people communicate their identities in this kind of public and culturally heterogeneous place. The main phrase to know in a bazaar is 'how much?' which in the Tashkent dialect is *nechi pul*. In literary Uzbek it is *qancha turadi* or *narhi qancha* and the Khorezmian version is *nicha som*. So instead of *pul* (money), Khorezmians use the word *som* which is the name of the local currency. All the above versions will be understood by non-Khorezmians, with the exception of the Khorezmian version of 'how much?'. So an average Khorezmian buyer and a non-Khorezmian seller conversation looks like this:

21 KH: *Nicha som?*
 (How much? [in Khorezmian]).
22 NKH: *nima dedingiz?*
 (What did you say? [in literary Uzbek]).
23 KH: *Qancha?*
 (How much? [in literary Uzbek]).
24 NKH: *Yigirma ming*
 (Twenty thousand [in literary Uzbek]).

Khorezmians often try to hide their identity in public by speaking the Tashkent dialect if they know it. Yet, often they are discovered. Consider the following fragment of a dialogue in the same bazaar between a Khorezmian customer speaking the Tashkent dialect and a non-Khorezmian seller:

25 KH: *Nechi pul **akan bu***?
 (I wonder how much it is? [in the Tashkent dialect with mistakes marked in bold]).
26 NKH: *Khorazmlimisiz? Qatllisiz?*
 (Are you from Khorezm? Where are you from? [in the Tashkent dialect]).
27 KH: ***Qayoq**dan bildingiz.*
 (How did you know? [In literary Uzbek with mistakes again marked in bold script])
28 NKH: *Shevangizdan.*
 (From your dialect [in the Tashkent dialect]).

Mistakes the Khorezmian made are marked in bold script in the dialogue (lines 25, 27). The incorrect form *akan bu* instead of *ekan byningiz* is the result of systematic vowel change in the root of the word, a > e in the Khorezmian dialect. Another word, '*Qayoqdan*', with mistakes marked in bold is a typical mistake Khorezmian speakers make. The literary Uzbek correct form of it is '*qayerda*', the Khorezmian version is '*nedan*'. The suffix '*yok*' comes from the form '*qayoqqa*', which is a literary spoken form.

29 KH: *Uchisi nitcha boladi?*
 (How much will three of these be? [in Khorezmian]).
30 NKH: *Uch**tasiga** besh ming bering*
 (Give five thousand for the three [in the Tashkent dialect the same in literary Uzbek]).
31 KH: *Yoqqey, **buni** sal **k**alishtirib_b**e**ring*
 (No, no [Khorezmian exclamatory] make it a little less meaning 'lower price' in literary Uzbek with mistakes marked in bold]).
32 NKH: *Nima?*
 (What [in the Tashkent dialect the same in literary Uzbek]).

100 Identification and communication

33 KH: *Bahosini*
(The price [in Khorezmian]).
34 NKH: *Narhinimi*
(The price? [in the Tashkent dialect the same in literary Uzbek]).
35 KH: *Hava*
(Yes [in Khorezmian]).
36 NKH: *Khorazmlik bolsangiz kerak, Khorazmlila faqat hava deydi 'ha'ni orniga.*
(You must be a Khorezmian they all say *hava* instead of '*ha*' [in the Tashkent dialect the same in literary Uzbek]).

In the above dialogue the Khorezmian made efforts to speak at least literary Uzbek, partly correcting the mistakes (underlined in line 31) that were more systematic, but she failed to correct basic mistakes (in bold script, lines 30, 31) of unsystematic character, like replacement of words different in literary Uzbek or in other Uzbek dialects, such as *baho* (line 33) instead of *narh* (line 34), although the word *baho* exists also in literary Uzbek but has a different meaning such as 'score/note in school'. In the word *uchisi* (line 30) a Khorezmian interlocutor forgot to put the suffix *-ta* then a correct form would be *uchtasi* (line 31). Finally, a Khorezmian interlocutor just gave up and said *hava* (yes) which in literary Uzbek and other dialects means 'air'.

This type of mistake made by Khorezmians when trying to speak *Toshkencha* is a systematic linguistic phenomenon. It makes it difficult for Khorezmians to replace those phonetic and other differences systematically when switching into the Tashkent dialect. These types of frequent linguistic differences between Khorezmian and non-Khorezmian dialects and literary Uzbek create a certain kind of linguistic barrier for Khorezmian speakers. The described systematic errors made by Khorezmians come from linguistic backgrounds rather than from not knowing literary Uzbek or another dialect. Consequently, it has little to do with the mastering of literary Uzbek or *Toshkencha*. So the above described mistakes are very particular to Khorezmian speakers. Most of the time the efforts to speak the Tashkent dialect by non-Tashkentis (particularly Khorezmians) fail. This creates an uneasy situation for the one who wanted to go unnoticed using another dialect.

So far I have discussed sociolinguistic aspects of the process of communicating collective identities and analysed the linguistic barriers among various groups. Now I will turn to other features and factors, which are important in the process of collective identification. I will also introduce the reader closer to Uzbek groups in Tashkent as well as their interactions with each other.

Impact of linguistic differences on 'We' and 'They'

The degree of linguistic differences is important for the 'We' and 'They' distinction. When these differences are so great that speakers have difficulties comprehending each other then the differences are more salient. Linguistic attitudes of speakers play a tremendous role in exclusionary and inclusionary practices.

The factors affecting peoples' choices of codes include *pride* (for speaking or not speaking a certain dialect or language), communicative competence, and emotional attachment to a certain language in addition to pragmatic reasons. I have observed feelings of expressed pride by refusing to speak *adabiycha* or *tashkencha* and approving the act by saying 'why should I learn *their* language, let them learn *my language* instead' (their language and my language was originally emphasised by face expressions and intonation during the interviews or other informal talks by Khorezmian informants).[23] In other cases, Khorezmians speak *adabiycha* rather than *tashkencha* as a compromise and as *lingua franca*. But the Tashkent dialect differs from literary Uzbek and is the most attractive dialect to speak in Tashkent. It suggests that a speaker is a *tashkenskiy*[Ru] (from Tashkent), and this brings about privileges in socialising in public spaces of Tashkent city. Privileges, or rather 'conveniences', are subject to discussion. It depends who defines the situation and for whom or among whom it is a privilege or just a convenience. In a mixed group environment, it is a privilege to be a Tashkenti. However, among Khorezmians themselves it is only a convenience or pragmatic need in order to avoid the stigma of being a villager or further questioning of the place of origin followed by what one is doing in Tashkent. This questioning between strangers in Uzbekistan I would say is a norm because one would expect any stranger to ask questions starting from one's name, age, birthplace, occupation, etc. Questioning anybody by anyone whenever there is a chance (the chances are often high) is almost habitual for all Uzbeks. Therefore, avoidance of being questioned is a more general attitude.

Language attitudes of the second-generation Khorezmians and students

Linguistic attitudes and language choice, as well as communicative competence, differ in terms of generations of migrants too. The second generation Khorezmians (born in Tashkent) and children of migrant Khorezmian families (who came along with their families but are born in Khorezm) seem to adapt better to a new language environment than their parents.[24] The difference between the two is that the former (born in Tashkent) grew up socialising in the new language environment, whereas the latter (children who were not born in Tashkent) have to learn a new dialect (the Tashkent dialect) in order to become integrated into the majority.

There is a tendency among students to look for counterparts from the same region in their department or even across departments. With school children the situation is different. Friendship across classes (i.e. school classes) is not popular; it is rather more common to have a friend or friends within one's own class. This indicates that the chances of having Khorezmian friends within the same class are very low according to my young informants. These school children seem not to care so much about who is from where when it comes to socialising with their classmates. Some were even proud to have non-Khorezmians friends and be able to speak their dialect.

All Khorezmian children of migrant families that I have interviewed spoke Khorezmian at home and with their relatives and Khorezmian friends. They were quick to switch to the Tashkent dialect instead of switching to *adabiycha* when talking to Tashkentis and to other non-Khorezmians. As to speech attitudes of school children and university students, there was a slight difference in preferences and pride of speaking one or another language. Some parents indicated that their children often asked them not to speak Khorezmian in the presence of their school friends. Children used the word 'shame' (*uyalaman*) when answering the question why they did not want their parents speaking Khorezmian. Some parents did not like at all that their children were ashamed or hiding their 'own' (*ozini*) language while talking to 'others'. To the contrary, children found it normal to be ashamed of speaking Khorezmian since it was different than the one (Tashkent dialect) spoken by the majority at school. Parents did not mind and even encouraged their children to learn and speak the Tashkent dialect as something very practical. However, when it came to the general attitude towards the Khorezmian language parents preferred that their children value their 'mother language' (*ana dili*) and use other languages only for practical necessity. When the children were asked why they were ashamed or hid their language, they answered that they did not want to be pointed at as somebody coming from a village (*qishloqi*). When I asked how they hid their identity, they answered that they did not necessarily tell their classmates where they were from and always stated that they were born in Tashkent. Many also stated that they did not have to hide their identity and even were proud to be Khorezmians.

There are not so many occasions for the children to socialise with their school friends outside of their school. This makes it easier to hide their place of origin. The only occasion would have been their birthday celebration, though usually a birthday cake and drinks are brought to the school by a parent, and the birthday is celebrated there. After school at home it is rather a family event where friends and relatives of their parents gather, making the birthday an excuse to get together.

University students do not have problems with switching dialects, but they still prefer to find other Khorezmians within the faculty and even outside of it. As many of my informants indicated: '*biza darrov topishamiz*' (we quickly find each other), 'Khorezmians quickly find each other for example if two [Khorezmians] are speaking to each other: and if a Khorezmian passes you by, he joins and that way we meet each other'.[25] I asked if they have also non-Khorezmian friends as well and asked about the criteria for making friends. I have not directly asked if they have non-Khorezmian friends but the questions were formulated in the following way: 'Who are your friends? And please describe them. What is important when making friends?' Most of the answers I got were positive to the question of whether they have non-Khorezmian friends as well. In the cases where the friends were mostly Khorezmians I continued asking whether there were also non-Khorezmian friends. I also heard remarks such as 'I feel myself more comfortable to express myself in Khorezmian than in any other language, although I do not have problems to speak the Tashkent dialect' or 'Khorezmian is closer to my soul [*konglima yaqin*] and when you want to talk to a friend you want to enjoy it [*hazzatib gaplshasing galadi*/one wants to talk with pleasure]',[26] 'when I talk the Tashkent dialect I feel always constrained in order not to make a mistake so it is different from talking relaxed [*qiynalmi*/without difficulties/efforts] in our *own* Khorezmian'.[27]

Language attitudes in mixed families

I have interviewed four mixed families. In three cases the wives were non-Khorezmians and in one case the husband was a Tashkenti. In the three families with non-Khorezmian wives, two of the wives learned Khorezmian but did not speak it. In one case the wife almost perfectly spoke a particular Khorezmian sub-dialect of the region where her husband came from. The Khorezmian wife from the mixed family with a Tashkenti husband learned the Tashkent dialect in her in-law family and spoke it in Tashkent. She spoke Khorezmian only with her relatives and her children. The children of the three families where the wife was a non-Khorezmian spoke Khorezmian at home and the Tashkent dialect at school. The children of the Khorezmian wife and Tashkenti husband spoke the Tashkent dialect but understood Khorezmian. There was one 'exceptional' case in the perspective of my informants in which a Khorezmian step-daughter of a non-Khorezmian mother learned to speak the Tashkent dialect after she came to Tashkent with her father and spoke it to everybody. Her brother spoke Khorezmian at home. This family had an 'unusual' (*boshkacha*/different) history of family-making according to Khorezmian standards. The Khorezmian man of 48 who was rich and had a very good position came to Tashkent with his son and daughter after an unhappy marriage.[28] In Tashkent he married a young woman (unmarried before) who was from another region working in Tashkent. The daughter of this man who grew up in Khorezm spoke the Tashkent dialect to me as well, although I started the conversation in Khorezmian. I was not sure how to react in terms of language choice as I was used to the fact that if one is Khorezmian, one automatically speaks Khorezmian to another Khorezmian. So I spoke mixed Tashkent dialect and Khorezmian during our interviews with her.

There is a certain discourse on linguistic choice among Khorezmians, often expressed by informants of different ages during the interviews and informal talks. It is negatively described when a person opts to speak the Tashkent dialect 'instead of speaking normal comprehensible Uzbek language [means some kind of literary version of Uzbek mixed with Khorezmian in order to make oneself comprehensible]' and it is considered to be 'showing off' (*ozini gorsatish uchun*). 'Showing off' here does not refer to the prestige of the Tashkent dialect. Rather, the phrase carries a negative connotation. In view of the generally negative attitude of Khorezmians towards Tashkentis, the phrase bears two different negative connotations. First, 'showing off' is not a modest feature of one's character. Second, the willingness to be like Tashkentis or attempts to become a *Tashkentskiy* is not welcome among Khorezmians, who frequently had a negative view of the 'natives' of the capital.

104 Identification and communication

Not all Khorezmians who are willing to learn Tashkenti dialect would necessarily like to become Tashkentis. Khorezmians who learn the Tashkent dialect and are eager to become Tashkentis are not appreciated by other Khorezmians: they are considered to be 'betrayers [*sotilgan*/was sold to]'.

In this context the verb '*sotildi* [have been sold to]' and its attribute form '*sotilgan* [was sold to]' is used by Khorezmians to describe a Khorezmian who speaks the Tashkent dialect. It was mostly the language choice that determined a Khorezmian with such a negative term. There is another expression used by Khorezmians, which is '*Tashkentni suvini ichgan* [the one who drank Tashkent water]' to describe a Khorezmian's other features than linguistic ones. It is used to indicate a Khorezmian who became more nimble and cunning after he has adapted to a new environment in Tashkent. This expression often has negative connotations in regards to the fact that *Tashkent suvi* (Tashkent water) is a metaphorical phrase to indicate 'the ways of doing things in Tashkent ways' or 'the way Tashkent people do it', which is usually described in negative tones. So the phrase '*Tashkent suvini ichgan*' indicates double reference of characteristics or pejorative description of, first, a Khorezmian who has adopted the bad aspects of a Tashkenti and, second, of a Tashkenti who has those bad qualities that are implied by the phrase '*Tashkent suvi*'.

The strategies mentioned above, when employed through certain degrees of emphasis on linguistic differences and other means, are indicative of what Gumperz (1964) called 'we-code' and 'they-code' in the process of code-switching.[29] The examples given above, such as code switching when addressing and distinguishing a member or a non-member, can be explained in terms of we-code and they-code. Having done research in urban settings, Gumperz became interested in the multiplicity of language varieties and codes in especially inter-ethnic settings. He argued that:

> Outsiders who enter the urban scene may learn a new language or dialect well at the level of sentence grammar, and this knowledge may be sufficient for the instrumental contacts that fill up much of the working day. But the situations of persuasion, where speakers are evaluated on their ability to explain, or to provide adequate descriptions which do not assume shared knowledge, or to produce complex narratives, are often difficult to manage. Here breakdowns lead to stereotyping and pejorative evaluations and may perpetuate social divisions.
>
> (Gumperz 1999: 210)

The breakdowns pointed out by Gumperz as crucial moments and causes for social divisions can explain certain social behaviour of various regional groups in Tashkent. They can also explain the cases where certain groups do not intermix or do not assimilate to majority groups or speech communities. The use of 'we-code' and 'they-code' is the linguistic means to communicate collective and social identities in multi-ethnic contexts like Tashkent. Schlee (2008: 102) has also drawn attention to the importance of linguistic variations in speech acts in a 'plurilingual and culturally heterogeneous setting'. He refers to what he calls an 'ecology of languages' (ibid.) that includes a variety of variables which are important to take into account for studying inter-ethnic context such as

> status of a language and institutions in which it is used ... communicational mobility and degree of multilingualism of speakers, specialisation of the functions of speech varieties in diglossic and polyglossic settings, and routines of interactions between ethnic groups/speech communities; ... predominant/exclusive use of language in the public/private sphere, and the linguistic distance between language in contact.
>
> (Ibid.)

These codes used by Khorezmians in Tashkent are not observed in a 'home' context where the population is more or less 'homogeneous' – for example, by Khorezmians in Khorezm. The intra-group differences within Khorezmian groups occur on the basis of district division such as *Khivali, Khonqali, Gurlanbet*,[30] *Boğotli, Urganchli* and *Shovotli*. This subdivision usually occurs in Urgench, which is a central town of Khorezm region. The Khorezmian dialect is divided into sub-dialects. They belong to one of two groups of dialects in Khorezm, Oghuz and Kypchak (see Figure 4.1). The latter is closer to the Karakalpak, Kazakh and Kyrgyz languages and the former is close to Turkmen and Azeri languages. These intra-group differences among Khorezmians are less visible in Tashkent as everybody is Khorezmian and strives to 'stay together' despite the regional differences mentioned above. The differences are not pronounced, under the cover of everybody being a Khorezmian. But the division is along district lines and can be still observed within Khorezmian networks themselves.[31]

Defining 'They': group names and stereotypes

There are many ways to define a group (when a group identifies itself) and of group ascription (when a group is identified by others) (Jenkins 1996). They are differently accepted or not accepted by both those who define and those who ascribe a group. I will discuss the groups and the ways they are differentiated and how they organise their social and economic lives in later chapters (Chapters 5 and 6).

The labels ascribed to different groups of people as well as dialects or languages used for naming those groups are no less important in the perception of the group which is being labelled. The ascribed names carry different connotations and stereotypes. There are two major group distinctions in Tashkent – between Tashkentis and non-Tashkentis and between Khorezmians and non-Khorezmians.[32]

In the capital city, the main distinction is between Tashkentis (*Toshkenli/ Tashkenskiy*[Ru]) and non-Tashkentis (*qishloqi/oblast'noy*[Ru]). In the labelling of groups various language varieties are employed. *Toshkenli* is the Tashkent dialect version for a 'Tashkenti', whereas *Tashkentskiy*[Ru] is a Russian version used by non-Tashkentis, particularly by Khorezmians. *Qishloqi* (from a village [in the Tashkent dialect]) is often used by Tashkentis. The second version of the same group name is *oblastnoy*, which is a Russian word for 'a regional'; it is mostly used by non-Tashkentis.

The discursive stereotyping of non-Khorezmians by Khorezmians is made on the basis of language differences in addition to physical features. The derogatory word *osha* is used by Khorezmians towards 'them' that pools together all non-Khorezmian Uzbek groups *even* including Tashkentis under this name.[33] The emphasis on 'even' is not accidental. According to the 'general' hierarchical division of groups in Tashkent, Tashkentis are in 'no way' associated with any of the groups of non-Tashkentis (neither by Tashkentis themselves or by non-Tashkentis, excluding Khorezmians).[34] There is another derogatory term, *quruq* (the word is from the Tashkent dialect, literally means 'dry'), used for Tashkentis by Khorezmians.[35] It means that they (Tashkentis) do not have anything 'good' left in them. When Khorezmians are asked why they use this word and what it means, they generally describe them as 'those from whom you cannot expect support or anything good'. The phrase was used during the informal talk with my female Khorezmian informants on the way back home after a small event, International Women's Day celebrated in a small Khorezmian café on 8 March 2006. The topic on Tashkentis started from discussing a small scandal made by a Tashkenti owner of the café with a Khorezmian renter. The landowner (a well-known national actor) yelled at the renter in front of his (the renter's) clients, complaining about the dirt next to the café, leading the Khorezmian renter to move to other premises. His popularity as an actor (the Tashkenti landowner) was emphasised by my informants during the discussion as a good example that 'even those Tashkentis with such a reputation are able to fall down and are unreliable'. In this context the owner was criticised and pooled under the general term for all Tashkentis.

As an example their (Tashkentis') poor hospitality is often brought up in explanations by Khorezmians. Khorezmians many times used rhetorical questions like 'Have you ever heard of Tashkentis organizing their *gap*s [parties] at home? You always see them in *choyhona*s [tea houses].' *Choyhona* is a most popular place visited usually by men for all kinds of social gatherings. As we (I and my female informants) were coming from a *choychona* ourselves, I used the chance to say 'but we are also coming from a *choyhona* instead of celebrating at our places?' One of the girls was very quick to answer 'but our usual gatherings [*tashkil*] take place in our homes and are not we going to continue at your place, Rano?' I just nodded and we indeed continued the party at my place. However, I observed that more and more Khorezmians themselves follow their Tashkenti counterparts and celebrate many events and smaller social gatherings in cafés and restaurants in Tashkent.[36]

These examples point to the bad hospitality of Tashkentis in the views of Khorezmians. Hospitality is a very important variable used for emic definitions of 'good', 'bad' person/family/house in the Central Asian countries. There is even a well-known proverb used among not only Uzbeks, but also other Central Asians as well, which says: '*Mehmon otangdan ulug*' (a guest is greater than your father).

I can only speculate about the reasons why the Tashkent dialect version is used for the following names of the two groups such as *osha* and *quruq* instead of the literary Uzbek form or the Khorezmian dialect form. There is an anecdote told by Khorezmians about the word *osha*. It says:

> During the Uzbek literature lesson pupils are reading an Uzbek novel *Otgan Kunlar* and a teacher reads: '*siz oshami*' [are you that one] and one pupil answers: '*osha bolmin Khorazmli bolsinmi* [should he be a Khorezmian (rhetorical question) of course he is *osha*]'.
>
> (Furqat, a Khorezmian young man, 2 May 2006)

Word play in '*siz* [you] *oshami* [that interrogative marker]', the derogatory word *osha* is a literary form of demonstrative 'that one'. This demonstrative pronoun in this phrase ('that one') serves both its own demonstrative function as well as the joke in the meaning of a group, namely 'osha', which refers to non-Khorezmians used by Khorezmians. The emphasis is made not on the content of the novel, although the popular expression from the famous novel is comparable with the expression 'to be or not to be' from Hamlet by Shakespeare. The expression is a climax of the novel where finally two lovers meet each other and one of them asks 'are you the one?' stressing that the lovers cannot believe that the meeting took place. The moment is ridiculed by an answer, the meaning of which reads like 'of course she is *osha* and not a Khorezmian'. This word play in the emotional context of the novel emphasises the dichotomy of an *osha* and a 'Khorezmian' through the meaning of the joke which is 'a Khorezmian cannot be an *osha*'.

The names used by Tashkentis towards other groups differ in the usage of derogatory terms and language varieties. There are several pejorative names used by Tashkentis towards regional migrant groups and these are: *harib* (no translation was given, they [Tashkentis] use it as a general pejorative similar to 'uncouth'), *qishloqi* (from a village), *kelgindi* ('comer/newcomer' in the derogatory meaning [because usually this form of the verb is not normally used in literary Uzbek, and the correct form of a newcomer is *yangi kelgan*]), *indeecsy*[Ru37] (red Indians), *negry*[Ru38] (Negros, Russian plural form) and the phrase '*ohirgi vagonga osilib kegan'a*' (those who came hanging [free riding is implied] on the last wagon of the train).[39]

When analysing these terms linguistically it becomes obvious how various linguistic techniques are (mis)used in the politics of difference. There are two types of linguistic differentiation in the use of the terms: first, different languages and codes are used such as Russian and Uzbek dialects. Second, various morphological means are also used such as suffixes and endings in the above terms in order to give a term derogatory meaning.

These terms pool together several or all regional groups under one label. The term *oblast'niye*[Ru] (regionals) is, so to say, supposedly neutral and used in the cases where it is not appropriate to use derogatory terms. *Oblastniye* is employed by both Tashkentis and by regionals themselves in order to be polite.

The second type of linguistic technique of differentiation that is applied in these terms concerns morphology. The term *qishloqi* is a humiliating form for 'a villager' with an ending *-qi*. This ending forms a noun from a noun and carries the meanings of 'rude' and 'uncivilised'. The correct form of this ending in literary Uzbek and other Uzbek dialects is *-dan/qishloqdan* where *qishloq* for a 'village' and *-dan* is a locative case ending, meaning 'from'. The same applies to an ending *-di* in the word *kelgindi*, the word formation mechanism is the same as in *-qi* as well as semantic quality.

These attitudes towards non-Khorezmians by Khorezmians and vice versa create certain manners of discursive behaviour that derive from the perception of the 'Other' in Tashkent.

Figure 4.3 represents different types of identification and making differences in terms of language use. The oval circles depict We-group identification. The squares contain the language of the We-group. We-groups are connected by their language and their relation is marked with a straight line. The Other is a group in circles. The position of each geometrical form indicates the hierarchical position of each form in relation to each other. The arrows indicate an act of pointing to 'the Other' whereas a straight line indicates direct relation and connectedness.

In part C of the group differentiations, there are two kinds of relations between the groups which are indicated by an arrow and a direct line. Even if they do not learn the Tashkent dialect, the group (real Tashkentis) is seen by them (non-Tashkentis born in Tashkent) as a point to reach, as the next upwards step on the social ladder. The idea of accepting the differences between them (non-Tashkentis in C) and Tashkentis is based on the belief that they (the differences) are a short-term phenomenon which fades with time (this relationship is shown with an arrow). Many non-Tashkentis state that 'at the end of the day Tashkent has been built by traders as a trade station', which is why it had no indigenous population which means everybody is an outsider anyway. Thus by learning the proper Tashkent dialect and getting 'properly' based in Tashkent (which is defined in terms of time and intermarriage as well as acquiring social status) one might have a good chance of becoming a 'real Tashkenti' and being accepted by Tashkentis themselves.

Two other types of distinctions are the extremes of identification and pointing to the significant Other; one from the Tashkentis' perspective (A) and the other from the Khorezmians' perspective (B). In both cases, the basis of identification is defined in relation to the groups' dialects. In type C, the We-group relates to its dialect as a variety of literary Uzbek. Its members do not necessarily see themselves at the top of the hierarchy, but strive to reach the top sooner or later.

The three types of distinctions are based on the linguistic competence of speakers of various Uzbek dialects. The fact that Khorezmian is a particularly distinct dialect of Uzbek creates a group of speakers that is different from other

Linguistic means and rhetorical strategies 109

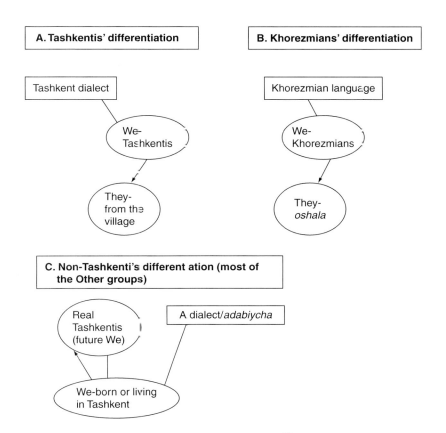

Figure 4.3 We and They distinctions among Uzbeks.[40]

Uzbek dialect speakers. The Tashkent dialect is not very different from literary Uzbek, but has specific phonological features that make the dialect an outstanding one to a certain degree. In addition to the language specificity of the Tashkent dialect, its speakers have certain privileges and advantages as members of a Tashkenti group, since they are the 'majority/native'[41] population of Tashkent city. Other Uzbek dialects are close to literary Uzbek, and there are no barriers or obstacles when speaking literary Uzbek. These three principles of linguistic differentiation explain the existing ways in which groups are distinguished and in which they identify themselves. These principles often coincide with the principles of distinction of groups on the basis of non-linguistic factors. I will come back to non-linguistic factors defining the same groupings later in this book.

From rhetoric to identification

The ethnographic material presented so far has dealt with language attitude towards language varieties of Uzbek and paralinguistic features of everyday communication. Before indulging in further ethnographic examples of communicative practices, I will briefly highlight some important rhetorical aspects of communicating one's identity and being identified as the Other.

When analysing linguistic practices in every day communicating of collective identities it was useful for my purposes to simplify the span of the process of communicating one's identity through focusing on the following:

- individual or collective consciousness ('being aware') about their identities;[42]
- communicating this 'awareness' to the Other; and
- further perception of the communicated message by a receiver.

I am aware that there are other factors and aspects when explaining the phenomenon of identification process. These are considered in other parts of this book. Conscious knowledge about one's identity ('being aware') influences the intention and strategies to be employed by an actor when communicating oneself to the Other.[43] Certain ways of speaking, and intentionality while making a speech, has a long tradition in the field of the art of rhetoric. The basic principles and notions of how to organise and deliver speech in public were established more than two millennia ago by Greek and Roman rhetoric. An essential feature of this rhetorical tradition is the connection of the art of speech with wisdom and virtue. Mastering the skills of speaking in public and wisdom in philosophy were signs of good education and social status. Aristotle, for example, expressed his thoughts about the existence of power in certain learned ways of speaking when done with a special art of speaking. The special art of speaking included three main components: *logos* (logic reasoning), *ethos* (mastery of cultural heritage) and *pathos* (emotions, force and passion). These components were necessary for a true orator who could persuade the audience and who was a polymath of his time (Garver 1994).

The new rhetorical has switched the focus from a speaker to the relationships of the speaker with a listener. This significant turn in rhetorical theory was marked by a great philosopher and critic, Kenneth Burke. He extended the term persuasion to identification and distinguished them 'by foregrounding the possibility of the unconscious, the dreamlike, and the nonspecific yearning in speaking subjects seeking to compensate for "real differences and divisions" that, in turn, prompt further identifications' (Burke 1950). Another important volume in this regard is *Rhetoricals of Selfmaking* (Battaglia 1995). The authors in this volume problematise the self and argue that self is not given but 'made' (ibid.: 2), focusing on agency and performance and turning away from the traditional approach to rhetoric. The argument is that '[rhetoric] is not about the commanding dominance of the individual personality in some consummate performance

Linguistic means and rhetorical strategies 111

or text' but it 'is taken as an uncertain, and provisional social project' (ibid.: 2). This approach to studying identities, the authors argue, is '[a]n approach to selfhood as an embodied and historically situated practical knowledge in other words, prompts a larger question of rhetorical, namely what *use* a particularly notion of self has for someone for some collective identity' (ibid.: 3). This turn in the studies of rhetorical theories considered communication as a two-sided process rather than a one-sided view of the speech deliverer and the art of his speech towards the respective audience. Now the focus is more on the internal reflection of a speaker and his intentions towards a listener that is closely intertwined with the process of identification and communicating it to the Other. While delivering his speech, a speaker makes use of various strategies employing different rhetorical means, such as comparison or metaphors, and becomes in a way creative to communicate himself on to the Other. Before he starts to communicate it is important to look at the notion of intent. Intent is a crucial notion in rhetorical strategies and discourse production when negotiating collective identity (Cook-Gumperz and Gumperz 1997; Gumperz 1977; Hymes 1964).

Recent studies of discourse, speech and communicative practices have widened the horizon of the research on language use and speech events in general. These are now increasingly studied in a situated manner without extracting the phenomena from their original local context. Sociolinguists, linguistic anthropologists and others considered long-term ethnographic methods in order to study lively everyday communication within its context of social organisation of the speech communities. New concepts and analytical frameworks have been developed to analyse discursive strategies and communicative practices by means of situating them into the local context. Gumperz (1997) and many others (Hymes 1974; Gumperz 1964, 1997, 1999; Gumperz and Hymes 1964) studied the discursive strategies and rhetoric in ethnically and culturally heterogeneous communities. Their aim was to find out whether certain values are shared and common knowledge of social cultural norms exists. They focused on understanding the differences that might hinder communication. They also looked at different aspects of communication barriers at the social, cultural and economic level. They were interested in cases of miscommunication. Their methodology included the analysis of everyday speeches on different levels, starting from the knowledge of the speakers (end in view), the communication flow including the analysis of the linguistic and rhetorical means and finally the analysis of the outcome of communication (ends as outcome). Hymes described it as 'end in view' and 'ends as outcomes' (Hymes 1964) when analysing speech events. Gumperz introduced the term 'communicative inference' which helps to explain the aspect of the speech outcome. He points to the importance of the intent of the speaker while analysing the effect of the speech on the listener.

Cook-Gumperz and Gumperz (1997: 16) argued that it is not only the speaker's 'intent' which matters but also how it is perceived and accepted in the interaction and other forms of contact. Misperception of the intent produces the stereotypes and pejorative discourses.

Cook-Gumperz and Gumperz (ibid.: 17) repeatedly pointed to the importance of the mutual knowledge of cultural background and context when studying different communicative events in order to understand how ethnic and other cultural differences are negotiated and how 'communicative flexibility' (ibid.: 14) is reached. Gumperz (1997 [1982]) defines 'communicative flexibility' as negotiating the differences during inter-ethnic communication.

I will consider below some paralinguistic features of communication that differ in the ways they are perceived by a listener and, as a result of miscommunication, certain stereotypes are created as the above authors argued. There is another aspect in this miscommunication which remains unclear in the above-discussed scholarly debate. Namely, it is the impact of already-existing stereotypes and a-priori discourses on the interpretation of the intent of a speaker by a listener. When analysing the mutual knowledge of cultural background which was discussed above (Cook-Gumperz and Gumperz 1997), it is crucial to look at what I refer to as 'perceived intent'. Perceived intent can be defined as an aspect of perception which a listener perceives, interprets or understands to be the intent of the speaker. The relation between intent and perceived intent implies the understanding of the speech event, its heterogeneity and its possible inherent contradictions. If it is taken that intent implies something planned and directed to some purpose, then it is perceived not always as intended or planned. This makes the Gricean equation of meaning to intent inapplicable in this case from the perspective of an interpreter.[44]

Consider the following example of an interpretation of a 'smile' or smiling – facial expression while talking. A smile giver wanted to be or at least look friendly. Yet, a receiver, due to certain stereotypes about the group to which the speaker belonged, did not receive the intent as it was initially planned by the speaker. I often observed Khorezmians perceive the appearance of non-Khorezmians such as looking friendly, smiling, using endearing words when talking as superficial and not sincere. They are perceived and interpreted as '*Bula yuzinga qarab gulsa habardor bolish garak. Bir gappi bomasa gulmidi. 'Ishim bitincha eshakim suvdan otincha* [These people, if they smile into your face one must be careful. If there is nothing they would not smile. 'Until my donkey crosses the water and until my business is done' (proverb)].'[45] This means if they smile and are nice to you then it must be because they want something from you. Sometimes it is also interpreted as a kind of trap. A metaphoric expression often used by Khorezmians in this regard is: '*Jonim, jonim dab jon-ingni aladigan hilisinan bula*' (word-for-word translation will be like 'by saying my soul, my soul these [people] are the types who take your soul away') meaning 'they can hurt you by saying nice words'.[46] Therefore, the smile is in fact not taken as a gesture of being friendly but as a lie and/or bad intention. Another example is the serious looks of Khorezmians while they (Khorezmians) talk, or the directness in the way they (Khorezmians) talk, which is negatively perceived by non-Khorezmians and considered to be rude (*qopol*). Khorezmians consider them (directness, serious looks) as something positive. For Khorezmians the intention behind these are the ways of communicating things directly without hiding anything as a sign of friendliness or friendly attitude. Khorezmians consider it to be honest and serving good purposes.[47] The term 'perceived intent' serves to display the outcome of the intent and to show its reflection by others to whom the intent was directed.

Paralinguistic means such as facial expression, tones, gestures and others are of crucial importance in the process of interpretation of intent and its outcome. They are particularly important in those speech events in which a speaker and a listener do not share the same cultural conventions and norms of social behaviour.

Notes

1 '*Qatdansan*' is a Tashkent dialect form which in Khorezmian will take a form '*nerdasan*'.
2 '*Shōtdanman*' is a Tashkent dialect form which in Khorezmian is '*shōrliman*'.
3 The joke was told by a Khorezmian in a small party where Khorezmian students gathered for a birthday celebration on 22 May 2006 in Tashkent, as well as in the interview with Adolat or 12 March 2006.
4 *Tashkencha* is 'the Tashkent dialect' in Khorezmian and *toshkencha* is in the Tashkent dialect.
5 Comments to the joke by Tashkentis are my own interpretation drawn from the comments made on the real-life situations of failure to speak the Tashkent dialect.
6 Adolat, a young Khorezmian woman, 12 March 2006.
7 I have published a detailed linguistic analysis of Uzbek literary language and its dialects in Turaeva (2013, 2014, 2015).
8 Linguistic competence is not used in the meaning as defined by Chomsky (1965) as perfect knowledge of grammatical structure. Rather in this context, 'linguistic' refers to enough knowledge to be able to speak a certain dialect or language.
9 The author of this saying is unknown. Most often, it is ascribed to Otto Jespersen or to Max Weinreich. I am grateful to Prof. Wolfgang Klein for prompting me with this proverb.
10 *Sheva* in a local linguistic scientific terminology denotes a sub-dialect, whereas a 'dialect' is '*dialekt*' in literary language, but people use the word '*sheva*' for both a dialect and a sub-dialect.
11 As I spoke the Tashkent dialect with all non-Khorezmians one can only speculate about the perception of non-Tashkentis of me. If they think that I am a Tashkenti then I could be seen as a member of a desired group, if they are aware of my birth place then I can be viewed as one of the newcomers to Tashkent.
12 Russian and local scholars studied the Uzbek language and its dialects with comparison to other Central Asian languages as well as other languages of the Turkic family as well as a few Western scholars who studied the Uzbek language and old Khorezmian (Begmatov 1935; Borovkov 1946; Kanonov 1960; Madrahimov 1999; Menges 1933; Polivanov 1927; Radjabov 1996; Samoylovich 1910, 1928; Shermatov 1978; Usmanov 1948; Yudahin 1939 and others cited in this book). There are only few scholars who systematically studied Uzbek language and its structure and its depth (Bidwell 1955; Bodrogligeti 2003; Boeschoten 1993; Eckman 1959, 1996; Henning 1956, 1965; Henning and MacKenzi 1971; Sjoberg 1962).
13 *Natskollektiv* is an abbreviated form from *natsionalniy kollektiv* in Russian and can be translated as 'national collectivity'.
14 Abdulğozi (1992 [1658–1661]) wrote that the written language was not accessible for the broad masses – see his 'Shajarai Turk'.

114 *Identification and communication*

15 See also Saparov (1988) for comparative studies of the Oguz family of dialects of Khorezm region with the Turkmen language.
16 See Fierman (1991) on language planning and nation in Uzbekistan, as well as comparative studies on politics of language and state in Central Asia and North Africa by Thomas (1999). See also Grenoble (2003) for the general language policies and nationality questions in the Soviet Union.
17 By 'people' I mean those who know Russian and spoke Russian not only to Russians and Koreans but also among themselves in the capital city or other urban contexts.
18 See also Mahmudov (1997), an Uzbek scientist who writes about national identity and ways of speaking the national language where he discusses identity as equal to the language of the speaker.
19 See also other works of Bourdieu (1977, 1990, 1998, 1999), developing his ideas further.
20 The biggest parts of marriage celebrations were held in Khorezm.
21 *Marhamat* (from Arabic *marhama* superlative degree of 'mercy'/*rahma* in Arabic) is not used in the meaning of the given context in spoken Khorezmian. Other forms of 'please' used in Khorezmian such as '*arzimidi*' as a reply to 'thank you' or 'please' as plead '*iltimas*' (from Arabic '*eltimas*'/a humble request whereas '*talab*' in Arabic is 'request', the same word in Uzbek).
22 Of course the guests did not express the 'perceived intent' verbally around the table. It is generally depicted in describing Khorezmians as being rude in general.
23 Adolat, Khorezmian informant, 12 March 2006.
24 Almost all the children of my informants of school age were interviewed with the consent of their parents. Students of different universities were interviewed partly by my research assistant and myself in the form of individual interviews as well as group discussions in private houses and in hostels.
25 Interview with a student (Shuhrat) on 20 April 2006.
26 Interview with Dilnura 18 January 2006.
27 The expressions were extracted from various interviews with students.
28 It is very important to note here that it is mostly unlikely that a man with two children at a certain age is able to marry a young woman who has not been married before, since unmarried young women marry out early and usually marry young men unmarried before. So he had to find a woman outside of the group in a place like Tashkent. This explanation was given to me when I was referred to his family by Halima, 57, during our informal talk in May 2006.
29 I have already briefly discussed general sociolinguistic research done in this field earlier in this book.
30 *Gurlanbet* is a derogatory term used for people who come from *Gurlen* district of Khorezm region by Khorezmians from Urgench, the central town of Khorezm. Instead of using the form '*gurlanli*' with ending -*li* as in other group names, ending -*bet* is used which is a Gurlan dialect form.
31 See Chapter 6 for analysis of the politics of Khorezmian networks.
32 I have briefly observed other group distinctions like Bukharans and others, but I have not been able to do more systematic research among this group. They speak the Tadjik language among themselves, which is a different language than Uzbek.
33 *Osha* can be translated from Uzbek as 'that one' but I do not have enough data on the etymology of the term used by Khorezmians. The explanations that were given during the interviews are mostly descriptive and do not explain the etymology of the word and why this word is used to pool together all the non-Khorezmian Uzbeks.
34 The term 'general' is used here to describe the views of the majority of the different Uzbek groups including Tashkentis and non-Tashkentis.
35 Interviews with Khorezmian Olima 23 February 2006.
36 Interviews 8 March 2006.
37 Abror, a young Tashkenti man, 25 May 2006.

38 Laziza, a young woman from Namangan, 15 August 2006.
39 In the interview with Olima (a young woman from Khorezm who grew up in Tashkent) conducted on 23 February 2006 the meaning of the phrase was interpreted differently from that of Tashkentis. Olima explained the meaning of the phrase as everybody wants to come to Tashkent even on the last wagon of the train. The maximum use of the chances available was implied.
40 I do not intend to draw boundaries around certain groups, or to put them into a neat order of boxes and forms. My intention is rather to visualise my analysis to see certain correlations and distinctions brought together in one picture in order to proceed with further arguments. The distinctions and differences were taken from the informants themselves and different perspectives of different groups and people were taken into account.
41 Majority or minority does not necessarily imply the statistical meaning these terms carry. First of all, it is difficult to define or describe a certain collectivity because groups' ascription and identification often do not coincide. And if even it would be possible to name a certain group it is always difficult to indicate their number. So these two descriptive terms are more symbolic and not fixed.
42 In other words '"being aware" [...] is a precondition for the use of a cultural element as an "identity marker"' (Schlee 2008: 72).
43 See Finke (2006) for a more detailed theorising of mental processes influencing identities. He introduces the schema model to the approaches of studying consciousness and behaviour.
44 Grice (1957) analysed intent, equating it with the meaning intended by a speaker as something like '*A* meant something by *X*' which is roughly equivalent to '*A* uttered *X* with the intention of inducing a belief by means of the recognition of this intention.'
45 This advice was given to a son by one of my informants during an informal gathering of relatives in her house in the context of discussion over non-Khorezmian friends – acquaintances of his (18 May 2006).
46 See Schlee and Sakado (2002) for more detailed analysis of proverbs and sayings in their social and cultural meanings and their functions.
47 The perception of these features of Khorezmians by non-Khorezmians was drawn from Khorezmians themselves from their experiences of being misunderstood by non-Khorezmians. This came out during small gatherings when discussing a non-Khorezmian friend in a group discussion of Khorezmians. It was a small family event at the place of my Khorezmian informant on 7 April 2006.

References

Abdulgozi, B. 1992. *Shajarai Turk*, Toshkent: Ilm.
Abdullaev, F. 1960. *Khorazm Shevalari* [Khorezmian Dialects]. Tashkent: Ozbekiston SSR Fanlar Akademiasi Nashryoti.
Barth, F. 1969. *Ethnic Groups and Boundaries: The Social Organisation of Culture Difference*. Bergen: Universitetsforlaget. Allen and Unwin.
Batmanov, I.A. 1934. *Voprosy Klassifikacii Uzbekskih Govorov: Problemy Yazyka I* [Classification of Uzbek city dialects. Language issues]. Tashkent: Nauka.
Battaglia, Debbora (ed.), 1995. *Rhetorics of Self-making*. Berkeley, CA: University of California Press.
Begmatov, E.A. 1985. *Hozirgi uzbek adabiy tilining leksik qatlamlari* [Lexical Layers of Contemporary Literary Uzbek language]. Tashkent: Fan.
Bidwell, C.E. 1955. *A Structural Analysis of Uzbek*. Washington, DC: American Council of Learned Societies
Bodrogligeti, A.J.E. 2003. *An Academic Reference Grammar of Modern Literary Uzbek*. München: Lincom.

Boeschoten, H. 1993. 'Chwaresmtürkisch asl z-Türkisch', *Journal of Turkology*, 1 (2), 183–193.
Borovkov, A.K. 1946. 'Alisher Navoi kak osnovopolozhnik uzbekskogo literaturnogo yazyka [Ali-Šir Navāi as the founder of the Uzbek literary language]', in A.K. Borovkov, (ed.), *Alisher Navoi*. Moscow and Leningrad: Nauka, pp. 92–120.
Bourdieu, P. 1977 (1972). *Outline of a Theory of Practice*. Cambridge: Cambridge University Press.
Bourdieu, P. 1990 [1980]. *The Logic of Practice*. Cambridge: Polity.
Bourdieu, P. 1998 [1994]. *Practical Reason*. Cambridge: Polity.
Bourdieu, P. 1999. *Language and Symbolic Power*. Cambridge: Polity.
Burke, K. 1950. *'The Range of Rhetorical': A Rhetorical of Motives*. Berkeley and Los Angeles, CA: University of California Press, pp. 3–46.
Chomsky, N. 1965. *Cartesian Linguistics*. New York: Harper and Row.
Cook-Gumperz, J.J. and Gumperz, J. 1997 [1982]. 'Introduction: language and the communication of social identity', in J.J. Gumperz (ed.), *Language and Social Identity*. New York: Cambridge University Press, pp. 1–21.
Eckmann, J. 1959. *Das Tschagataysche. Philologia Turcicae Fundamenta I.D. e. al.* Wiesbaden: Steiner, pp. 138–160.
Eckmann, J. 1996. *Harezm, Kipçak, ve Çagatay Tükçesi Üzerine Arastirmalar. Atatürk Kültür, Dil ve Tarih Yüksek Kurumu*. Ankara: Turk Dil Kurumu.
Fierman, W. 1991. *Language Planning and National Development: The Uzbek Experience*. Berlin: Mouton de Gruyter.
Finke, P. 2006. Variations on Uzbek identity: concepts, constraints and local configurations. Habilitation thesis, Leipzig University, Leipzig.
Fishman, J.A., Ferguson, J. and Dasgupta, J. (ed.), 1968. *Language Problems of Developing Nations*. New York: John Wiley & Sons.
Fishman, J.A. 1991. *Language and Ethnicity*. Manchester: Manchester University Press.
Garver, E. 1994. *Aristotle's Rhetorical: An Art of Character*. Chicago, IL: University of Chicago Press.
Gozi Olim 1936. *Özbek Lahchalarini Tasnifida Bir Tajriba* [One Experience of Classification of Uzek Dialects]. Tashkent: Nauka.
Grenoble, L.A. 2003. *Language Policy in the Soviet Union*. Dordrecht: Kluwer Academic Publishers.
Grice, P. 1957. 'Meaning', *The Philosophical Review*, 66, 377–388.
Gumperz, J.J. 1964. 'Linguistic and social interaction in two communities', *American Anthropologist*, 66 (6), 137–153.
Gumperz, J.J. 1977. 'Sociocultural knowledge in conversational inference', in M. Saville-Troike (ed.), *28th Annual Round Table Monograph Series on Languages and Linguistics*. Washington, DC: Georgetown University Press.
Gumperz, J.J. 1997 [1982]. *Language and Social Identity*. Cambridge: Cambridge University Press.
Gumperz, J.J. 1999 [1982]. *Discourse Strategies*. Cambridge: Cambridge University Press.
Gumperz, J.J. 2005. 'Language standardisation and the complexities of communicative practice', in S. McKinnon and S. Silverman (eds), *Complexities: Beyond Nature & Nurture*. Chicago, IL: University of Chicago Press.
Gumperz, J.J. and Hymes, D. (eds), 1964. *The Ethnography of Communication*. Washington, DC: American Anthropological Association.
Haugen, Einar 1966. 'Linguistics and language planning', in William Bright (ed.), *Sociolinguistics*. The Hague: Mouton, pp. 50–67.

Henning, W.B. 1951. 'The Khwarezmian language', in: Z.V. Togan, *Documents on Khorezmian Culture, pt. 1. Muqaddimat al-adab, with the Translation in Khorezmian*, Istanbul: Sucuoğlu Matbaası, pp. 421–436.
Henning, W.B. 1965. 'The Choresmian documents', *Asia Major*, 11 (2), 166–179.
Henning, W.B. and MacKenzie, D.N. 1971. *A Fragment of a Khwarezmian Dictionary*. London: Lund Humphries.
Hymes, D. 1964. 'Introduction: Toward ethnographies of communication', *American Anthropologist* 66, 6, 1–34.
Hymes, D. 1972. 'Models of the interaction of language and social life', in J. Gumperz and D. Hymes (eds), *Directions in Sociolinguistics: The Ethnography of Communication*. New York: Holt, Rinehart and Winston, pp. 35–71.
Hymes, D. 1974 [1964]. *Foundations in Sociolinguistics: An Ethnographic Approach*. Philadelphia, PA: University of Pennsylvania Press.
Hymes, D. 2001. 'On communicative competence', in A. Duranti (ed.), *Linguistic Anthropology: A Reader*. Malden, MA: Blackwell Publishers. pp. 53–73.
Jackson J. 1974. 'Language identity of the Colombian Vaupés Indians', in R. Bauman and J. Sherzer (eds), *Explorations in the Ethnography of Speaking*. New York: Cambridge University Press, pp. 50–64.
Jenkins, R. 1996. *Social Identity*. London: Routledge.
Johanson, L. 1998. 'The history of Turkic', in L. Johanson and Éva Ágnes Csató Johanson (eds), *The Turkic Languages*. London: Routledge, pp. 81–125.
Johanson, L. 2002. *Structural Factors in Turkic Language Contacts*. London: Curzon.
Johanson, L. 2005. 'Converging Codes in Iranian, Semitic and Turkic' in E.A. Csató, B. Isaksson and C. Jahani (eds), *Linguistic Convergence and Areal Diffusion: Case Studies from Iranian, Semitic and Turkic*. New York: RoutledgeCurzon.
Johanson, L. 2008. *Turkic Languages*. Chicago, IL: Encyclopedia Britannica.
Kanonov, A.N. 1960. *Gramatika Sovremennogo Uzbekskogo Literaturnogo Yazyka* [The Grammar of Contemporary Literary Uzbek Language]. Moscow: The Academy of Sciences of the USSR.
Laruelle, M. 2008. 'The concept of ethnogenesis in Central Asia: political context and institutional mediators (1940–50)', *Kritika: Explorations in Russian and Eurasian History*, 9 (1), 169–188.
Laruelle, M. 2010. 'National narrative, ethnology, and academia in post-Soviet Uzbekistan', *Journal of Eurasian Studies*, 1 (2), 102–110.
Madrahimov, O. 1999. *Ozbek Tili Oğuz Lakhjasining Khiva Shevasi* [Khiva Sub-dialect of Oguz Dialect of the Uzbek Language]. Urgench. Obdolov Regional Press.
Mahmudov, N. 1997. *Uzimiz va sozimiz* [Ourself and Our Words]. Tashkent: Gafur Gulom Press.
Menges, K. 1933. *Drei özbekische texte, Der Islam. XXI*, Leipzig, pp. 141–194.
Polivanov, E.D. 1927. *Vvedenie v izuchenie uzbekskogo yazyka* [Introduction to the Study of the Uzbek Language]. Tashkent: Turkpechat.
Polivanov, E.D. 1933. *Uzbekskaya Dialektologiya i Uzbekskiy Literaturniy Yazyk* (K sovremennoy stadii uzbekskogo yazykovogo stroitelstva) [Uzbek Dialectology and Uzbek Literary Language (Modern Stage of Building the Uzbek Language)]. Tashkent: Oqituvchi.
Radjabov, N. 1996. *Uzbek Shevashunosligi* [Uzbek Dialectology]. Tashkent: Oqituvchi.
Reshetov, V.V. 1946. *Sovremenniy uzbekskiy yazyk* [Modern Uzbek language]. Tashkent: Gosizdat.
Reshetov, V.V. 1966. 'Uzbekskiy Yazyk (The Uzbek Language)', in *Yazyki Narodov SSR* [Languages of the Peoples of the USSR], vol. 2. Moscow: Nauka.

Reshetov, V.V. 1978. *Uzbek Dialectologiasi* [Uzbek dialectology]. Tashkent: Uqituvchi.
Samoylovich, A.N. 1910. 'Dva Otryvka iz "Khorezm-name" [Two passages from "Khorezm-name"]', *Zapiski Vostochnogo Otdelenia Imperatorskogo Russkogo Arheologicheskogo Obshestva* [Notes of Eastern Russian Imperial Archeological Society], 19, 78–83.
Samoylovich, A.N. 1922. *Nekotorie Dopolnenia k Klassifikacii Tureckih Yazykov* [Some Additions to Turkish Language Classifications]. Petrograd.
Samoylovich, A.N. 1928. *K Istorii Literaturnogo Sredneaziatskogo Tureckogo Yazyka* [To the history of Central Asian Turkish language]. Leningrad: K Istorii Literaturnogo.
Saparov, M. 1988. *Khorazm vohasidagi turkiy tillarning ozaro munosabatlari: uzbek va turkman tillari materiallari asosida* [Turkish Language Relations in Khorezmian Region: On the Basis of Materials from Uzbek and Turkmen Languages]. Tashkent: Uzbekistan SSR, Press 'FAN'.
Schlee, G. 2008. *How Enemies are Made: Towards a Theory of Ethnic and Religious Conflicts*. New York: Berghahn Books.
Schlee, G. and Sahado, K. 2002, *Rendille Proverbs in their Social and Legal Context*. Cologne: Rüdiger Köppe Verlag.
Shermatov, A.S. 1978. *Uzbekskie narodniye govory Kashkadaryinskoy oblast'i* [Uzbek Folk Dialects Kashkadarya Region]. Tashkent: Fan.
Shoabdurahmanov, S. 1962. *Ozbek Tili va Ozbek Halq Shevalari* [The Uzbek Language and Uzbek Fold Dialects). Tashkent: Fan.
Sjoberg, A.F. 1962. *Uzbek Structural Grammar*. Bloomington, IN: Indiana University Press.
Thomas, E.H. 1999. 'The politics of language in former colonial lands: a comparative look at North Africa and Central Asia', *Journal of North African Studies*, 4, 1–44.
Turaeva, R. 2013, 'From rhetoric to identification: miscommunication in inter-ethnic contact', *Anthropology of Middle East*, 8 (2), 21–45.
Turaeva, R. 2014, 'Linguistic and social contradictions within Uzbek national identity', in Birgit Schlyter (ed.), *Historiography and National-Building Among Turkic Populations*, Istanbul: Swedish Research Institute in Istanbul.
Turaeva, R. 2015, 'Linguistic ambiguities of Uzbek and classification of Uzbek dialects', *Anthropos*, 110 (2), 463–476.
Usmanov, A. 1948. *Mukhakamat-al-Lugatajn*. Tashkent: Fan.
Woolard, K.A. 1998. 'Introduction: language ideology as a field of enquiry', in B.B. Schieflin, K.A. Woolard and P.V. Kroskrity (eds), *Language Ideologies: Practice and Theory*. New York: Oxford University Press, pp. 3–47.
Yudahin, K.K. 1939. 'Uzbekskiy Yazyk'. In: *Literaturnaya Encyclopedia* [The Uzbek Language: Literary Encyclopaedia], vol. 11. Moscow: Nauka.

Part III
Identification and belonging

5 Who is a Negro and who is not?
Sub-ethnic groups of Uzbeks: Khorezmians and others in Tashkent

Qorami. Aqmi, Kazakmi hammasi Õzbak.[1]
[Be he Black, White or Kazak all are Uzbeks].

Ozi negr bogannan keyin regrni himoya qiladi da.[2]
[Because she herself is a Negro of course she will defend a Negro].

Bizanikila baribir bashqacha.[3]
[Whatever is said our people are anyway different].

The above epigraph is in the form of a 'dialogue' compiled from the statements of various actors and contexts, and points to interactions between different groups. Members of these groups talk in different languages (in a metaphorical sense), but still 'talk' to each other, sending the same, constant message: 'Everybody is Uzbek, just different ones.' In what follows, I will bring those differences to light. The chapter explores various discourses and practices of sub-ethnic groups within Uzbek ethnicity. There are different resources and values at stake in the identity politics played by these groups. The chapter aims to show the inherent contradictions of these identity discourses and practices involved in the processes of defining the We and defining the Other. Contradictions imply the heterogeneity, flexibility and situationality of collective identities.

Uzbeks as a nation is a young creation, the basic 'raw material' of which was composed of numerous tribes and tribal confederations living in that territory.[4] After independence, the Uzbek state promoted an ideology of nationalistic politics. The historical heterogeneity of Uzbek ethnicity implies internal subdivisions into sub-ethnic groups based on cultural and territorial distinctions, which foreground identity politics among Uzbeks. Identity politics here denotes the games of inclusion and exclusion played by actors, which comprises the processes of identification and categorisation of the Others. The identity politics of non-Khorezmians partly takes the form of autochthony discourse opposing autochthons to allochthons. Conversely, Khorezmian identity politics proceed along other lines more related to dynamics of ethnicity. Autochthony-based identity politics of non-Khorezmians engage two perspectives. Tashkentis' authentic discourses stem from a sense of belonging to a symbolic place such as, for instance, Eski Shahar (the old part of Tashkent), whereas non-Tashkentis lay claim to Tashkent as a place of birth. Khorezmian identity politics emphasise identification with people coming from Khorezm, a distinct culture, as well as a language. Khorezmians neither enjoin autochthony discourses, nor claim Tashkent as their own. They refer to their homeland (Khorezm region) as a 'real' home (*oy yan*^{Kh}), unlike others. In this context autochthony discourses are only relevant for non-Khorezmians.

I will present the perspectives of different actors on collective identification by focusing on various variables which contribute to identity politics. Various distinctions are made and categories are used by the actors involved, which do not necessarily match, and are often in conflict. These are: from the perspective of Tashkentis two groups exist, namely Tashkentis vs others (regionals); from the perspective of all non-Khorezmians there are Tashkentis who are on the top and other groups (regionals); for Khorezmians there are Khorezmians and non-Khorezmians.

Further analysis of identity politics shed light on the ways different Uzbeks make sense of themselves and others. On the basis of this analysis I will present patterns of collective identifications and categorisation of Others among the groups in question. The primary argument of the chapter concerns different scales or layers of identification and belonging, which seems to be important for different Uzbek groups. I will follow Harneit-Sievers (2006) in my analysis of Uzbek groups and their construction of belonging. Harneit-Sievers (ibid.) examined the constitution of the construction of the Igbo 'community' in Nigeria from within and from outside. The main goal of this book is to examine the ways of constructing belonging and identity politics in the context of a post-colonial state. These discourses and practices of identity politics indicate a constant renegotiation of both *content* (ways of defining 'We') and *boundaries* (defining 'the Other'). Both processes do not take place independently from each other, but are rather in a continuous relationship, through interaction, dialogue or, in fact, any human activity involving the Other. During these processes of renegotiation contents and boundaries are constantly reshaped (Barth 1994).

Uzbeks and Uzbek sub-ethnic groups: introduction

The discussion of the dimensions of identification and its taxonomies can shed light on the heterogeneous character of the content of collective identities. In this context, ethnic identity is not monolithic, comprising a homogeneous group. There are different dimensions and scales of identification. I will support this statement by bringing examples of variations of Uzbek national identity.

After Uzbekistan gained its independence, the Uzbek government strengthened national emphasis in all political and socio-economic aspects of life in the country. *Uzbek Milliy Goyasi* (Uzbek National Ideology) policy was introduced as a leading ideology in constructing Uzbek national identity. Finke and Sancak (2003–2004) argue that '*uzbekchilik*' has been to some extent successful but Finke (2006: 18) also notes that

[t]he concept of Uzbekness is *more flexible* in this respect and includes a *definition of locality* that acknowledges *regional variation* and the possibility of membership by voluntary decision. Depending on the respective setting and ethnic configuration, *the boundaries of being Uzbek vary*, and therefore almost by definition take on a *different shape* in each setting, incorporating elements of local languages, cultures, and social organisations. Within each locality people share specific cultural patterns irrespective of their ethnic affiliation. Thus, members of other groups living in the same place are usually considered closer to oneself than co-ethnics settling in other parts of the country [italics mine].

Finke (ibid.) carefully examines how people identify themselves in different regions of Uzbekistan. He provides a detailed analysis of Uzbek national identity politics based on the data derived from four different parts of Uzbekistan. His analysis is helpful in understanding various contexts and variations of Uzbek national identity in Uzbekistan. My data fully support the argument of Finke (ibid.: 18) in that 'Uzbekness ... includes a definition of locality' which is distinguished by 'specific cultural patterns' and incorporates 'elements of local languages, cultures and social organisation.' These variations which Finke (2006: 18) recollects are the focus of this book and in this chapter the task is to 'measure' the degree of variability and define the basis of these variations. There are several possibilities of grouping or several variations made by Others which serve as a source of self-identification.

Carlisle (1986: 96) stated that studies in the former Soviet states with 'artificial nationalities' where

Soviet nationality policies and the tactics applied vis-à-vis republics such as Uzbekistan would recommend attention to how local *ethnic groups* [italics mine] were played against each other *within* and *between* [italics in the original] republics.... Thus personal cliques and factions conceptualised on *an intra-Republic regional axis* [italics mine] might be used to divide and re-divide native leadership.

Uzbekistan is administratively divided into 12 *oblasts*. However, there is also a verbal, informal distinction among Uzbeks into the following five groups. The first group is *Bukharalik/Bukharskiy*[Ru] and *Samarkandlik/Samarkandskiy*[Ru]. Many people who are not from these two regions speak of these two groups as one, calling them Tadjiks. This is ascribed identity. I am not sure if they would identify themselves as Tadjiks. Bukharans tend to distinguish themselves from Samarqandis. The second group, *Khorazmlik/Khorezmskiy*[Ru] is both ascribed and also a collective self-identification. The third group, *Tashkentskiye*[Ru], is at the top in the city hierarchy of sub-ethnic identities in Tashkent. The fourth group, *Vodiylik/Vodiy* (from Uzbek, meaning 'valley') is a more ascribed category which is based not only upon administrative division as Fergana Valley, but is also defined as a more religious sub-ethnic group. The fifth group, *Surqash* (a derogative term used for the people from *Sur*hondarya and *Qash*qadarya regions, the nickname itself consists of the first syllables of the two region's names '*sur*' and '*q/kash*'), is also more an ascribed identity than one of group self-identification.

Carlisle (1986: 92–96) also makes five regional distinctions among the members of the Uzbek elite; the North-eastern region refers to what I mentioned above as *Tashkentskiye*; the Eastern region refers to *Vodiy*; Central refers to Samarkand/Bukhara; the Southern region refers to *Surqash*, and the North-western region refers to *Khorezmskiy*, including Karakalpakstan. He briefly describes the distinction of the five regions by cultural, geographical and economic differences (Carlisle 1986).[5]

The division that has been suggested by Carlisle concerns the elite and government level of interactions. The division among elite members along regional lines is similar to the group divisions I observed among ordinary people. However, I do not have enough data and knowledge to state whether or not there is some connection[6] between the two parallel and similar divisions of the above-mentioned groups on two different levels – namely the elite and ordinary people. I can only recall several examples where students from Khorezm went directly to a certain well-known member of the Khorezmian elite to ask for funding a Khorezmian event at the University in Tashkent. I will present more details on this event later in this chapter, since it is an interesting case to show how representations and performance of collective identities often function.

Uzbek ethnicity can be regarded at the same level as other ethnicities in Uzbekistan, such as Russians, Turkmens, and others within the ambit of Uzbek citizenship. Hence, the term sub-ethnicity within Uzbek ethnicity makes sense in order to talk about the above-mentioned categories in Tashkent. According to the qualities of these sub-ethnicities, it is clear that each sub-ethnic unit has its own peculiarities, and what unites them under the category of sub-ethnicity is that the categories are, for instance, used by the Others and known to most of the members of these groups, although often the categories do not match the groups' self-identification.

Considering the above examples of the relation between ethnicity and sub-ethnicity, the definition of sub-ethnicity comes also quite close to the definition proposed by a Russian popular thinker, Gumilev (1989), whom I briefly mentioned in the introduction of this book. He described sub-ethnicity as part of ethnicity and emphasised that it does not damage the unity of ethnicity. He also showed that these sub-ethnicities can be further investigated as webs of relations. His sub-*ethnos* is a

> structure which is the second feature of *ethnos* and is always more or less complex, but this very complexity is what gives the stability to *etnos* to live through years of perturbation, revolt and world withering. The principle of the ethnic structure can be called hierarchical subordination of sub-ethnic groups, the latter being understood as taxonomic units (*taksonomicheskiye edinitsy*) [situated within the *etnos* (as visual totality) without breaking its totality/unity].

I do not agree with Gumilev's primordial argument on ethnicity. He mentions the qualities of *ethnos* as stable and equates *ethnos* to a living organism. Nonetheless, his observations on the existence of sub-ethnicities and their relations within a larger group are relevant to my analysis.

Defining the 'Other'

It is important to know how differences are produced and acquire different meanings for different actors. The differences make sense to the authors themselves: as to how they are perceived is another matter. In this section I will use various categories shaped on the basis of various perspectives of actors of both opposite sides (We and the Other). Hence, while looking at the discourses of constructing difference, I will try to represent the perspectives and opinions of both sides, so far as my data and my local knowledge allow.

The definition of the terms *chujoy*, *chet*, *negr* and *boshkala* is necessary before I go into their meanings in various contexts of their use. Whenever I encountered the terms I asked my informants to define them. Although I was constantly asked if I did not know them myself and confronted with the question 'why?', I justified my questions by saying that I knew the definitions but argued that different people use the same words differently and that I was interested to know the ways they used and understood the terms.

The Other is defined by using various terms and categories depending on the context and the subject of making the definition. There are inter-ethnic and intra-ethnic definitions of 'Them'. Khorezmians, for example, use different terms to make inter-ethnic and intra-ethnic distinctions. For a general distinction of the We from Others, Khorezmians use a pair of opposite terms – *chujoy* for 'a stranger' (They/the Other) and *ozlarimizniki* for 'our own' (We/one of us). In order to distinguish a non-Khorezmian from a Khorezmian they use terms such as *oshala, boshkaia ozlarimizniki*/one of us, *oy yanli*/from home. *Boshkala* can literally be translated as 'Others' and is used synonymously with *chujoy*.

There are also spatial terms such as *chet* (an edge) used by Khorezmians to describe the boundaries of 'home' in a wider sense of this term, which is also used to denote the boundaries of the Khorezmian community. For example, in the context of describing marriage out of the group, the expression *cheta chiqdi* is used, literally meaning 'went beyond the edge', and can be translated as 'crossed the border'. I already gave more detailed information about the existing stereotypes and names which define the Other in the linguistic part of this book. Here, my aim is to focus on the applications and meanings which influence the shaping of the everyday practices of boundary drawing and self-identification. Since I have already shown the ways verbal differentiations are made, I will go on to consider the practices of these identity politics.

Non-Khorezmians are usually engaged in autochthonous discourses when differentiating between 'Us' and 'Them', namely between autochthones and allochthons. The main dichotomies are represented by Tashkentis through derogative

126   *Identification and belonging*

terms such as *harib/kelgindi* to refer to *oblastniye* (regionals)/allochthons. Autochthones' (those considering themselves as being 'true' Tashkentis) usual statements and arguments against allochthons are pronounced in the following manner:

> *Hamma yoqni haribla bosib ketdi (Haribla* (pl.: a derogative term for allochthones) have occupied everywhere [in Tashkent]), *Indeyesla kopayib ketdi Toshkenda* (Indians [meaning indigenous population of America] have become numerous in Tashkent), *Toshkenni pigmeyla/indeyesla bosib ketdi* (Tashkent is invaded by pigmeys/Indians), *Haribla kopayib ketdi Toshkenda* (*Haribla* [pl.] have become numerous in Tashkent).

These statements have similar content, though differently phrased, and using various derogatory terms. Interestingly, the term 'everywhere' (*hamma yoqni*) in the above statement is used to denote only the territory of Tashkent city, which implies an expansionist character ascribed to allochthons, by autochthons. This kind of categorisation towards each party creates particular attitudes among ethnic groups of Uzbeks in Tashkent. These attitudes often lead to confrontations in public spaces such as bazaars, where conflicts of interest take place. In those conflicts between two main groups, namely *Tashkentskiye* and *oblastniye*, racist terms were used by *Tashkentskiye* against *oblastniye*. A 43-year-old woman from another region told the following story of the conflict in which she had interceded in the *Farhadskiy* bazaar in Tashkent. She said:

> These *Tashkentskiy*e have gone beyond all boundaries. Who do they think they are? [...] in the bazaar a local woman (*mestnaya*[Ru]) [Tashkenti] seller of grapes insulted and made another poor *oblastnaya* [a regional] woman move away from her selling place. The *mestnaya* made her vacate the place she was selling her fruit. Besides losing her place, this poor *oblastnaya* had to listen to her [*mestnaya*] insults in public. The *mestnaya* verbally said '*Negrlar hamma yoqni bosib ketdi* [Negroes have occupied everywhere here]'. Then I interrupted by asking her why she was insulting the woman and said that being from Tashkent did not give her the right to insult her, and being from another region did not make someone a Negro. I said that it was only because these 'Negros' work hard that she could make money and eat fruits. In reply that local woman said without any shame in public that '*Ozi Negr bogannan kein Negrni himoya kiladi da* [because she is herself a Negro of course she will defend a Negro]'. I was shocked and said that when she becomes sick she will come to me [the speaker is a medical nurse], to a Negro, and I left.
>
> (Laziza, 43, Tashkent, 15 August 2006)

The above conflictual exchange in the bazaar shows that 'naturalness' in discourse or 'racial' vocabulary used in definitions of the Other is quite striking. The use of racial terms to define the 'Other' and drawing the boundaries between

'We and They' is not a new phenomenon. The knowledge about division of human beings into races was taught in schools during the Soviet Union. The secondary school textbooks had 'enlightened' people on the distinction of the world population into three major races: white, black and yellow. The history of black slaves has been associated not with any politics and economics but with skin colour and social and ethnic division, that are also applied above in the Uzbek context. I will dwell on differentiations based on appearance and dress codes in more detail later in this chapter.

Besides such conflict situations as described above, there are also fields of inter-ethnic interaction. In everyday life autochthony discourses take different forms and meanings, depending on the context. During social gatherings, occasional conversations, bazaars and other business negotiations, as well as talk in all public spheres, the language of autochthony entails the vocabulary of purity and biological argumentation, race and physical distinctions, as well as kinship belonging.

If conflicts of interest arise, the question of *who is who* and *who belongs where* – that is, who is local/*an autochthon* and who is a stranger/*an allochthon* – is at stake. In the incident in the bazaar, the conflict was over the place to sell fruits. The *mestniy* ordered the *oblastnoy* to vacate the place since it was obviously a good place for customers, and both sold the same wares.[7] When the conflict started it was about the *place* to sell the fruits, which immediately turned into the *politics of belonging* to Tashkent. This, in turn, was followed by an insult based on racial and physical pejorative in order to distinguish and diminish the regional competitor as a stranger/allochthon. Although it is prohibited by the national law to differentiate groups (*tabaqabozlik*[Uz]/tribalism), the autochthony discourses can also be witnessed in the contexts of 'official' publicity such as local movies, concerts, and media, to which I turn now.

Performing the Other

Another similar field of expression is show business. Movies, concerts and public performances are all possible spaces to perform identities. Topics of movies are devoted to this, the texts of songs sung by Tashkentis for example, as well as traditions, customs and music displayed to represent the groups in question. Although all programmes, texts for songs and movie scripts must go through a special committee from the *Philarmoniya* that checks content and conformity to national ideologies, loyalty to the regime and political character, popular art is another sphere of enquiry for similar discourses of belonging.

A national version of 'show business' in Uzbekistan has been developing since the Soviet period, and has taken a move away from the Russian, towards an Uzbek national style of art in its repertoires and content. Show business by now is highly developed in terms of large-scale performances and has the highest income by comparison to other spheres of economic engagement. Khorezmians say '*kimni karama artis*', literally 'everybody is *artis*' (*artis* refers to singers, dancers, actors). Listening to music is a fashion in Uzbekistan, and regardless of

128 *Identification and belonging*

age, all listen to the same national stars. Consequently, the competition for being the number one national singer is very high, which underpins numerous power games in Uzbek show business. It is not very expensive to go to the theatre or the cinema in Uzbekistan. Concerts are relatively expensive, and those featuring national stars are very costly in relation to the average income. This notwithstanding, one can see crowds attending performances of famous stars and at the cinema entrances in Tashkent city.

Khorezmian musicians, particularly singers, are known to become national stars very soon after coming to Tashkent. The relatively quick success of many Khorezmian musicians has not gone unnoticed by other artists in Uzbekistan and has, accordingly, prompted professional jealousy and other negative reactions in show business circles. At the time of my field research, the 'number one' pop star of Uzbekistan was notorious for using her power to keep new upcoming stars out of the scene and limiting their popularity. In 2006, during my field research, she organised a very large concert attracting tens of thousands of people. I visited her concert in September 2006. As usual, she opened her performance with a speech on music as art and about the Uzbek nation. She went on to mention 'fake' performers who come to Tashkent and dishonour the 'real' (*haqiqiy*)[8] and 'pure' (*sof*)[9] art of singing. She continued that '*Khorazmlik bosib ketdi Toshkentimizni*' (Khorezmians have invaded *our* Tashkent) and proceeded to insult 'Khorezmian girls', impugning their flirtatious behaviour. Most of the Khorezmian fans in the front seats stood up and made to leave the concert. The singer, however, ordered the guards on the doors to refuse anyone exit. After the concert, all Khorezmian discourses against *oshala* (derogative term used by Khorezmians for all non-Khorezmians) were directed towards the singer, and she was criticised that she herself was *Vodiy* (valley from Uzbek; here it means people from Fergana Valley). In public and private gatherings, Khorezmians had fierce discussions and anticipated that she would sooner or later be punished.[10]

There were other cases where regionals were depicted in a poor light, showing them as the dirtiest, poorest and most uneducated types in national movies (particularly a movie called *Dev va Pakana*/A monster and a dwarf [metaphorical names that depict a tall and fat person vs. a small and thin person]). In this movie they depicted a young Khorezmian woman, distinguished by her broken Khorezmian language (the actress was not a Khorezmian), mouthing usually Khorezmian words which do not exist in the Uzbek literary language. She was an adulteress and was shown as being not a 'decent' girl. This, of course, carried a negative message for Khorezmians, and implied all Khorezmian girls were biddable and promiscuous. Khorezmians told stories of the beatings of actors who had played the roles of 'insulters': producers, I assumed, were further from reach.

Now I will turn to smaller performances of the same identities and bring an example of the Khorezmian event organised by Khorezmian students at a university in Tashkent as part of a cultural programme in which regional cultures are performed. It is similar to the cultural events at the universities in the West, where a week is devoted to Africa and there one can eat African food and see exhibitions with performances and art. Unlike this format, the cultural programme of the universities in Tashkent devote one day per region. In this day students coming from the relevant region perform highlights of their culture, be it local cuisine, cloth or other traditions.

I have already referred to this case earlier in this book, mentioning Khorezmian students seeking funding for organising their events from Khorezmian patrons in Tashkent. Usually these kinds of events require little finance, only the time spent for the organisation of the event by the students involved in the project. The funding was necessary, as one of the students argued, because the students wanted to come up with a very special and impressive presentation of the Khorezmian culture. They took the task very seriously. I participated in the meetings during preparations for the event. Different ideas about presenting Khorezmian culture were brainstormed. Differing ideas among the students on how to represent the exceptional nature of Khorezmians constituted the main dilemma. I did not contribute any ideas as I preferred to listen to them. I agreed to contribute by filming and photographing the event. The students found one sponsor, a Khorezmian in Tashkent who had a very influential position in the sphere of show business. They raised some finances for cooking Khorezmian *palov*, and also used connections to bring a Khorezmian singer who had established her career as a successful pop star in Tashkent. She sang several songs at the end of the performance; her show represented the climax of the event. The programme consisted of the very popular Khorezmian dance *Lazgi*, some Khorezmian jokes, and a short video, shot in Khorezm by the student-organisers. The film itself started with a scene in which some Khorezmian students take a non-Khorezmian student friend to Khorezm. They arrive by aeroplane and are met at the airport. With the exception of the non-Khorezmian friend, everybody wears black sunglasses. A Nexia car meets them at the airport and the driver helps them with their luggage. Modern Uzbek rap music is played constantly, and even after the arrival in Khorezm the music does not change. The characters in the short film reach home and are met by a 'mother' who puts a *chapan* on the guest (which is actually a Bukhara *chapan*). The guest is brought to a very large luxury house where a very good-looking young woman greets the student with tea. Then, *tuhum barak* and *palov* are served (on such occasions, these do not normally go together, I was told). *Tuhum barak* was shown in order to emphasise it as a non-existent dish in other regional cuisines, meaning it has a symbolic value. The guest shows pleasure at the excellent food, while in the background Khorezmian classical music is played. After that, the guest is taken to one of the pearls of Khorezm – the historical town of Khiva – and he looks around with astonishment (it is true that non-Khorezmians, much like some rural Khorezmians, have never visited Khiva in their lives). The film continues: the guest falls in love with the Khorezmian girl who served him tea, and who obviously played the sister of the Khorezmian host. There are no words in the film, only faces and emotions, and the whole visit of the non-Khorezmian guest is overshadowed by his suffering for the Khorezmian girl. He imagines her next to him in traditional clothes, longing for her as his bride. The non-Khorezmian student calls his father. The father's sad expression shows the trouble his son has brought, falling in love with a Khorezmian girl. In the following scene, the father talks to his wife. Both lament where they will find the finances to secure this girl for their son. The story ends sadly. The non-Khorezmian visitor's dreams about the local girl do not come true.

As a Khorezmian myself, and also as an analyst, I trace several stereotypes about non-Khorezmians and Khorezmians performed in this short video. The film featured Khorezmian food, particularly showing those food items which do not exist in the rest of Uzbek cuisine, combined with classical Khorezmian music in a luxury Khorezmian-style house. Furthermore, the astonishment of the guest at the beauty of the Khorezmian girl and also at other things is not accidental. This perspective of Khorezmians on non-Khorezmians derives from the knowledge about the Other and awareness about Khorezmian identity, as well as from the existing and partly shared stereotypes about one another. The significance of the film is the end, which is a clear message to non-Khorezmians which would most probably say 'You do not get our Khorezmian girls easily', which is depicted in the sad ending of the story. This was further exaggerated by the scene in which his puzzled and sad parents were shown. According to marriage traditions, a groom's family takes on most of the expenses, whereas in other regions the bride's family is burdened with obligations which require considerable expenses.

After the film, the famous Khorezmian singer sang several songs and all were invited for free Khorezmian *palov*. These and other student events, be they traditional performance or inter-regional competition of institutes, all provide a stage for students to perform their 'culture', and everyone competes to present their best in order to make the best impression. After all of these examples of identity politics among various ethnic groups, one wonders how, if they are all Uzbeks, one can differentiate one from another. Are these groups so distinct that one can easily point to who belongs where, and who comes from where? In what follows I present various fields of distinctions made among the groups in question. These include physical appearance such as clothing, cuisine and strategic inter-marriages as signs of differences.

Identity markers

I systematically asked my informants from different regions including Tashkentis about how they distinguished *Tashkentskiye*, *oblastniye* and other categories of people. In the following I will summarise the answers I got to that question.

Physical appearance

Hammasinanam (before all/first of all) physical features are said to indicate the regional background of a person. The skin colour of *oblastniye* is usually dark from spending too much time in the sun, which partly was the cause of the emergence of the pejorative term *negr*. This association is corroborated by the knowledge or belief that those who come from rural areas do the 'black work' (*chyornorabochiy*[Ru], literally 'black worker' meaning unskilled labourer). Another aspect related to the skin is about general skin care, especially applied to women, and is described as the skin with poor care (*neuhojenniy*[Ru]/not cared, *ozina karamagan*/not looked at oneself) meaning a woman who neither uses crèmes nor showers regularly. As described by a regional who herself grew up in Tashkent, when one meets people from rural areas one may also notice hard hands. She also stated that differentiations based on the physical features were unfair, saying that,

> people from rural areas are under hard environmental conditions, often without access to running water, working with cattle in fields under an open sun. Of course their skin and their hair becomes very different from those who sit around in their small flats in Tashkent and do nothing apart from washing dishes, doing laundry and cleaning the house.
> (Laziza, 43, Tashkent, 26 April 2006)

On the question of difference in skin and hair, Laziza answered that I should know myself how it is when hair and skin are always under the sun and wind and what becomes of hair and skin when using all kinds of cheap shampoos. Then the skin becomes dark and rough with cracks. Hair, in turn, loses its silky appearance and lustre.

Another pronounced physical feature was the facial structure and particularly the form of the eyes (this was only stated by the Khorezmian informants as a marker to distinguish non-Khorezmians). Khorezmians believe that all others (non-Khorezmians) have small, mongoloid or Kazakh (*yumuq*/closed) eyes, whereas Khorezmians have bigger, rounder eyes. It should be noted here that these markers, together with language differences, are made within Khorezm region itself to distinguish Kypchak speakers of Uzbek from Oghuz speakers, who are also believed to have facial differences, with 'a face like *kapkir*[Kh]'. *Kapkir* refers to a kitchen tool which is flat. The term derives from a joke that these people's faces were stamped/hit with the *kapkir*, which accounts for their faces being so flat (*yempiq*[Kh]).[11]

Alongside physical appearance, linguistic differences are the most important markers of ethnic identities in Tashkent. I have already described linguistic differences and interactional peculiarities of these differentiations in Part II of this book. Another important marker was stated to be clothing, and that in Uzbekistan a person's regional origins may be identified in this manner.

Dress code

Clothes

Even the Tashkenti police use particular conventional stereotypical distinctions on the basis of appearance when they 'fish'[12] in the metro for naive regional

132 *Identification and belonging*

victims. My metaphorical representation of police activity is also shared by victims themselves, who use additional analogies depicting police as those who goes hunting for *ôlja* (booty).[13] After long observation, the type of person usually stopped for passport checks more or less conformed to existing stereotypes on appearance, classifying people as either regionals or Tashkentis. Below I will describe different clothing styles that usually differentiate the two separate groups.

There are recommendations on dress code given by the headmen of construction teams to their new team members who come to Tashkent in order to prevent them from being apprehended in the metro stations or streets by the police. The basic recommendations (for men) include: 'Do not wear sport trousers and sport shoes (*krossovka*[Ru]), do not carry big bags or plastic bags, do not go out unshaved, do not use perfume, do not wear white shirts, do not look around at things as though you saw them for the first time in your life.'[14] Husan, one of the headmen of a construction team I studied, formulated these recommendations. He was tired of constant dealings with the police to secure the release of his team members, as well as having problems himself from time to time.

Non-Tashkentis who come from different regions of Uzbekistan try to follow these and other recommendations made on the basis of existing conventions about dress code. The aim was to avoid identification as regionals and seizure by the police. As people in general, both non-Tashkentis and particularly Tashkentis themselves believe that Tashkentis are the most 'Europeanised' (*yevropalashgan*) in terms of dress and other aspects of social behaviour (personal conduct, table manners, etc.). However, as far as I could observe, this depends on which part of Tashkent one lives in. In the central parts of Tashkent close to Amir Timur Square and other central parts of the city, one can encounter young women wearing modern dresses such as miniskirts, T-shirts, shorts, tight shirts, jeans, suits in different styles (formal, casual, evening, classic). In *Eski Shahar* especially (the old part of the city) and more in suburban regions of Tashkent, one can still see a modern style of clothing, but also more conservative styles of dressing like long skirts, long dresses, some not so tight, some a bit wider, as well as more covered styles of clothing, both modern (youth) and traditional (older women).

Both Khorezmians living in Tashkent and Tashkentis agreed that the female clothing elements indicated a distinction between Tashkentis and other regionals. This distinction of dress code of regionals was positively approved or described as a decent way of clothing by regionals themselves, which is different from the dress code of 'Tashkentis who shamelessly show everything possible' (*hamma yoqi ochiq*), as many regional women described it. These types of clothing include: wearing 'too long' dresses or skirts (from Tashkentis' perspective), especially by young women; wearing men's shirts over the dress; wearing scarves by young women unless the scarf is put on with a particular style, for example, if it is worn like *hijab*;[15] wearing a *halat*[Ru] (the form is like a gown) with many buttons in front and usually made by dressmakers; traditional dresses, dresses made by a dressmaker, especially if worn by young women, too colourful dresses or tops, wearing fabrics that glitter, the wrong sized cloth and so forth.

Who is a Negro and who is not? 133

Bukhara and Samarkand women were distinguished by Khorezmians, stating that one could recognise them by their liking for dresses made from very glittery fabric. Male regionals were described by Tashkentis and Khorezmians as wearing: not-ironed shirts new from the package, where one may still see lines from the packaging. They (urban members referring to regionals) explain it by saying that

> these poor *oblastriye'* before coming to Tashkent bought a new shirt and just before going out downtown took this shirt out of the package and put it on without bothering to iron them as they never do, especially since the shirt was new and looked very nice to their eyes.

Sport trousers were also included, as well as white shirts, shirts of the wrong size (usually bigger), cheap shirts made out of *sintetika*[Ru] (synthetic fabric), trousers made at a dressmaker, cheap trousers from black, soft fabric unlike the dark jeans trousers that look more stiff and of better quality in comparison to others, not wearing *mayka*[Ru] under a shirt, especially when visible in the summer. Older men who came to Tashkent do not try to match the clothing style of Tashkentis, especially men from Fergana Valley and other regions who wear parts of traditional clothing items such as *döppi* (an Uzbek cap), and *chapcn* (a long, handmade, two-layered coat-like covering mostly worn in winter instead of a coat).

In winter the winter jackets are the most important marker because they are the most expensive accessory. Different jackets are worn. Leather jackets are up to style, so there are real leather jackets and *dermantin*[Ru] (artificial leather-like fabric). Real leather jackets are very expensive and start from $150. *Dermantin* can be of good quality *kojazamenitel*[Ru] (leather replacer) or a plastic of bad quality (*kliyonka*[Ru]).

Bags

Bags are also important accessories of clothing. Tashkentis tend to wear fancier bags (counterfeit bags using expensive brand names such D&G, Gucci, etc.). It is important that bags should not be too old or worn out. Bags for older women can be a bit bigger and the latest trend, for example (2005–2006), was the bags called '*indiskiy*[Ru]' (Indian) for older women. This is a nice quadrate bag with two elephants in a decorative Indian style embroidered on the leather half of the fabric bag. The main interdiction concerns the carrying of plastic bags or big bazaar bags, especially those used by shuttle traders, which are square in form with a plastic zipper

Jewellery

Large amounts of jewellery is one of the signs to recognise a regional; gold teeth, or no jewellery at all, are also not 'good'. Hair accessories also have meanings. Large flowers are inadvisable or other big or colourful hair styles. Too much gold is generally not advisable due to increased street crime. Wearing too much gold and having golden teeth is ascribed to Khorezmians and stereotypes them as being rich.

Shoes

Shoes are a very important part of clothing. They must be well polished, and it is best to buy oneself a pocket shoe cleaner that can be carried in the pocket or bag. They are very practical for cleaning the shoes *en route*. Dust is unavoidable and happens within two to three hours of leaving the house.

Shoes should not be worn-out, and the stitches of repaired shoes should not be seen. When one visits a shoe maker (usually repairer) and sits there a while, one may observe a large pile of shoes waiting to be repaired and people constantly bringing their shoes for repair. Most of the shoes are repaired several times: the heels especially break, or the shoe opens up on the front or sides, requiring stitching, glue, and nails.

It is difficult to find shoes of good quality in Uzbekistan, so everybody must buy new shoes at the beginning of each season. Another option is to prolong one's shoe for at least two seasons (*sezon*), needing constant repair, which finally becomes all too visible.

Another observation I myself made was that Tashkentis wear very high heels and other 'daring' accessories. I have never seen my informants wearing high heels or display any desire for local shoes such as those adorned with jewellery, or with many straps or other accessories. Some of my young Khorezmian female informants did wear these shoes and other clothes, saying they could avoid being taken as regionals – talking, in turn, was also avoided.

Regional varieties of food

Another very important aspect of regional and cultural differences was food. The primary item of food to be differentiated is bread and *osh* (the main Uzbek dish made out of rice, carrots, onions, meat and oil).

Bread is made differently in the various regions of Uzbekistan. Famous and popular in Tashkent is one specialty of Samarkand bread which is very thick, round and has the form of most bread made in Tashkent. Other regions stamp a flower ornament in the centre of their bread. Khorezmians have a very particular type of bread distinguished by its thinness and is more decoratively floral; one flower in the centre and two or three rows surrounding it. Khorezmians do not like the bread of other regions and consider the quality too thick. Consequently, Khorezmians who come to live and build a house in Tashkent first construct their own *tandir* (a self-built oven usually in the garden) in order to bake their own bread. Otherwise, their families send them Khorezmian bread along with other food items from Khorezm. Khorezmians consider Tashkent bread as being 'empty' (not nutritional) and meagre. They say '[i]t is better to buy a Russian *buhanka*[Ru] [loaf of bread] than this Tashkent bread' (Adolat, 35, 12 March 2006).

Every region is proud of its way of making *osh* (Khorezmians use the word *palov*). Khorezmian *palov* is distinguished as being white and Khorezmians do not like others' *osh* as, depending on the regional variety, it is too dark and spicy for them. The differences in the recipes for *osh* (all other Uzbeks) or *palov*^{Kh} (Khorezmians, Bukharans) are insignificant to a non-specialist of this dish. For example, the *osh* of Tashkentis is distinct as they add beans and the onions are burnt, giving the rice its dark colour and specific taste. *Osh* from Fergana Valley includes sheep fat instead of normal oil, giving a different flavour. Bukhara and Samarqand *palov* is known to be served separately, and the rice is cooked independently and added at the end. These are the most distinct varieties of *osh* or *palov*. Khorezmian *palov* is considered to be very special from the Khorezmian point of view and 'strange' for non-Khorezmians. It is distinct from others in that Khorezmians use less oil, do not burn onions in the frying, and use nothing but rice, carrots, meat, oil, garlic, salt and *zira* (cumin seeds). Khorezmians say that their *palov* is *diyeticheskiy*^{Ru} (dietary) in comparison to others, as the rice is cooked well, with less oil and no burning in the process.

Members of ethnic groups can go to great lengths to promote their regional specialties. One can, of course, find cafés with a cuisine specific to the region. One may find Khorezmian, Bukhara or Samarqand cafés which claim to offer specific food from their region. Khorezmians are very proud of their cuisine since they have dishes that are not found in other regions; *tuhum barak* (dumplings filled with eggs and boiled in the water) is the most cited. I was also asked to cook *tuhum barak* when I was a guest at my informants' places from Namangan, Andijan and Tashkent, but cooked only once, which took the whole morning. Unfortunately, judging from the amount they ate, and from their faces, they did not seem to like it so much, although they were very curious about it and were sampling it for the first time.

Witnessing the discussions over bread and *osh* and whose food is tastier, better and more popular, one wonders why these differences are so often discussed, compared and competed over. As I mentioned above, although sometimes the dishes in question might not be so excitingly tasty for others, they are still promoted with great enthusiasm, and one may be led to believe it is done only for the sake of making a difference. Conversely, it may only be a matter of dietic habit, and an inability to accept alternatives.

Marriage strategies as contexts of relevance in politics of belonging in Tashkent

Marriage strategies are one of the main mechanisms of inclusion and exclusion and also an important method to classify who identifies with whom.[16] With the exception of Tashkentis, non-Khorezmians' marriage decisions are closely related to both belonging to a place and collective identification. As I mentioned, other regional groups do not see any problems in inter-marrying with Tashkentis or with members of other regional groups. The criteria for choosing a partner do not restrict the group affiliation of the future partner. Rather, the place of his/her residence is more important, and possession of a *tashkentskaya propiska*^{Ru} (Tashkent registration). It is even better if the prospective partner owns a flat or a house in Tashkent. For many non-Khorezmians, marrying a Tashkenti is seen as a step up on both the social and ethnic ladder, whereas among Khorezmians it is viewed as a betrayal (*sotilgan*).

Gulchehra is 34, a young woman, and a rice trader who comes from Guliston, a region not far from Tashkent. She is married to a man from Qoqand who lives in Tashkent and works as a policeman. He has, of course, no problems with *propiska*. He also owns a small flat. *Propiska* and housing are the most important things in the life of a newcomer to Tashkent. Gulchehra also has a 'good' income in addition to security provided by her husband. Neither Gulchehra nor her husband see their different regional backgrounds as an impediment to their marriage and, as she stated, their parents were of the same mind. She emphasised that her husband had a stable job and registration in Tashkent, so their family was secure.

Sadoqat is 44 years old and grew up in Tashkent, but her parents come from Namangan, Fergana Valley. She is married to a Khorezmian. She indicated that his family was strictly against their marriage, adding that it was always difficult to get into this 'pack of wolves' (*staya*^{Ru} *volkov*^{Ru}). She has been married to her husband for 22 years, and said that she is still not accepted in his extended family as one of them. She also indicated that she avoids the relatives of her husband as much as possible, or is afraid that 'they will eat her up' (*yeb koiyadi bula mani*). She learned the Khorezmian language, and even the specific dialect of her husband; yet she still has problems being integrated into the group. She said that when they married she did not care about his cultural background, and knew him from the same university. She also indicated that she did not expect that Khorezmians would be so exclusively related to their relatives and co-ethnics.

Tashkentis, like Khorezmians, are endogamous, and try to marry only other Tashkentis. I asked some members of this group how this was possible, since so many inhabitants of Tashkent had come from other regions of Uzbekistan, and a second generation had grown up in the city. To my mind they were difficult to distinguish from Tashkentis themselves. Both young and older female Tashkenti informants indicated that this is avoided by arranging marriage with the children of friends and acquaintances, people whom they or their parents have known well for many years. The most important criterion was that the parents and/or grandparents of a future candidate for marriage should be Tashkenti.

Khorezmians have 'isolated' themselves from non-Khorezmians, and socialise within their own 'circles', or with other Khorezmians.[17] Khorezmians, unlike the Others, 'usually' try to stay endogamous. Parents in Tashkent are more alert about their children in order to prevent them from a 'wrong path' (*natoģri yol* [a wrong marriage candidate]) or as Khorezmians often phrase it 'we [parents] say that they [children] should not cross the line drawn by their parents [*biza chizgan chiziqdan chiqmasin dimiz*]'.

In Chapter 6 I will talk in more detail about how marriages are organised within the Khorezmian community and their strategic and non-strategic ways of socialising and networking. There, I will also present a biography of a Khorezmian ethnic entrepreneur, Sayora, a woman of 47, who is involved in establishing numerous Khorezmian networks around herself, and creating a relatively extensive Khorezmian community in Tashkent. Sayora organises and arranges many of the marriages of Khorezmians in Tashkent and is very well known for that. I have been present in more than eight instances where requests about finding a spouse were made, both in face-to-face meetings and on the telephone. I have taken part in four marriage parties arranged by her, and soon after I left she was on the way to two arranged marriages which I missed. Sayora said: 'I do not want our girls to go outside; good girls should not be married to strangers (*chujoylara*[Ru] with Khorezmian suffix) [bizani kizlar cheta getib kolmasin ozlarimizdan, yahshi kizlar chujoylara getmasin diman].' She said that in her life she wants to do good things for people, and help them as much as she can. One of the marriages I witnessed that was arranged by Sayora concerned the daughter of a divorced woman (Maryam). Sayora had a strong relationship with Maryam, having helped her to get established in Tashkent and build her own house. I did not witness the negotiations between the two sides for the marriage but I attended the ceremonies and interviewed the *kelin* and her family. Sayora was very proud of the match she had made and told me that she 'had chosen a very good match [*ozlarina mos*]'. The groom was a Khorezmian and she referred to him as 'one of our own boys [*ozlarimizni bollardan*]'. Sayora said that she knew the parents of the groom and that they had asked her about a possible wife for their son. Sayora said that she was very quick to suggest Manzura (the *kelin*) and told others that her family was very nice and *ozlarimizdan*/from ours. Manzura's view of the marriage was characterised by disinterest. She was not planning to marry as she wanted to go to university and dreamed of travelling abroad at least once before her marriage. The *kelin*'s mother, however, said that she must hurry to marry her daughter because

> who knows what will happen [with her daughter] in a big city? What if she falls in love with someone who is not a Khorezmian? In Khorezm there are other worries – you are always afraid what kind of family he [the groom] comes from. But here [in Tashkent], in addition to that you have a bigger problem which is the danger of losing your daughter to Others [*boshkalara*].

The main arguments against inter-marriage between Khorezmians and other groups refer to the major differences in traditions and ritual practices, as well as rules of reciprocity. It is very 'expensive' to marry a girl in other ethnic groups, including Tashkentis. Tashkentis, in particular, employ a strict rule of financial burden on the side of the parents of a *kelin*. If they have many girls in the family, Tashkentis and many other non-Khorezmians are required to save everything to marry their daughters, which demands very large expenditure and obligations. Khorezmians, however, have the opposite tradition. The parents of a groom have the financial responsibilities, and not the family of a bride.

From an economic point of view, the rationale for a Khorezmian man would hence be to marry a non-Khorezmian girl, since the groom's family would thereby profit. Then the question of pride comes in, however, by saying that Khorezmian men are not so 'low' (*pas* is a local term used for 'low' denoting moral status) 'to get a girl from *oshala* for the sake of money' (it is low or diminishing to manly pride if one takes a girl from *oshala* for money). In most of the cases I have observed it is generally so, that they do inter-marry, and claim to belong to Tashkent. Besides Khorezmians, all other regional groups have a general traditional pattern that is a financial burden to the bride's family. This has an effect on the status of the women and parents who have many daughters. This traditional pattern is economically and socially very important. In terms of intra- and inter-group relations, it also affects marriage strategies and the principles of status-making.

Among Khorezmians, belonging to a group carries more weight than belonging to a place. Other regional groups in Uzbekistan, however, tend to identify with place (Tashkent). They prefer to be assimilated to a 'major' population of Tashkentis in the capital city. This creates specific dynamics in the politics of belonging among different groups in Tashkent. In the next section I will present these dynamics in more detail.

Defining the 'We'

There are several ways Uzbek groups identify themselves, and all do not necessarily fit with the categorisation presented above. This is the main reason I will group the cultural differences and analyse them without reference to these aforementioned five categories of Uzbek groups. I will take the content and meaning of self-identification as a point of departure in my analysis, rather than starting with existing categories of grouping Uzbeks. The pattern of self-identification of various Uzbek sub-ethnic groups consists of autochthony discourses about Tashkent, construction of 'home' by Khorezmians, and their deconstruction of the autochthony discourses stated by Tashkentis, which undermines Tashkenti authenticity.

Autochthony discourses of non-Khorezmians

The main question is: who identifies with whom, and how? This question is a summary of several questions. I already briefly presented some kind of answer to how people determine who they are. I will analyse the 'how' part of the question in this section. To answer all parts of the question it is important to note here the fact that Tashkent city is the centre of the whole country in the sense that resource allocation is based on a one-city centralisation principle. The interaction of the sub-ethnic groups described in this chapter is relevant for the capital city of Tashkent where everybody strives to come to live. That is the main reason I start this section by describing Tashkent city and the motivations of migrants who come exclusively to this city from all over Uzbekistan (Bartlett

2001). For example, for Khorezmians it would have been much easier to go to the closer Samarqand and not to Tashkent, which is at the other end of the country. Furthermore, I will explore the motivations built into the choices of identification, and how these senses of belonging are produced in everyday interactions.

Tashkent is the capital city, where most of the economic and other resources are allocated due to the centralised system of government. For reasons of practical access to government bureaucracy, all of the international NGOs, state agencies and business companies have situated at least their head offices in Tashkent. All of the major institutions and educational, business and medical centres are also situated there. This attracts many students, employees seeking career advancement, businessmen looking for an already well-established infrastructure and commodities, and people in need of medical help. Nevertheless, there are universities, hospitals, bazaars, etc. in each regional centre of all 12 regions of Uzbekistan. I asked why people still prefer to migrate to the capital. To my questions in this regard, I was given the following answers (dialogue between me (R) and Zuhra (Z)):

Z: Look, you know very well yourself and I do not have to tell you because you also came to Tashkent to work didn't you?
R: Yes I had to finish my studies and there was no such department outside Tashkent.
Z: OK, let me explain to you then. I am a trader and trade rice; I could go just to Urgench and trade my rice there which is only 30 minutes by bus and 20 by car. But I came here to Tashkent: why, because the price of rice is not the same, there are not as many people in Urgench, even in the whole Khorezm region as there are in Tashkent, and these people are the number of clients for people like me who sell something. If I am sick, which is often the case, I will pay the same amount to the doctors in Khorezm and I do not know if they have good technical equipment to make proper treatment or to diagnose me. And even if I am fortunate enough to find the best medical centre in Khorezm with all the equipment then it is all in vain (*bir tiyin*) as our ecology and water is very bad. The same is with my children. If I have enough money and want to provide them with good education I must find a good school which may not need to be perfect [*zorinan bomasaam*] but at least a normal one where they teach something to my children. Do you think that well-educated teachers will be looking for jobs in our local schools? Of course not, they will try to stay in Tashkent after they graduate, and if they have graduated, from our universities in Urgench, at least the good ones, like you, will seek to continue their further education of course in Tashkent. Because there are more opportunities in Tashkent than somewhere else, and maybe they will have more students who are able to pay. I sell more rice in Tashkent than I would sell in Urgench so I have more money to pay to the teachers if they teach my children. Everything is connected.
(Zuhra, 29, 12 May 2006, Tashkent)

It becomes clear that striving for resources and betterment of lifestyle and education is the reason for migrants to establish themselves in Tashkent. I have heard similar stories and explanations from migrants from other regions such as Fergana Valley, Bukhara, Surkhandarya and Qashqadarya. Members of other regions often mentioned that their grandfathers or their relatives are from Tashkent and therefore they came to be reunited with members of their families. They try not to mention the fact that they are migrants by saying that they were born in Tashkent or they are married and have a family in Tashkent.

What about the reaction of Tashkentis to this influx of newcomers who even claim to be from the city? *Toshkenli* is a very attractive group to belong to, considering its place at the top of the hierarchy in terms of both regional and national belonging. Being *Toshkenli* grants first of all access to all sorts of resources, not only in Tashkent city itself. Its power goes beyond the territory of the city. Particularly this concerns those who work in lucrative, high-rank positions within the state administration. All of the state agencies are hierarchically organised in a way that the main offices are in Tashkent and their representative offices are in the 12 districts (*oblast'*) of Uzbekistan. Those representative offices are called *oblastnoy* (district) department of so and so; then comes city office; and then in rural areas one sub-district office. All of the regional offices, including their sub-offices, are randomly checked for their performance by so called *Tashkentdan komissia* (assessment board from Tashkent, which is usually made of the members of Tashkent main office). The board comes usually without prior notice. The head of the regional office is mostly nervous since he is responsible for all his sub-offices. Usually these checks are abused and are the main source of power and resource – and not only for individual members of the board. This kind of over-centralised hierarchical system grants limitless power to state agencies in Tashkent.

To be from Tashkent means to have *tashkentskaya*[Ru] *propiska*, which grants the holder the right to buy real estate in Tashkent, which has the highest value in Uzbekistan, and to find employment opportunities that are better than in peripheral parts of the country. In addition to all the other advantages, holding a *tashkentskaya propiska* makes a person an attractive candidate for marriage and somebody who can grant particular opportunities.

However, there are differences of being a 'real' Tashkenti (*girt Toshkenli*) and being only a holder of *tashkenstkaya propiska*. Not all of the mentioned resources are freely available to all in possession of *tashkentskaya propiska*. 'Real' Tashkentis have had their networks established in the city for many years, often inherited from their parents, as well as access to particular resources, which might not be available to others.

Girt Toshkenli can be translated as 'very much from Tashkent', which refers to those Tashkentis whose parents and also grandparents are from Tashkent. The notion of a 'real' *toshkenli*, who claims to be an autochthon of Tashkent city, is authenticity for Tashkentis. A sense of 'who came first when Tashkent was founded' is the main topic discussed when claiming autochthony. So autochthonous population of Tashkent, or *girt toshkenli*, has well-established networks in the city at its disposal and enjoys easier access to the most attractive resources in the sphere of employment, real estate, business and other services, including better education and medical services. This group is, of course, exclusive, and has its own methods of recognising whether or not a person is *girt toshkenli*. Principles of exclusion are based primarily on descent; second on place of birth; and third on important linguistic elements of '*toshkencha*' dialect, which must include good knowledge of slang and specific accents and intonations.

Tashkentis entertain also a myth about the origin of the 'real' Tashkentis who allegedly have been born in an old part of Tashkent known as Eski Shahar (old city). Eski Shahar is currently in the process of demolition by the government, and modern multi-storey buildings are being built instead. Many people have moved out of Eski Shahar because conditions in other parts of Tashkent have improved in terms of roads, proximity to other places or the economic centre that has obviously vacated Eski Shahar. Now, it is difficult to define the centre of Tashkent, since it fully depends on the speaker who defines it. The cultural and political centre is, of course, the area around Independence Square, where most theatres, government buildings, museums and parks are situated. The business centre is around the highest concentration of shops and other business-related administrative buildings. For rice traders, *Chilanzar* is the centre, as *Farhadskiy* and *Chilanzar* bazaars are situated there.

Thus the connection to Eski Shahar cannot be defined as loyalty to the most attractive place to live or visit Tashkent anymore. Eski Shahar is a more symbolic place to appropriate as a place of birth when claiming autochthony as *Toshkenli*. Eski shahar is viewed by Tashkentis as a place where the history of Tashkent began. The discourse is not about who is the indigenous population of Tashkent, but instead who came first when Tashkent was founded. It is also not about who was living in the territory of present-day Tashkent. Thus the *girt toshkenlis* identify themselves as growing up in *Eski Shahar* and being born in that part of Tashkent. In contrast, the *Chilanzar* district of Tashkent city is defined as a place of migrants.

As regards the Tashkentis who are not considered 'real', what are the ingredients and forms of their identification? As mentioned, those who come to Tashkent try to avoid the label *oblastniye*, or an even worse form used by Tashkentis, which is *harib*,[18] and eventually also become part of the group. They also join the autochthony discourses but in a different way than 'real' Tashkentis do. The latecomers state that they were born in Tashkent. When they are further interrogated they state that their parents also live in Tashkent. In further interrogation with an eye to revealing the allochthon, the usual question concerns the origin of the parents, which is difficult to evade. The interrogations are performed by both autochthones and allochthons.

Asking this kind of private questions can be considered part of the Uzbek 'culture' in general. Simultaneously, this way of asking questions is often ascribed to the 'uncultured regionals who do not have any manners of conversation'.[19] This is not only the position of many Tashkentis, but also of urbanised Khorezmians. Actually this aspect of conversational culture was an advantage for me as I could ask many private questions from strangers without any problems.

Comparing autochthony in Africa and Uzbekistan

Coming back to the autochthony discourses between autochthones and allochthons, it is worthwhile to connect them with the existing academic discussions of these matters in other regions of the world. This can shed light on the comparative possibilities of my examples within, for instance, the African context. There is also an insightful theoretical discussion of the link between autochthony and ethnicity in the example of Irish identity, which is directly linked to the theories of nationalism and ethnicity (Zenker 2013: 254).

The politics of belonging and the concept of autochthony, which derive from the colonial and postcolonial context in Africa, offer a useful analytical framework for comparing similar types of processes elsewhere in the world. Important scholarly contribution in this field has been made by Arnaut (2004), Englund *et al.* (2004), Geschiere (1997, 2004), Geschiere and Gugler (1998), Geschiere and Nyamnjoh (1998, 2000, 2001), Nyamjoh (2005, 2007), Jackson (2006), Marshall-Fratani (2006) and Yuval-Davis (2006). I largely draw on the theoretical models of those authors in my analysis of the discourses on autochthony and belonging. Stephen Jackson's (2006) analysis of autochthony politics in the Democratic Republic of Congo is useful in considering different scales or layers of autochthony discourses among the groups with different cultural and historical backgrounds. He (ibid.) offers a multi-scaled and complex framework to examine autochthony politics and discourses. Jackson (ibid.: 95) considers the dualities and binary oppositions of autochthony and allochthony through different lenses informed by 'pre-existing identity polarities at particular scales of identity and difference: local, provincial, national, regional'. He carefully examines the spheres or spaces of autochthony discourses by dividing them into various scales and levels. His 'successive scales' of autochthony discourses include 'ethnicity, geographical divisions, nationality and mega ethnicity' (ibid.: 100). He argues that autochthony discourses depend on their level or scale, and can have different meanings and content. They can provide means and ways to make difference and exclude the Other or a stranger. Jackson (ibid.) describes the language of autochthony as a jargon in which the stereotypes and special terms are used for differentiating 'purity' versus 'impurity' and 'infection'. Jackson's (ibid.: 100) distinction of 'successive scales' of autochthony discourses helps to explain the differences in content and meanings of these discourses among real Tashkentis and others who hold only *tashkentskaya propiska*.

Although analytical models developed on the basis of African examples partly fit the examples from Uzbekistan, there are, of course, fundamental and historical differences in the content and dynamics of the politics of belonging between the African continent and post-Soviet Central Asian countries. Regardless of these similarities and differences, in fact the government of Uzbekistan does not support autochthonous movements or discourses of this kind, and even prohibits them by law.

Politics of belonging in the context of Tashkent city are based on the local discourses over who belongs where and to which group one belongs, as well as the very making of the significant Other. All these processes of making difference stay on the local level without extending into the national political space. Therefore, the adjective 'political' in my case does not only refer to the state of affairs in the sphere of government, but rather defines the set of practices and set of relations among groups in the local competition for resources and the power struggle among them (Barnes 1969).

The restriction of autochthonous discourses by the state does not point to its weakness or debility, but implies that autochthony discourses are limited to particular spaces that are outside the state discourses. National state policies and ideologies about national unity do not allow any space for expressing difference, or claiming autochthony or other group belonging within the realm of official politics. Any expressions or implications that are connected with notions of ethnicity or cultural difference within the same nation are considered to be illegal, and are prosecuted by law. Having said that, it becomes obvious that the spheres or contexts for autochthony discourses are observed outside of state policies and on a different level than suggested by Jackson (2006: 100).

Autochthony discourses are not the only constituents of the self-identification of non-Khorezmians. Other elements or aspects of their identification include discussions of the degree of Uzbekness as a tool/strategy for differentiating themselves from other ethnic groups, which is particularly relevant for those who come from Fergana Valley. They claim to be more real Uzbeks than any other, since their dialect form makes the basis of official Uzbek literary language. This argument, of course, applies to the rights to the capital city of Uzbekistan, and automatically makes them autochthones in their own eyes, a view not necessarily shared by Tashkentis. Tashkentis do not necessarily have to very much engage in discussions as to who is more Uzbek, and it is not so important to them, since their Tashkent identity is already high enough in the ranking of local hierarchies of identities. Likewise, Khorezmians do not join these discussions of who is more Uzbek, since for them – and this is particular about this group – their Khorezmian identity prevails.

Deconstruction of the autochthony discourses by Khorezmians

As I mentioned above, different groups negotiate their belonging differently. Khorezmians strongly identify with their group and do not attach very much symbolic meaning to their new place of residence (Tashkent). Counter to the autochthonous claims by Tashkentis, they argue that Tashkent was a place where traders came and went to trade, and the town was always known as a place of migrants. Khorezmians conclude that Tashkent cannot be claimed as an autochthonous place with an indigenous population. These counter-arguments made by Khorezmians in a way downgrade the symbolic and historical power of the place as asserted by Tashkentis and others. Khorezmians do this by, for example, enquiring about the origin of the great-grandparents' generation of their

Tashkenti counterparts to prove contrary to autochthonous discourses about belonging to Tashkent advanced by non-Khorezmians. These forefathers may in fact have come from elsewhere and settled in Tashkent as traders or for other reasons. This, of course, can lead to conflict situations as a result of fierce discussion concerning the real indigenous population of Tashkent, and when it was founded. On several occasions I have encountered this questioning of Tashkenti authenticity. These counter-arguments, however, are restricted to Khorezmians, as other regional groups in Tashkent avoid entering conflicts.

Khorezmians have their own myth about their history. They claim to have lived in a separate state prior to the annexation of Khorezm into contemporary Uzbekistan during early Russian occupation. The myth elaborates also on the treasury left by the Khorezmian khans in a legendary Swiss bank account. 'The money has become so big, it could feed the whole population of Khorezm for the next 50 years' one informant told me. Many Khorezmians added that 'the condition for the withdrawal of the money from the Swiss bank is to become an independent state'. This kind of discourse would legally mean several years of imprisonment for the speaker, so one has to be very careful to whom one talks about this myth. Khorezmians also have their own way of relating to their 'home' which is not Tashkent. Below I will present some ideas about 'home', and how 'home' is constructed by Khorezmians.

The Khorezmian mode of belonging to a place or space[20] can be well described as a 'deterritorialised' translocal mode of belonging (Englund 2004: 293; Geschiere and Gugler 1998).[21] Khorezmians have very strong connections and attachment to their 'home' in Khorezm, even if they reside in Tashkent. Constructing home includes several patterns I am going to discuss below. The major patterns include striving for residential proximity with other Khorezmians, building or designing the interior in a Khorezmian style and ensuring a supply of Khorezmian food products brought from Khorezm such as rice, bread and often even meat in winter.

I often observed and heard of Khorezmians' efforts to reside in proximity with their relatives, or their co-ethnics. This calls for imagination of the 'home' not at home. The best example for 'making home' at a place that is not home is the migrants' efforts to establish residential proximities with 'people from home' (*oy yandakila*/those who are from home). People from home include relatives, friends and acquaintances.

Those who are lucky enough to be able to build their own house naturally build them in the 'Khorezmian style'. Khorezmian-style houses differ from those of non-Khorezmians by the architecture and land planning of the house plot, which mainly concerns private house plots. The difference between a Khorezmian and non-Khorezmian house is in the location of the entrance door. The entrance gate in non-Khorezmian houses leads directly to the inside yard/garden, whereas in a Khorezmian house one enters directly into the house and the garden is located behind the house. The houses of non-Khorezmians are usually built around the garden. Those Khorezmians who cannot afford to build their own houses in Tashkent limit themselves to the interior design of their homes in the

Khorezmian style. In other words, Khorezmians in Tashkent strive to create a Khorezmian environment in a new place of residence. This new place is still not called home as they refer to Khorezm when they speak about home (*oy yan*). Khorezmians in Tashkent strive to produce a newly made space as a formal continuum of 'real home': 'home' itself is an imaginary, as well as a product of the day-to-day practices of making a new place *part* of 'home', since home itself refers not only to the actual place of residence, but to their place of origin as well.

Khorezmians' definition of 'home' goes beyond their place of residence and connects to their natal village. Sayora even stated that she has a secret desire 'to create a Khorezmian oasis here [in her neighbourhood in Tashkent], carefully and step by step [*astan-astan*]'. The word 'oasis' represents a metaphor that is related to a particular image of Khorezm. In the past this region was located between several famous oases, such as the ones of Khiva and Bukhara. Simultaneously, the use of the geographic term 'oasis' conveys the speaker's efforts to create a 'real' physical place.

By applying hermeneutic tools one can assume that the fact that the speaker intends to create this physical place 'carefully and step by step' emphasises its tangible, not metaphorical, character. It also demonstrates that Sayora is aware of how others, e.g. the state and other ethnic groups, may perceive such a Khorezmian place. It is very probable that these other actors would hinder the flourishing of a Khorezmian oasis in the capital city. The state is interested in controlling and enforcing a national identity that tolerates cultural diversity only in the sphere of folklore. Other groups in Uzbekistan, particularly native Tashkentis in the capital, perceive Khorezmians with ambiguity. They admire their arts but also look down upon them as 'regionals', which is synonymous with 'backward' and, in some ways, 'uncivilised'.

In spatial terms, 'home' for internal migrants (and others) involves both physical and symbolic components of construction. The 'home' of Khorezmians in Tashkent cannot be defined as a physically existent place with fixed physical boundaries. It is, rather, a socially constructed and, to some extent, 'culturally bounded' and simultaneously trans-local space, which is typical for migrants and transnational actors anywhere in the world (Glick-Schiller and Levitt 2004). The way in which Khorezmians imagine and relate to 'home' can be compared to what Englund (2004: 293) refers to as 'deterritorialised modes of belonging'. He (ibid.) described Pentecostal Christians in Malawi in impoverished townships who identify themselves as belonging to their imagined 'world down here' in contrast to the 'world out there' (ibid.: 293). The mode of belonging in their case is imagined. Englund (ibid.) describes this mode of belonging as 'deterritorialised' due to their interpretations of the world and localities in terms of religious belief and myths without fixed borders or territory. He (ibid.) uses Ferguson's (1999) model of 'local and cosmopolitan', which challenges the dualistic urban and rural distinctions. Ferguson (ibid.) exemplifies both 'localism' and 'cosmopolitanism' of urban dwellers originating from rural regions of Zambia by emphasising their 'rural belonging despite their urban existence' (ibid.: 212).

146 *Identification and belonging*

These ideas are similarly theorised by Henri Lefebvre (2004), who combined what he understands as objective and subjective realities with cognitive processes and everyday lived experiences in order to bridge the gap between, on the one hand, pure subjective or metaphysical definitions of space, and lived experiences and practices on the Other. For him (Lefebvre 2004), objective reality is lived experience of everyday life; in turn, subjective reality comprises perceived and conceived experiences of human ecology. Conceived experiences of subjective reality include external influences of power, ideology and knowledge. And the perceived experiences of human subjective realities include the influence of images, memories and symbolic forms of representations. Lefebvre (2004) defines spaces as produced and reproduced and a consequence of interrelationships between different spheres within different spaces.

Making of 'We and They'

I have already partly explained in Chapter 4 collective identifications in terms of differentiation of different groups by language varieties, autochthony discourses and belonging to a group. The material of this chapter on identification strategies complemented the previous chapter on similar issues by means of adding practices, whereas the previous material was based on discursive practices. I depicted other aspects of collective identification derived not only from discourses of identification, but also practices and representation of collective identities. In this context the symbolic place as a reference for identity politics served the main point of departure for understanding this complex taxonomy of social relations and identity politics. The symbolic place is different for each group: for Tashkentis it is Eski Shahar (old part of Tashkent which is being destroyed at the time of research); for Khorezmians it is 'Khorezm'; and for the rest it is 'Tashkent city'. These differences also led to different autochthonous discourses about belonging to a place. Considering all the aspects highlighted so far on collective identification and ethnicity I come to the following conclusions.

First, ethnicity is not homogeneous. The notion of heterogeneity, flexibility and situationality of collective identities is not new in the academic debate. The contradictory content of collective identities and the flexibility of their boundaries do not necessarily deny the existence of particular forms of collective identity, but rather point to the constant contact between various forms of collective identification. In the process of numerous contacts, ethnic groups renegotiate the content of their identities and boundaries.

Second, there are contradictory discourses among Uzbek sub-ethnic groups in Tashkent. They vary in content and form depending on the context of interaction. Tashkentis and most of other groups (except Khorezmians) join the autochthonous discourses over who belongs to Tashkent and who does not. Tashkentis compound the discussion with arguments over their degrees of Uzbekness making their autochthonous claims stronger, or more authentic, than the claims of Others. Tashkentis authenticate themselves as *girt Toshkenli* by reference to a certain part of the city (Eski Shahar), which was known to be the oldest part. This automatically strengthens the historical 'depth' of their identity. Khorezmians, by contrast, not only refute these discourses but deconstruct the autochthonous claims of Tashkentis by citing the history of Tashkent as initially a place for Silk Road traders, as *Karavan Saroy*, and that Tashkent has always been a city of migrants. Khorezmians have their own stories and myths to tell concerning their authenticity, identity and pride in their difference.

Third, this process of interaction and renegotiation of the content and forms of collective identification leads to the dialectical relationship between the 'We group' and 'They group', implying the inherent contradictions within the content of both, as well as the boundaries drawn between each other. In this chapter I showed the contradictions within the domain of the 'We vs They' relations and the very making of this domain. In the following part of the book I will look into what makes the We domain and how the We is constituted in the example of social relations among Khorezmians within their communities.

Notes

1. Rahim, 47, a Khorezmian, Tashkent, 11 January 2006.
2. A Tashkenti seller of fruits to another regional seller in the bazaar in Tashkent.
3. Sayora, 47, a Khorezmian, 15 March 2006.
4. See more details on the early history of populations' movements and region in Chapter 2 of this book.
5. See also Bohr (2004) for analysis of regionalism in Central Asia.
6. I mean the connection in the sense of elite members seeking to mobilise their members from below to engage in the politics of difference.
7. There are designated places to sell in the bazaar where sellers have to pay taxes and there are also random places where the sellers simply stand with their product on the ground.
8. From Arabic '*haqiqat*'/truth.
9. From Arabic '*safi*'/pure.
10. The last news about her is that she left Uzbekistan for Turkey, married a Turkish man and continues her professional life in Istanbul. I am sure the fact of her leaving Uzbekistan is conspicuously connected with the punishment for her last performance which contributes to the common belief about Khorezmians and their unity as well as their power in Tashkent.
11. Before, this term was widely used for Koreans so any resemblance to the face of Koreans was also the reason to apply the term.
12. Fishing is the term I use metaphorically in order to present my views of policemen's attitudes towards their victims. I have often been one of those fishes myself in the past. It is most obvious in the metro stations in Tashkent. Policemen are like real fishermen who are very patient, waiting for their fish to be caught. Only small fish are usually caught in the metro stations since big fish (who have some money in their pockets) prefer taking a taxi to avoid being caught by policemen. The metaphor I am using is not to compare people to fish but rather to present the view on policemen and their attitudes towards their victims.
13. More details of this story by Husan are in Chapter 3.
14. Husan, 38, December 2005.
15. From Arabic '*hijab*'/cover, veil. This term locally is used for describing a particular style of wearing the scarf, covering the forehead and neck, and pinning the end of the scarf on top of the head by 'very religious' women.

148 *Identification and belonging*

16 I will talk more on marriage strategies inside Khorezm and matchmaking services by Sayora later in the following chapter.
17 See Chapter 6 for more details on the social organisation of Khorezmians.
18 See Chapter 4 for the discussion of derogative terms and other rhetorical strategies.
19 Adolat, 35, a Khorezmian, 12 March 2006.
20 I will use the terms *space* and *place* interchangeably; I am aware of the differences between them and will discuss these concepts below in the context of Lefebvre's theoretical framework (2004).
21 Geschiere and Gugler (1998) studied belonging and identification of persons who migrated from rural to urban settings.

References

Arnaut, K. 2004. 'Performing displacements and rephrasing attachments: ethnographic explorations of space, mobility in art, ritual, media and politics'. PhD, Ghent University.
Barnes, J.A. 1969. 'Networks and political process', in J.C. Mitchell (ed.), *Social Networks in Urban Situations: Analyses of Personal Relationships in Central African Towns*. Manchester: Manchester University Press.
Barth, F. 1969. *Ethnic Groups and Boundaries: The Social Organisation of Culture Difference*. Bergen: Allen and Unwin.
Barth, F. 1994. 'Enduring and emerging issues in the analysis of ethnicity', in H. Vermeulen and C. Govers (eds), *The Anthropology of Ethnicity: Beyond Ethnic Groups and Boundaries*. Amsterdam: Het Spinhuis.
Bartlett, D.L. 2001. 'Economic recentralisation in Uzbekistan', *Post-Soviet Geography and Economics*, 42 (2), 105–121.
Bohr, A. 2004. 'Regionalism in Central Asia: new geopolitics, old regional order', *International Affairs*, 80 (3), 498–501.
Carlisle, D.S. 1986. 'The Uzbek power elite: Politburo and Secretariat (1938–83)', *Central Asian Survey*, 5 (3/4), 91–132.
Englund, H. 2004. 'Cosmopolitanism and the devil in Malawi'. *Ethnos*, 69 (3), 293–316.
Englund, H., Nyamnjoh, F.B. and International Centre for Contemporary Cultural Research. 2004. *Rights and the Politics of Recognition in Africa*. London and New York: Pantheon Books.
Ferguson, James. 1999. *Expectations of Modernity: Myths and Meanings of Urban Life on the Zambian Copperbelt*. Berkeley, CA: University of California Press.
Finke, P. 2006. Variations on Uzbek identity: concepts, constraints and local configurations. Habilitation thesis, Leipzig University, Leipzig.
Finke, P. and Sancak, M. 2003–2004. *Variations in Social Identity and Ethnic Differentiation, Report*. Halle/Saale: Max Planck Institute for Social Anthropology.
Geschiere, P. 1997. *The Modernity of Witchcraft: Politics and the Occult in Postcolonial Africa/Sorcellerie et politique en Afrique: la viande des autres*. Charlottesville: University Press of Virginia.
Geschiere, P. 2004. 'Ecology, belonging and xenophobia: the 1994 Forest Law in Cameroon and the issue of "community"', in H. Englund *et al.* (ed.), *Rights and the Politics of Recognition in Africa*. London: Zed Books, pp. 237–259.
Geschiere, P. and Gugler, J. 1998. 'The urban–rural connection: changing issues of belonging and identification', *Africa*, 68 (3), 309–319.
Geschiere, P. and Nyamnjoh, F.B. 1998. 'Witchcraft as an issue in the "politics of belonging": democratization and urban migrants' involvement with the home village', *African Studies Review* 41 (3), 69–91.

Geschiere, P. and Nyamnjoh, F.B. 2000. 'Capitalism and autochthony: the seesaw of mobility and belonging', *Public Cult*, 12 (2), 423–453.

Geschiere, P. and Nyamnjoh, F.B. 2001. 'Autochthony as an alternative to citizenship: new modes in the politics of belonging in postcolonial Africa', in E Kurimoto (ed.), *Rewriting Africa: Toward Renaissance or Collapse?* Osaka: The Japan Center for Area Studies (JCAS) in The National Museum of Ethnology, pp. 209–237.

Glick-Schiller, N. and Levitt, P. 2004. 'Conceptualizing simultaneity: a transnational social field perspective on society', *International Migration Review*, 38 (145), 595–629.

Gumilev, L.N. 1989. *Etnogenez i biosfera Zemli* [Ethnogenesis and biosphere of the Earth]. Leningrad: Izdatel'stvo Institut DI-DIK.

Harneit-Sievers, A. 2006. *Constructions of Belonging: Igbo Communities and the Nigerian State in the Twentieth Century*. Rochester: University of Rochester Press.

Jackson, Stephen 2006. 'Sons of which soil? The language and politics of autochthony in Eastern D.R. Congo', *African Studies Review*, 49 (2), 95–123.

Lefebvre, H. 2004. *The Production of Space*. Malden, MA: Blackwell.

Marshall-Fratani, R. 2006. 'The war of "who is who": autochthony, nationalism, and citizenship in the Ivorian crisis', *African Studies Review*, 49 (2), 9–43.

Nyamnjoh, F.B. 2005. *Africa's Media, Democracy, and the Politics of Belonging*. London: Zed Books.

Nyamnjoh, F.B. 2007. *Insiders and Outsiders: Citizenship and Xenophobia in Contemporary Southern Africa*. London and New York: Zed Books.

Yuval-Davis, N. 2006. 'Belonging and the politics of belonging', *Patterns of Prejudice*, 40 (3), 197–214.

Zenker, Olaf, 2013. *Irish/ness is all around us*. New York and Oxford: Berghahn books.

6 Networking strategies of migrants

Khorezmian community in Tashkent

'bir dorohtni atropindo uzini kushlori buladi'
[Every tree has its own birds]
(Rahim, 7 January 2006)

I started this chapter with an epigraph, a citation from an informant (one of the main characters of this section) who metaphorically describes social networks of individuals. Answering my question about the people surrounding him, Rahim, a medical doctor and owner of a private clinic, once said: 'every tree has its own birds' (*atropingizdaki odamla*). In local parlance, this means 'the people around him who are friends, relatives and acquaintances'. He explained the saying as: 'every person gathers or is gathered by the kind of people whom he or she likes to share something with'. In other words, the saying lends itself as a good description of personal and social networks.[1]

This explanation leads me to the aim of this chapter, which is to describe the social organisation of a Khorezmian community in Tashkent. I will bring several examples that describe various ways and strategies by various ethnic entrepreneurs within Khorezmian communities which are part of community-building projects and the social organisation of Khorezmians. In this section I will focus on the Khorezmians and their networking strategies to create a space which accommodates Khorezmian newcomers in Tashkent. These strategies are particularly characteristic for leaders and actors who are actively involved in the process of community building. I will use the terms 'network' and 'networking' in their metaphorical sense, without going into formal network analysis.

First, a few words about how I came to know about Khorezmian networks in Tashkent. I started fieldwork in Tashkent with a solid working plan in mind; namely, to focus on professional clusters since the hypothesis was that migrants are professionally grouped. My first contact persons were Khorezmian rice traders and construction workers. I used the snowball technique to gain access to other members of these groups. Soon my networks extended and included Khorezmians grouped together not on the basis of professional belonging, but rather connected through family and kinship ties. Profession mattered in the formation of collectives but the base of initial social organisation was family or kinship belonging. Networking strategies were not limited to co-workers, but rather crosscut many other existing networks and groups. The only prevailing criterion was connection along ethnic lines. Learning about the various forms of social organisation of Khorezmians and their different purposes prompted me to reorient my focus from professional clusters to the systematic enquiry of networking strategies of Khorezmians in Tashkent.

The knowledge about the social organisation of Khorezmians in Tashkent derives from the participation in three kinship networks and visiting their members, or going out with them. From one network to another, and through different individual links, I found myself entering a web of complex relations, which I had to make sense of at the end of my fieldwork. The life in this 'jungle' made me aware of how the contacts work, get established and sometimes break. When engaging with individual actors in their everyday lives, I found out that it was possible for me to observe how people related to one another. Socialising within these Khorezmian networks also provided me with insights into the feelings and ways of perceiving the social outside/the Other from the perspective of Khorezmians. I had to test these internal perspectives by engaging with non-Khorezmians. This feeling for the 'outside' was a result of not only discourses and opinions I had heard from Khorezmians, but also came from the ways Khorezmians handled their everyday life in a big city like Tashkent. Networking was vitally important. I could see how the outside was in a state of continuous making within Khorezmian networks and communities.

One of the main purposes of networking is marriage, which is the main concern of Khorezmians after they have left their homes and started their 'new' lives in a big city. Marriages often happen by the initiative of parents and their agreement with each other. In this context I will present a 'school' for future brides, grooms and mothers-in-law organised by Sayora, where marriage strategies are successfully employed.

Besides marriage planning there are also essential problems one has to solve after relocating to a big city. This includes the economic and legal aspects of everyday life of Khorezmians in Tashkent. Employment, affordable accommodation, or local registrations (*propiska*) are among other things to consider in an environment where state welfare provisions are completely non-existent. The case study of a private medical clinic and its medical networks serve as a good example of how various services are accommodated within one institution and/or networks. For these reasons, it is important to be a member of some Khorezmian network (*danish-bilish*) in Tashkent, as my informants explained.[2]

In the following I will start by introducing the ways Khorezmians secure future marriage plans within their own networks and groups. This is presented by various means: namely, the autobiography of a leader (Sayora) of several networks, her matchmaking services and brides' school. Furthermore, I will describe several *krug*s that I have attended during my fieldwork. Finally, I will present a case study of a medical network and a private medical clinic.

Finding the right partner: Sayora and the brides' school

Sayora: a 'big woman'

Before I consider marriage-planning, and presenting the school for future brides, grooms and mothers-in-law, it is very important to introduce Sayora, who is one of the outstanding 'leaders' of several types of Khorezmian networks in Tashkent. Her life story and her activities will show why I describe her as an outstanding leader of Khorezmian networks. While presenting Sayora's life story, I will try to focus on her ability to generate varieties of capital in order to use it to raise her status among the same or higher social 'classes' to which she belongs. I will also focus on her abilities to exercise her power in all spheres and levels of her interactions with people. It is also necessary to note here that Sayora has been very successful in establishing herself financially and socially, as well as in creating a big Khorezmian community around herself, which I think is an outstanding achievement considering the short period of time she has been living in Tashkent since her first arrival (2001).

These achievements have been the result of not only her primary social capital within the elite community of Khorezmians, but also her own abilities as a charismatic leader, additionally supported by her religious knowledge and mystic spiritual possession (her annual illness). She usually was one or two months in which she is ill. There was a common belief that all healers or persons with extraordinary abilities had to pass a lengthy period of sickness until they would be granted a supernatural gift from God. To accept this gift was a difficult task which needed to be skilfully approached, since the sickness would otherwise continue, leading to death. In Sayora's case this gift lent her great authority and respect in the community. Sayora did not offer an explanation of her sickness. It is my own interpretation based on the local knowledge and discourse about people with extraordinary abilities given by God. She said that she did not know what had afflicted her, but did not seek medical advice because she thought 'it was not an illness [treatable by] "for doctors" [*dohtorlik amas*]'. In the popular view, this kind of illness afflicts only to the 'chosen ones' and endows them with a certain kind of power. People fear these chosen ones because their curse can be dangerous and their blessings are effective.

Her illness resembles the classical pattern of possession by spirits which strike only chosen ones. Lewis (1971: 79) describes female spirit possession as a strategic act to gain material benefits from their husbands. Schlee (2008: 85) talks about syncretic practices among a Sufi community in northern Kenya where pre-Islamic beliefs and practices took place. This includes spirit possession and healing practices which might also have the strategic intention of gaining symbolic and political power.

Sayora is a woman in her early fifties, and has two daughters and a son. She was the seventh *kelin* in a huge family. Before moving to Tashkent, Sayora recounted her extraordinary[3] activities, organising collective events in various locations for different people. She pointed to the fact that all *kelin*s lived in the same huge house as their parents-in-law, which was very challenging for her. She spoke at length about the difficulties of coping with her 'very strict' (*dim*[4] *strogiy*[Ru]) mother in-law, and living together with 'very different' women under the same roof (the women are the other *kelin*s of the house). She was a very 'exemplary' (*obratzoviy*[Ru]) *kelin* and was respected for that. She had been well educated, was open-minded (*achiq*) and very active in organising a social life together with the people around her. Her experience of being one of many *kelin*s and learning diplomacy to 'keep peace' in such a big family had given her much of the knowledge she chose to share with other young women around her. As a result, she initiated social gatherings of young girls among her relatives and friends to talk about different matters that were of primary concern for any future *kelin*. Parents – especially mothers – were very happy to send their daughters to attend those social gatherings organised by Sayora. First of all, girls would get to know each other better; second, they would be noticed in the environment of families with 'good standing', such as the in-laws of Sayora herself. In turn, being seen in 'good' (here it is meant as elite/higher class) circles of families and learning such 'important' matters would offer good chances for successful marriage. Finally, the knowledge they would acquire could only be of benefit for the girls where this task was otherwise an extra burden for busy mothers, especially those living with their parents-in-law in the same house.

Sayora was also interested in enhancing her reputation among the parents of the girls, which would gain her recognition as somebody more than a *kelin* in a family within her immediate social surroundings. A few words about the social status of any *kelin* in a Central Asian context are necessary here. A *kelin* has a very low, if not the lowest, status, not only in the family and kinship networks but also in her residence neighbourhood. She is never called by name and only recognised as a '*kelin* of so and so', (of somebody who is known by his name in the neighbourhood, kinship or other networks). Later, when she lives separately from her in-laws, she will be called a wife of so and so. Only after she has already married off her daughters and sons, and became a mother in-law herself, will she finally be called by name and given a full social status.

Besides being recognised as more than a *kelin*, her new social engagement also gave Sayora incentives to spend her free time in a more interesting way than merely sitting at home and serving her parents-in-law, deprived of a job. In addition, she did not have her own children for more than ten years, which made her freer than others who were busy rearing children from the first year of their marriage. Sayora had to adopt a child after a long 10–12 years. Immediately after the adoption, she became pregnant and gave birth to a daughter. After some five or six years she gave birth to a son.

Her and her husband's health became poor from the bad environmental situation in Khorezm region; she said this was the main reason to move to Tashkent. Sayora and her husband had persuaded another family (her husband's brother) to move with them to Tashkent, since her *avsin* (her husband's brother's wife) also had health problems at the time.

Sayora moved to Tashkent in 2001 with her husband and her son. They came to live in a three-room flat together with her in-laws. Sayora first moved with only her son, leaving her daughters in Khorezm with her in-laws. Her *avsin* had also left her two children back in Khorezm and waited for half a year until they settled down.

They started to build their house right after they moved to Tashkent. They bought an old and shabby, almost ruined, house from emigrating Russians which was equal in price to a small plot for building a new house. Sayora also managed to buy an adjacent house in her backyard, which was in similar condition and made good financial sense. From then onwards she started to acquaint herself with the neighbourhood and bought several houses not far from each other. She started out by buying and reselling one house at the very beginning; in one month she made large profits from resale. Since she was renovating the houses prior to sales she decided to recruit her own construction team. She got to know her headman (Dilmurad) while he was working on her first (own) house; Dilmurad was recruited with the help of her relative (HB). I will talk in more detail about the relationship between Sayora and Dilmurad in the next chapter. After her house was completed she brought her daughters to Tashkent and married them to two brothers – sons of Sayora's relative (MBDS).

She made an agreement that her daughters would be living in her house on a rotating basis; one week one daughter lived with her husband and children in her (Sayora's) house while the other daughter lived in the house of the parents-in-law (both daughters had the same parents-in-law). In this way both daughters avoided serving their mother-in-law (who also lived in Tashkent, not very far from Sayora's neighbourhood) full-time.

After the second year, the agreement was still working. The agreement would end with the marriage of Sayora's son, which would take at least five more years. This agreement is very unusual for local residential arrangements for women after marriage. 'Normally' a *kelin* goes to live in her husband's house together with his parents until they (a young couple) are *otde'lno*[Ru] *chiqincha* (literary 'exit separately') or live separately in a house or a flat provided by the parents-in-law. This happens when a younger male sibling gets married. However, in the case of the youngest son he must stay in the house of his parents for his lifetime. The parents-in-law of Sayora's daughters had only two sons, which meant that one of the daughters of Sayora would have to stay in that house for her lifetime and serve her parents-in-law for the rest of their lives. I anticipate that this would not be the youngest daughter of Sayora (which would have been correct according to tradition), but rather the older one who had originally been adopted by Sayora from her in-law relatives. This will work out in the following way: Sayora would build a house for her daughter, taking up the responsibilities from her daughter's in-laws. This would automatically decide the future residence of her daughters, leaving no space for the parents-in-law of her daughters to make that decision.

In the meantime Sayora got to know many people from Khorezm living in Tashkent, both old friends, new acquaintances, and other Khorezmians who had been recruited to her construction team. The team consisted of drivers and other helpers around both her house and the properties she had acquired in and around Tashkent. At the time of my fieldwork she had bought three more houses in addition to her own home and adjacent outhouse. Dilmurad's family was living in the outhouse at that time, where Sayora's cow, a big dog and several chickens were kept by his wife. It also served as storage for construction material brought for building and renovation. I knew only of Khorezmians as her building clients, though, according to Dilmurad, there were obviously also clients who were not Khorezmian. According to my informants from that neighbourhood, four houses had been built by Sayora for more than four families. Sayora promises to provide support for settling in Tashkent by finding a good deal for an old house in her neighbourhood and building a house at an affordable price. She showed me a very nice catalogue of houses with interior designs, from mini two-storey houses to large mansions. She explained to me that one can build a very small house that will not take up so much land, such as a two-storey home, for an affordable price. She argued that it is better to build a small house than buying a small flat without a garden. She also offered to help my parents to sell their house in Khorezm and build a new one in her neighbourhood, which I personally would find very convenient.

She stated that she knows 15 different networks and named 15 'leaders' for each of the networks. As far as I understood, by 'leaders' ($lidery^{Ru}$/leaders) she meant a person who would be a kind of group initiator of social events. For Sayora, in turn, a leader was a contact person for the network – to mobilise it, invite its members to events, spread information or disseminate knowledge that Sayora would find useful for its members. She stated that she knew each member of each network personally, but saved time by contacting the leader, instead of contacting individuals in cases concerning the network as a whole. She called those networks '$kampania^{Ru}$', from Russian 'a company' as in 'a company of friends'. For her these *kampanias* were divided according to professions or length of residency in Tashkent. The oldest *kampania* consisted of people who came from Khorezm to Tashkent 20 years ago, then, respectively, 15 years, 10 years, or newcomers as Sayora classified them. There was also *artisla kampaniasi*, which was people involved in show business and singing. This group obviously, at least to my mind, was useful for events to find live Khorezmian music and dancing for a good price. It was also very interesting to socialise with these people who devoted their lives to the art of music and dancing, and with whom, according to Sayora, 'one spiritually relaxes' (*dushevniy^{Ru} otdyh^{Ru}*/'soul rest').[5] The rest of *kampanias* were either professionally connected or were simply another kinship network.

Sayora continued her school for *kelin*s in Tashkent, having widened her networks, as well as the profile of the school itself. Her school was now open not only for girls but also for boys and mothers. The school aimed to prepare good *kelin*s, husbands and mothers-in-law. Although the school widened its range of listeners or attendees they consisted exclusively of Khorezmians who belonged to one of Sayora's surrounding networks (*kuri ozlarimiznikila*/only our own people).[6] In the below I will present the school.

The brides' school

Marriage of children is an important task for parents in the Central Asian context. It is an important institution that involves various aspects of social life such as status, economic resources, security, kinship and descent. Therefore both parents and close relatives of future candidates for marriage, start 'thinking and planning ahead' for a possible union. For example, a small boy, a potential candidate for a future groom, will be permitted to literally bite an ear of a small girl, a symbolic act of early engagement. This is a specific tradition or at least often a phrase used among Khorezmians to talk about the early engagement/agreement between both parents at a very early age of their children. It is considered to be a very serious commitment because the superstitious belief says that if the marriage does not take place between the promised couple then the side that broke the 'holy' agreement will be severely punished by the curse of never being able to get married at all.

Arranging marriage in Tashkent has a different dynamic compared to the 'home' context in Khorezm. 'At home', there is no fear that one's 'son or daughter's head will be turned by a stranger [a non-Khorezmian]' meaning 'non-Khorezmians will make young Khorezmians in Tashkent fall into their love trap'.[7] So Khorezmian parents in Tashkent are more cautious and alert, and marry their children as early as possible, usually right after they finish high school at the age of 17 (*maktabni bitirganan*).

Sayora gained popularity as an organiser of the brides' school in Khorezm and the number of her listeners grew, as her 'students' later described. She organised a school for young *kelin*s, a grooms' school and one for mothers-in-law in her little office – a two-room flat on the first floor of an apartment house in Tashkent.[8] In that office she also ran a small business for delivering stamps. Sayora stated that 'there are no strangers [*chujoylar*[Ru]] in the classroom'. All students were the children of her friends and her class for the mothers-in-law consisted of her friends (*chiqanla*). I attended several classes for both girls and boys, but did not have a chance to attend classes for mothers-in-law, as Sayora became sick and later went to Khorezm for about a month.

The main idea of the school, which I realised only later, was to get the boys and girls to meet so that they married inside 'the group' (our own people). The schedule for classes was organised in a way that girls came at 10 a.m. and the next class for boys started at 12 p.m., which was exactly the same time the girls' class would end and boys would enter the office. The probability that young people would at least exchange glances with each other was very high. The classes for both boys and girls took place once per week or once every second Sunday. Sometimes there was a long break in between.

During classes both boys and girls learned how to write Arabic, what it were to be a proper Muslim, and the duties of children to their parents and husbands. She also explained (mostly to girls) how it was to live in a family and to take care of a husband and children and at the same time respect elders and please their parents-in-law (*qaynota-qaynana*). She often talked about the life stories of others in order to bring up bad and good examples. If she did not find a topic to talk about she would cancel the class. As far as I could observe, she did not have an exact curriculum for her classes and the topics were organised on an *ad hoc* basis. She asked me to give several lectures to both boys and girls about my experiences abroad. She instructed me to make them understand that not everything depicted in 'blue colours about going abroad is not true, and that it is a myth that if you go abroad you will become rich quickly'. She also asked me if I could teach boys English. However, young people were very serious about attending 'the school' as a potential space of opportunity to find a 'right husband' or a 'right wife'. The knowledge acquired during the classes was also very highly appreciated by the girls. One of the 'graduates' of this school, then (at the time of my field research) a proper wife and a mother of three children, stated that she very much appreciated and still used the acquired knowledge from the school in her everyday family life.

In the class for boys Sayora usually talked about how to maintain the balance between a mother and a wife. She also talked about how it was important to learn everything possible to be able to become flexible regarding jobs and earning money. She said '*Erkaka qirq hunar ham kam*' literally from Khorezmian 'forty professions/skills are still not enough for a man'. She would also urge respect for elders and parents, and shared information about the possibilities for the boys' future careers. In order to advise them about the possibilities and existing contacts in Tashkent, she would ask each student about his present studies and his professional aspirations.

I have talked to mother-in-law school attendees and asked about their classes. They said that they talked about how to keep peace at home and live together with daughter/s-in-law. That class (for mothers-in-law) provides many chances to chat and gossip since the students were Sayora's friends. This made the class the most interesting part of the school for Sayora. They met at her office, made tea, talked about their everyday life and children, planning events and gossiping about others. Sayora was in the car returning from an engagement party alongside another woman, a friend of hers who also attended her 'class' together with her daughter (17 years of age and not married yet). Sayora and the woman discussed the best possible candidate for the daughter. Sayora proposed the candidate and suggested that she would refer her daughter to the candidate's mother. She praised her qualities according to her behaviour in the school.

Once, we went out of the class with the girls and there was a mother standing at the entrance hall of the office, who was an attendee of the mothers-in-law class. Sayora introduced me to her briefly. I found out only later that she came to look at one of the girls as a possible *kelin* and a future wife for her son. She looked at the girl (possibly recommended by Sayora beforehand) carefully. Then the boys entered another classroom for their class. The mother waited for Sayora after the girls left and they talked in a separate room without me. At that time I was asked to talk to the boys as Sayora was busy.

158 *Identification and belonging*

Matchmaking services by Sayora

I could well imagine how the conversation went between Sayora and that woman. I experienced several telephone enquiries of that kind at Sayora's place. It usually started by consulting the astrological compatibility of the future couple, which, to Sayora's mind, partly guaranteed a 'successful marriage'. After the astrological signs were considered by Sayora, she would continue talking about the parents of a potential match – a young girl or a boy. Only afterwards would she go on to the character and social behaviour of the candidate, though only about the girl's. The order of description and recommendation given by Sayora to the enquirer depended on the gender of the potential candidate. If inquiries about a girl were made by a mother for her son, then after the astrological match and her parents' description, the girl's behaviour was carefully described in terms of obedience, decency and modesty, which were the most important features for a future *kelin*.[9] Girls' mothers usually would not enquire of a future husband for their daughters and would prefer that their daughters were sought after by the family of the potential groom. In this way, Sayora did a big 'favour' for mothers of girls by asking them about their daughter's marriage plans. Where the mother did not yet have a potential male candidate for her daughter, then Sayora happily recommended one from her list.

I saw her list as she came up with a candidate for me as well. She considered my living without a husband 'inappropriate' for 'such a girl' (*shunnin qiza dogri gamidi*). She asked me about my date of birth and knew exactly which signs would be a perfect match for me without even consulting her book. Then she took out her notebook, which had a blue leather hard cover and contained names and dates of birth ordered according to the astrological signs, along with names of parents and contact details. Other details included what one did or studied, as well as the occupation of their parents. She opened it and asked me about my ideal man. After I described him, she said that she did not have one yet, but as soon as she found him she would let me know. She also included all my sisters' details in her book as my sisters were all unmarried, which was bad in her opinion.

According to Sayora, the aim of having this school was to make something good in a religious sense (*savab*).[10] *Savab* in her understanding was 'to do something good for someone for free and to give something to someone who needs it'.[11] Furthermore, she explained that every Muslim should do *savab* as much as possible and that it was a duty of each Muslim. Another 'holy mission' (*niyat*)[12] she had was to educate people about Islam, as a devoted Muslim herself. She said that it was important for each Muslim mother to raise her children with awareness and good knowledge of Islam. I asked her if her own children followed all the rules of Islam and she answered with regret that she had not reached that aim as yet, but she would persist. She was the only person in her family who did not drink alcohol, prayed five times each day and kept *roza* (fasting).

According to my interpretation and understanding, the school had been created with the aim of keeping Khorezmians in Tashkent as an endogamous group, i.e. to make sure that young Khorezmians marry inside the group (*ozlar-imizniki*). Now I turn to various small groups and networks that have been created in order to socialise and maintain friendship and kinship relationships which also have more or less the same purpose as in the institutions I described above.

Forms of socialising

In the section above I introduced a more 'formal' way of establishing and maintaining contacts for certain strategic purposes. In the rest of this section I will highlight more 'informal' ways of socialising and maintaining various groups within a Khorezmian community. I will present *sumalak* events and smaller circles called *krug*s.

Sumalak

Sumalak events take place once each year, usually in early spring during Navruz. *Sumalak* is brown, sweet and has a consistency of soup puree; it is considered to be a holy sweet dish. It is made out of wheat, small amounts of oil, a small amount of white flour and water. *Sumalak* is prepared through 12 hours of boiling and non-stop stirring, plus a preparation period of about three to four hours of manual labour. At the bottom of the *kazan* (a big pot for cooking), small smooth stones are placed to avoid burning. It is important to constantly stir the *sumalak* while cooking. Preparation for the cooking begins as early as ten days prior to the celebration. For four days, moist wheat is kept in linen bags and frequently watered. After four days, the turgid grains are placed on trays and watered every four hours until sprouts appear. The cooking itself begins during the day and ends in the early morning of the next day. The sprouts are then cut, crushed or manually fed through the meat grinder several times until the juice has been squeezed out and the mash put through the grinder again. Due to the labour intensity and the length of preparation and cooking of *sumalak*, it requires many people to work together for more than 24 hours. This makes it a relatively big event for acquaintances who want to socialise, such as kinship networks, friends and co-ethnics (*zem'yak*[Ru13]/co-lander). *Sumalak* is one of the events in which one can see the core of networks getting together and also observe the status and role each member has in the given network. The *Sumalak* event becomes a lively space of interaction where there is time for important things to be discussed in a more relaxed environment, events planned, relations established and renegotiated, and where gossip is collected and spread, decisions made and future plans discussed.

I have attended four *Sumalak* events organised by Khorezmians in Tashkent. One was organised by Sayora in her house, another was organised within a kinship network I studied, one was organised within the neighbourhood of one of my Khorezmian informants, and another I attended was organised by a Khorezmian informant for her kinship and friendship networks, including several

160   *Identification and belonging*

*krug*s and families. *Sumalak* is a good opportunity to compare different networks socialising intensively. In these events one can see how status and social roles are negotiated, maintained and performed, as well as the hierarchies within these networks.

Sayora's house was full of different people preparing *sumalak*, consisting mostly of Khorezmians and only a few non-Khorezmians who were her neighbours. The division of labour was as follows: those who were helping around her house, including wives of her construction worker's team, the wife of Sayora's driver, a student living in their house, Sayora's younger brother's wife, and several married and unmarried relatives of both Sayora and her husband were involved in the kitchen work. The kitchen work included washing dishes, cutting vegetables, replenishing the tea, passing the wheat through the meat grinder and otherwise cleaning up after guests and refreshing the food table. Closer relatives and younger relatives of the more honoured guests were also busy in the service part of the work, but on lighter tasks such as bringing tea to guests, stirring and controlling the food cooking, watching out for smaller children and sometimes just enjoying themselves over a separate table, usually in the kitchen. The honoured guests and other guests of more elderly status, also including younger married women but with older children with the exception of young *kelin*s (*kelin*s are supposed to be with younger guests on service or over their table in the kitchen) were at the guests' table, usually in the living room, enjoying the food and beverages as well as the service of younger members in the house. Men's labour was also similar to that of the younger ones, doing tea service for other male guests or preparing the fire and keeping it alight or simply staying in the garden, so usually younger male guests could enjoy their company outside the house, chatting and smoking. When the *sumalak* is on the fire, the women take turns to stir it for another 12 hours as it burns quickly, and men look after the fire. The most critical moment of the *sumalak* cooking is putting it on the fire, first frying eggs, and taking them out of the huge pot, and then putting in all necessary ingredients until it starts to boil.

In this moment of high responsibility, elder women take the lead and control the pot. The rest is only making sure that stirring is continuous, and other older guests sometimes take turns to stir. The honoured female guests take the stirring stick only symbolically to make their wishes over the holy *sumalak* and make a couple of rounds of stirring.

But instead of fire in Sayora's house they used a more modern version, an extension pipe connected to the gas which was installed by the men, and a *samovar*[Ru] (a big water boiler outside to make tea for large amounts of guests), also kept by the men. Music was playing outside for those stirring the *sumalak*, and inside different music was playing for the guests over the long table. Music outside was mixed modern singing by Uzbek Estrada stars and Khorezmian dancing songs; inside there was Khorezmian folk music and some *halpa* singing on tape. There were no dances performed, which would have usually been the case around *sumalak* cooking. Sayora kept going back and forth, making sure everything was in order and everybody knew what and how to do things, sometimes instructing and spending time with the guests at the table, chatting with them.

Another *Sumalak* was organised by a kinship network from one of the regions in Khorezm. Members of this region were distinguished by particularly closed kinship ties, which was less strict among those who came from other regions of Khorezm. Membership of this kinship network add up to 22–25 persons, excluding children, and *sumalak* was prepared in the house yard of one of the younger members of the kinship network. This kinship network established itself well in Tashkent and the members of this network are very mutually supportive. Kinship network members support each other with finding jobs, taking care of children when one is sick, visiting them with some food products, etc. They meet regularly and cook *sumalak* each year together. The labour was divided by a similar principle as described above. The difference between Sayora's *sumalak* and this one was that elder women took more responsibility for the whole process of cooking, and central focus the cooking of *sumalak*, whereas at Sayora's *sumalak* the centre of the event was her guests. In this kinship *sumalak* there were more internal problems discussed in smaller circles, guests of honour were not gender-based and all guests of honour, both female and male, sat together. Guests of honour were the elders of the kinship. There were only eight of them that night and I also was partly joining them in the *Sumalak*. However, I enjoyed the company of the younger female circle consisting of *kelin*s and unmarried young girls, both inside at the table and outside over the *sumalak* fire, where the music played and Khorezmian dances were also performed. This *Sumalak* event within the kinship network was the most intense in terms of the relations and problems discussed during the whole event.

Events such as *Sumalak* are the best locations where one can see the status and role that members of networks possess and perform. The length of the event also creates a more relaxed atmosphere for discussing internal arrangements regarding social relations, solving problems and discussing others. Depending on who is organising *Sumalak* and for whom, the event had different purposes of gathering together as well as the character of the whole event. For example, the neighbourhood *Sumalak* was performed in the *mahalla* public yard where most of the neighbours attended and the group of attendees was heterogeneous in terms of cultural and regional background. There the exchange was very formal, and discussion centred around issues concerning the common problems of the households and neighbourhood, such as communal payments and taxes. The music was not specific and depended on who donated the player and CDs or tapes. Dances were not performed as everybody was shy. There was also a feeling that some women had been forced into this event in order to get to know their own neighbours and, if new in the neighbourhood, also to introduce themselves. At other Khorezmian *Sumalak* events (with the exception of a few neighbours) where the participants were solely Khorezmians, the exchange was more intensive and served as a forum for not only socialising but also planning things together and solving each other's problems.

Krugs

There are various types of *krug*s, membership of which is organised according to occupation, kinship, common interests and other criteria. During my fieldwork I attended several *krug*s where I was included as a member in accordance with binding rules and obligations rather than as a guest.

The word *krug* from Russian means a 'circle' and is used by Khorezmians to indicate a group of people who meet on a regular basis or at least socialise together on different occasions. Exchange of information, material things, and other kinds of symbolic exchange within these *krug*s vary depending on the principle of the organisation of a *krug*.

Non-Khorezmians use the term *Gap* to indicate the event where certain people gather on a regular basis. *Krug* for Khorezmians is more than the event itself. Though they do not have to meet on a regular basis, it does indicate a particular group of people who are united by various common principles from kinship, friendship, colleagues, or even just neighbours. Membership of any *krug*s is gender-based. Men and women have separate *krug*s. I would say *krug*s are usually organised by women, whereas men use the word *krug* for describing a circle of friends with whom they have parties (*tashkila girishmak*). Besides socialising within *krug*s, women's *krug*s are usually the basis of 'rotating savings'.[14] Most men find collecting money to be 'women's business and that men are too proud to collect money and find it embarrassing and inappropriate'.[15] Not all *krug*s are based on money saving. One person can have several *krug*s where she or he socialises. Often these *krug*s overlap in terms of the people and relationships inside and across them. If there is money involved in the *krug* the amount to collect varies according to the financial status of *krug* members. If the members of the *krug* are rich or members of wealthy families, the amounts can be accordingly high, which automatically excludes the poor from joining these kinds of *krug*s. Membership is usually closed after the *krug* is formed, although exceptions can be made. A *krug* can be initiated by one or several people who share the same values or have close relations in one or another realm of social life. I have known *krug*s where amounts to be gathered among members would reach a US$100–200 per a month, which would return to a contributor every 6–7 months, depending on the number of participants. For example, if I am a member of this kind of *krug* with seven members and we each contribute US$100 per months I receive 700 dollars every seven months. The principle of collecting money is seen as both negative and positive by members and non-members of such *krug*s. The money is collected on each gathering event of the *krug* and given to one member, who is in the queue to receive it. Basically the principle is that everybody contributes a little amount which makes at the end a 'big' amount for a receiver who can in turn solve a financial problem which requires a large amount, such as a big purchase, house renovation or organising a lifecycle event. In fact, it is like putting money into a savings account in a bank, though less secure, thus making the issue of trust a first principle in this kind of *krug*. Although it can become a burden to find the money every month, each member of such *krug*s benefits from getting a lump sum occasionally.

I myself joined the *krug*s of my female Khorezmian informants, and was part of six *krug*s altogether with my four informants. Two informants were part of the same kinship *krug*. One of them was a young woman, Nazira, aged 38, and another was a medical doctor, Halima, 46 years of age. I attended one *krug* of Nazira where Halima was not part. I also attended a friendship *krug* of Halima consisting of six women. Another informant, Adolat, 35, was a cosmetic products (Oriflame) distributor and had several *krug*s. I attended one of her friendship *krug*s consisting of 12 young women of different ages and also a *krug* of her neighbours. I often joined two *krug*s of Sayora. One was kinship-based and the other was friendship-based.

Another krug I attended was organised within the kinship network I described above in the *Sumalak* section. This *krug* was formed out of age-mates (young women) with common interests and the same social status. Members of this kinship *krug* met regularly outside of bigger meetings of the kinship network, such as holiday celebrations such as Navruz (8 March; International Women's Day) or any other fixed dates such as the last Sunday of each month or the end of every two months.

Nazira's kinship *krug* (*bir ikki karindoshla bir krug*) consisted of six women, all *kelin*s. This *krug* met at the end of each second month; the date varied according to the availability of its members. There was also money involved in this gathering, to the sum of 25,000 in the local currency (equivalent to US$20). When it was Nazira's turn to receive the lump sum of the monthly contributions, she just paid the debts that had been piling up for all kinds of small things she had needed for her household. The last time she received the money, she used it to buy some furniture for her flat, and several times she gave it to her husband to pay off debts (for a car).[16] I attended two of the planned four gatherings (until my departure from the field) of Nazira's kinship *krug*. Two were missed because of the summer break. Another time, the host fell ill.

Below, I will describe one of the events of the above *krug* in order to provide a reader with an approximate idea of the event. The event was organised by a young woman who lived with her husband and three children in an old house consisting of two rooms, a kitchen, a bathroom and a small hall. It was almost a ruined house, probably built in early Soviet times, as the woman indicated that it had belonged to an old Russian woman who had returned to Russia. There was a very old fence about 1.7 m high, made out of very thin, old wood with a small door without a bell. The door was open, and when we arrived together with Nazira others were already sitting around a small table about 25 cm high – the so-called *han-tahta*. A small dog greeted us with continual barking until a young woman hastily appeared to meet us. Three hens and a cock were rummaging for food in the empty 'garden' without any grass. We took off our shoes at the small entrance space and were shown to a room where guests were already sitting at the table. The table was full of two different Russian and Korean salads, Khorezmian bread and some baked sweets such as small round cookies and other

164 *Identification and belonging*

pastries. There were four women sitting at the table, their faces familiar to me from other events of a wider kinship network of which they were members. As we entered the room, all faces smiled and we greeted one another by kissing each other twice on the cheeks. There was Khorezmian music playing on a small music player.

Khorezmian *Palov* (*Osh* in Uzbek) was served after 20 minutes of chat and catching up on the latest news about each other's family members and what one was up to. There were all kinds of things discussed, from small, everyday problems to gossip about other members of the kinship network who were not present in this *krug*. The main things discussed in these kinds of circles or *krug*s are the basic everyday life of the family, along with children's issues such as schooling and babysitting. These kinds of problems are discussed and solved within close friend and kinship *krug*s.

After a couple of hours of chatting, eating and a round of dancing there were plans made for the next meeting. Towards the evening, with the husband coming home, everybody hurried to leave.

Kinship *krug*s among senior people take another format and dynamic in comparison to the kinship *krug* of young *kelin*s. They differ from each other by the contents of the discussion and the principle of organisation and mixed sexes. This type of senior kinship *krug*s have no binding rules or obligations and rather meet on an *ad hoc* basis. Another very important difference between the two types of kinship *krug*s is that alcoholic drinks, namely vodka, are served in the senior type of gathering rather than in the *krug* of young *kelin*s. Younger people do drink alcohol but maybe rather in their own friendship *krug*s where kin are not present, since drinking alcohol as a *kelin* would be an inappropriate image, especially if this reached the ears of the *kelin*'s parents-in-law. This also speaks about the status of women in the family – the more senior a woman is, the more power and agency she acquires.

The senior kinship *krug* consisted of three couples aged above 50 and all related to each other by kinship ties (besides Sayora, who was the only non-kin, but a good friend, and attended those meetings without her husband). This *krug* met irregularly as far as I understood from their conversations, and there were no binding obligations to maintain this very small *krug*. When I attended their evening gathering they exchanged recent news about each other and their families. There were also all kinds of small events planned, such as outings to the mountains and upcoming events; they discussed who was responsible for what and how one could organise something like that. There was also news exchanged about other members of the kinship group who were not present, and their families and children. Furthermore, they talked about other news concerning a newly arrived family to Tashkent from Khorezm, who obviously belonged to the same kinship group and whether he (the husband of the family discussed) had found a job and whether there were gatekeepers (acquaintance/*danishla*) that needed to be 'put to work' (*isha salish*). *Danish* literally means acquaintance or contact but also has another meaning of 'strategic contact', which is used more often. Here *danish* has a meaning of a 'strategic contact who can open some doors'. This term has a considerable weight attached to it. It can also be a measure of one's social capital, particularly important in places like Tashkent where Khorezmians are 'not at home' (*oy yandamas*). Other gatherings of the same people at the same house took place before a planned marriage in order to get advice about how to proceed with it.

As I mentioned earlier, the social ties within *krug*s crosscut. Sometimes kinship *krug*s can be composed of friends. Friendship *krug*s also exist between colleagues, which bring three or four people together to socialise outside of office hours. Friendship within kinship networks and friendship within colleagues vary in their intensity.[17]

Friendship between colleagues can also be intense and more intimate than friendship within kinship. The definition of closeness varies depending on the contents of what is shared and trusted. One can share many things with a non-kin friend and trust her in private matters, particularly those matters which one cannot share with kin friends in order to keep a 'right' image among kin. Among those shared things there can be, for example, romantic or other similar events of the 'prohibited kind' that must be kept secret from kin friends.

Trust and relatedness as a kin are very closely related in the general understanding of Khorezmians. Even if someone can trust some secrets with her best friend she cannot necessarily generally trust her. For example, members of kinship friendship *krug*s would do business together (trade or other business-related work) but they would not trust this kind of 'serious' (*muhim*) work to their friends, to whom they probably would only entrust a selective style of secrets. The latter kind of relationship is considered to be 'unimportant' and temporary (*vaqtincha*). Another very decisive aspect in defining trust is the exchange of girls, since one would not easily exchange girls without being able to generally trust a family or a member of the family in question.

Institutions of support

Private medical clinic and medical network

In the following I will present another aspect of networking strategies that involves purely financial interests, through accommodation of newly arrived migrants from Khorezm, as well as maintaining contacts with other Khorezmians living in Tashkent. This will be illustrated by the example of a private medical clinic and medical network, to which its owner, Rahim, is also a member (a member of the kinship network I described above in the *Sumalak* section).

At the time I started my field research, arriving in Tashkent as a migrant myself in 2002, I had been introduced to two Khorezmian doctors. Until I left Uzbekistan I used their services whenever I or one of my family members was sick. Both of them were surgeons, but they could refer me to another doctor, also a Khorezmian, but not always for a specialist I needed. At the time of my fieldwork, one of these doctors referred me to her colleagues when I told her about my research and topic.

First, she referred me to a female cardiologist who was working in the same clinic. I became close to her family and visited them often. There I met the relatives of this family and their friends who were living in Tashkent. Members of this network are all from the same district in Khorezm. I met many of the members of this network and attended most of their events (in a more general sense; significant dates or other important events) and social gatherings. What struck me in this network was the medical connections or medical networks set up for Khorezmians patients in Tashkent. Besides the doctors who were working for state hospitals, I also studied a private clinic owned by one of my informants, Rahim, an important member of this network. Rahim is a man of 47, a father of two sons and a daughter. His wife is also a *medik* (works in the field of medicine) – a nurse. Many of my informants, members of this network who had some kind of medical education, recollected and sometimes admitted that Rahim had helped them to get employment within the same clinic he worked in before opening a clinic of his own.[18]

The clinic: my impressions

I had an interview appointment with Rahim in his clinic in the morning at around 11. I had difficulty in locating the clinic from the given address, since it was located in one of the apartment houses in a prestigious residential area of Tashkent. It was an old and shabby apartment building of two stories. There was no number or any large sign announcing the private clinic, so one could not find it easily. Finally, I approached the building and there was a small wooden door with small glass windows covered with white curtains from inside so I could not see in. It was closed. The clinic did not look functioning to me. On the door I saw a small sign which said in Russian 'private clinic for laser treatments Dr. Rahim, office hours Mo–Sa from 9 to 18. Telephone numbers and mobile number of the doctor'. I dialled and Rahim's voice said: 'I am in the clinic'; I told him that I was also at the door of the clinic, but it was closed. He said that he would open the door for me. After one minute I heard sounds of a turning key and with some creaking noise the door opened. Rahim was in his white uniform, but one could see that he had been sleeping and that I had probably woken him up. He hurried to lock the door after me, as if he didn't want it seen that his clinic was open. He showed me into his '*kabinet*'[19] ('office' in Russian) and suggested I sit down on a chair. There was a small table in the left corner with approximately ten empty bottles – two were Russian vodkas and one empty bottle of *konyak*; the rest were two or three plastic bottles of locally produced Fanta and Cola and several bottles of mineral water. There were also unwashed glasses and *piola*s (Uzbek small cups for drinking tea). In the middle of the room there was a small, round, low table with a small plate of Khorezmian bread and another plate of two apples with some grapes on it. He comfortably put himself in a half-reclined position on the sofa in front of me, preparing himself for an interview which gave the impression that he felt he was about to become a known and popular person, someone worth interviewing. He was very serious about having an interview with me, so I asked questions about his life and his work. I asked him about his clinic and about the difficulties I had in finding and locating his clinic. He said that his clinic was closed down by the epidemiological inspectors on the basis of insufficient hygiene in the clinic. He said that the sanitation department had officially closed down his clinic for renovation. He did not want to talk about this matter as it seemed to be a most painful topic at that time. He expressed his frustration about all this, and nothing more, and I asked no more about it.[20] During our interview the old telephone rang very loudly about five or six times (during three hours). He spoke only once in literary Uzbek and the rest in Khorezmian. He did not cut anyone short, although we were in the middle of the interview. I did not interrupt because it was also interesting to be part of the everyday conversations Rahim holds on the phone from his clinic.

The business of the clinic

The next week when I came to his clinic it was, as usual, closed, so he opened the door for me. To my surprise the clinic was full of patients. Obviously my first impressions of the clinic and what Rahim told me were not so close to reality. In other words, the clinic was only closed officially, but in practice it was 'fully' functioning. I could only guess that maybe the last time it was the only day or half day that there was nobody scheduled – or even then there were people upstairs, which I did not notice.

The personnel of the clinic were exclusively Khorezmians. Even the dressmaker who saw to the medical uniforms was a Khorezmian woman. He showed me upstairs. There were three other rooms on that floor, one of which was an examination room as far as I could tell from the gynaecological chair and other things that looked like medical instruments. He said I should make myself comfortable and showed me into one of his patient rooms with two beds where a Khorezmian couple was staying. Rahim introduced me to his Khorezmian patients, and asked me to wait in the room. They were obviously living in this place as there were two beds with their things lying around. The patients were a young couple who came from Khorezm to receive treatment in Rahim's clinic. Rahim went downstairs where he had other patients from Tashkent waiting in his examination room. Rahim was a gynaecologist by training, so he had usually women patients with gynaecological problems.

I had been left with the couple in a small room with one small window, two beds and a small cupboard. The room was about $10\,m^2$, no more because there were two beds and just enough space for two people to stand in between the beds. So I sat on one of the beds, the woman made tea and offered me some Khorezmian bread with it. Her husband offered me *tör* (a special place in any public space for a respected guest, usually the place farthest from the entrance door) and I sat on the other end of the bed. I had some tea and bread. The couple said that the lunch would be ready soon. So we chatted while drinking tea. Personal introduction of me by Rahim to his patients obviously was a symbolic sign

168 Identification and belonging

by Rahim that would imply that I must be respected as a guest because these patients owe Rahim in various ways. Thus I was received as a respected guest in return of a favour of Rahim for his generous opportunities offered in the clinic for them.

The couple came from a neighbouring village of the same district in Khorezm as Rahim. They said they had heard of him through their relatives, who knew distant relatives of Rahim. The young woman (Orzigul) had 'problems' with her reproductive health; it was 'already' two years after marriage and she had still not become pregnant.[21] It was the first time they had ever travelled outside of Khorezm. To my question of how they liked it in Tashkent, they said they were advised not to leave the clinic because they were illegal (without *propiska*).[22] They stayed in the clinic both as patients and renters of the small room for an affordable sum, which was also secure from the constant police checks on passports and local registration. They seemed to be very happy to have had this opportunity to travel and see things, and at the same time to get some treatment. They said that Rahim had also offered them some basic medical check-ups, which they appreciated, since they had never been medically checked in their village. Orzigul said:

> Back at home [*oy yanda*] one does not go to the doctor if one is not seriously sick. We have only one hospital in a district and in a village there is only *medpunkt* [a Russian word for 'medical point'].[23] And even if one has to go to a district hospital they do not have such nice technical things to check your health so nicely. And all good doctors would not work in a district hospital, of course there are also good doctors in hospital in Urgench [the central town of Khorezm region] but we do not know anybody there. But anyway, of course the best things are in the capital because here the things are different, all the best doctors, best technological things are all modern [*zamonaviy*] here because it is the capital. You yourself know that if there would be a very clever doctor, what he would do in Urgench? They all of course study in Tashkent and stay here to work.
>
> (Orzigul, 12 January 2006)

This couple has sold one of their bulls to cover expenses for the trip. They also hope that, using this chance to come to Tashkent, they might find work or look for opportunities in Tashkent in order 'to step a foot there'. They would also like to go shopping in the big bazaar to bring some things home and maybe to sell them in order to cover at least their transportation expenses. This trip is not only for their treatment, but also a holiday which they have never had and 'who knows when again [they] will have this kind of opportunity in the future'.[24]

I was offered some noodle soup with chicken. I asked about who was responsible and how the lunch and other meals were prepared. The husband of the couple told me that it was included in the 'agreed package' so that they did not have to go out for shopping in the city, and could avoid the police. Food was brought to the clinic by Rahim in his car and one of the female patients in the clinic cooked lunch. In between, Rahim came by and asked if I was not bored as he was caught up with other things and had to let me wait; he said that he was running short of time. I answered I was not bored and did not mind spending more time in the room. I asked about other patients who were staying in the clinic. They told me about another woman of 35 who stayed alone with other medical problems. They said that Rahim also offers various medical specialists because he was well connected to other Khorezmian doctors in Tashkent. They told me that one doctor who specialises in kidneys came to visit the young woman and also checked Orzigul on the way. She said that it was very convenient because 'once you know one doctor you do not need to know the other one'. This was confirmed according to my own findings as well. The doctors, not only Khorezmians, but also others seem to be very well connected and send each other their patients as they have verbal agreements in order to keep their patients within their own network.

The clinic was a very comfortable destination not only to receive clients but also to offer them other services, such as a room secure from police checks. If not for this clinic, these patients would first need to have found friends or relatives to stay with, and then also secure local registration or constantly evade police passport control. Transportation expenses within the city are also saved because they do not have to travel to see a doctor and Rahim has even organised that other specialists when necessary can come directly to the clinic to examine a patient. Rahim himself never mentioned these kinds of arrangement when I asked about his clinic.

Khorezmian medical network

I had several discussions with Rahim and his family members. I got to know about his circle of friends and his co-villagers back in Khorezm. It was obvious that Khorezmian doctors had created a particular economic niche for themselves within the Khorezmian community.

Medical specialists in many different fields, including surgeons, therapists, neurologists, urologists, cardiologists, gynaecologists and even dentists have formed the so-called 'medical network' (*Danish dohtirla jorala*) that formed internal mutual agreements to send their patients to each other in order to keep clients inside.[25] Members of the medical network Rahim belongs to are all from Khorezm region but not necessarily from one village or district. One of them is Tahir, a general surgeon with a wide range of knowledge about various pathologies of the liver, gastroenterology and intestines. Tahir (36) met Rahim while working in the same clinic and he also had his own medical network independent of Rahim's. Another member of both medical networks (Tahir's and Rahim's) is Sapar, an anaesthetist who is from the same district in the Khorezm region. He found his job in the clinic with Rahim's help. They are also related affinal kin through Rahim's wife. The next member of this medical network is Madrahim, a physician in the department of intensive care. Madrahim comes from a neighbouring district in Khorezm to where Rahim is from. He also went to the same medical school as Rahim. He is part of this network together with his wife Halima, who is a cardiologist. Murad, another member of this network, a proctologist in the same clinic, with his wife (a nurse), make this network complete.

This small medical group meets for each other's birthdays, big holidays and also once every two months. This circle of friends and kin have established good working and social relationships within their own circle, in addition to their separate memberships in other *krug*s. Exchanging patients reaffirms the existing ties within this kind of circle or network of friends. Usually the fees for medical services are very flexible, varying from favours, small money, food or other services in return. The doctor's reputation back home was no less important to them, and all had an interest in keeping their names widely known in order to attract more 'clients', not only in Tashkent but also those coming from Khorezm. They would succeed in this through positive reports from returning patients with success stories which would serve as advertising. To keep the medical network functioning, member-doctors would send their patients or acquaintances to each other from time to time and also socialise together. For clients of this type of network, the offered services are very convenient and not that expensive compared to other ways to get medical treatment. As many patients indicated, one has to know a good doctor in order to get adequate treatment, since it is very difficult to find the right one. There is a myth about medical services in general that appeared after the collapse of the Soviet Union:

> Everything collapsed with the Soviet state, not only the state.... Nowadays one cannot trust anyone, everything is done according to capitalistic principles today. Even doctors became capitalistically minded. If you go to any doctor they tell you all kinds of things that you are seriously ill and you need all kinds of treatments only in order to take money from you. I even heard that they have special agreements with drug stores and prescribe all kinds of medicine so that you buy these things from the drug store and then the drug store can also make some money from you. And whenever you go to that doctor he tries to keep you as long as he can or as long as you have money. So it is very important to have your 'own' doctor whom you can trust and he will of course have his own friends – good specialists if your diseases are not his speciality.
>
> (Gulbahor, a patient of the medical network, 23 May 2006)

This statement made by one of the patients refers to the fact that trust is important when choosing a doctor. The trust is defined in terms of knowing a person well enough to be able to trust him. Trust is defined differently depending on what is being trusted. When it comes to trusting doctors it is important that one has heard about this doctor from friends or relatives. Second, one knows the family of the doctor so one may be confident that the doctor is decent enough (*ota onasi ma'lum*). *Ota onasi ma'lum* is a very often used phrase literally translated from Uzbek as 'parents are known' meaning 'we know the parents'; in other words, 'we know the person well enough because we know her parents', which is a positive sign. It is very often used in the context of describing a person and in the context of whether one can trust that person or whether he is worth have business with in a general sense. His acumen is usually confirmed by the stories of his patients. Once one finds such a doctor it is advisable to keep that doctor for a lifetime if possible.

Networking to sell: distributors of Oriflame *and* Mary Kay

Besides the case studies presented in this chapter, there are of course other kinds of employment arrangements to generate income. I will not discuss this form of networking strategy because of the limits of space here, but a brief mention will help to sketch a picture of it.

At the time of the research it was very prosperous to conduct networking business for distribution of cosmetic products where one could earn not only by selling the products but also by recruiting other distributor-sellers of the same products into this kind of network. These were mainly young women from 20 to 40 years of age, To my surprise I heard from my neighbours in Khorezm that our neighbourhood young male mullah (32) had also been attracted to join the so-called '*setevoy biznes*' (from Russian 'network business'), namely the job of a distributor-seller. My neighbours said that 'it is a profitable job and that he *even* bought a car'. As far as I understood, he sells food supplementary health products to his friends and acquaintances. He did not stop his job as mullah, as he can sell his products on the side, since his position in the central mosque as the second main mullah is also lucrative one. I saw his products but did not buy any – to his disappointment.

The most prominent brands are *Oriflame* (now replaced by *Faberlik*) and *Mary Kay*. The main supply office of all products of both brands is located in Moscow. Local distributors in Tashkent, Khorezm, and other regional centres use their networks to sell their products. Five of my female informants were working as distributors of the cosmetic products of *Oriflame* and *Mary Kay*. Whenever we visited friends where distributors were present, the distributors would use every opportunity to show their catalogues to get orders from friends or relatives who apparently cared for their appearance. The distributors would start talking about how one's skin became so dry and she had exactly the right crème against it, and so on.[26] Such distributors of cosmetic products and skin care of a known firm are said to be trusted because they have 'at least not fake Chinese rubbish'.[27] This kind of business made not only distributors some cash, but also the clients were glad to be offered 'good quality' products for affordable prices, which they could purchase in small increments over some time comfortably from home.

Institutionalisation of patrons and clients or ethnic entrepreneurship

In the above ethnographic material I showed the ways Khorezmians organise their social lives as well as the role certain actors play in the community-building

172 Identification and belonging

projects in Tashkent. There is an obvious pattern observed in all of these transactions and interactions. It is clear that there are two categories of Khorezmians in Tashkent: 'settled' and 'non-settled'. The settled provide certain services for the non-settled, such as cheap accommodation, *propiska*, employment and social security. These and other services are institutionalised in various formats from 'formal' organisations to institutions and networks. Certain actors and leaders play crucial roles in creating those institutions and networks as well as maintaining them. Membership is open to Khorezmians. The increasing number of Khorezmians in Tashkent is one of the incentives for ethnic entrepreneurs (often patrons) to create economic niches which open up various opportunities. Without a certain number of clientele, a patron cannot survive alone. In order to be able to extract resources from a network, one should connect people into a network and offer incentives. The patrons, leaders and other actors who are actively involved in the community-building in Tashkent often act with rational strategies in mind. They always belong to the category of settled Khorezmians who have already secured their *propiska*, have bought their own accommodation and have enough social capital to be able to help the new arrivals. Income and marriage of the children seems to be a primary concern of the people who belong to this category, whereas a primary concern of the non-settled is to establish themselves in Tashkent, meaning to secure first of all *propiska*, find employment and save money for buying their own accommodation.

As it was shown in the examples in the chapter, charismatic leaders or a patron like a big woman (Sayora) have created several simultaneous niches for various people from Khorezm. Her financial capacities allowed her to maintain those niches and invest in various types of businesses, from construction businesses to greenhouse enterprises, as well as other related services, for both the newly arrived from Khorezm and those Khorezmians who had already been living in Tashkent.

Another form of organising of similar services and businesses are represented in the case of private medical clinics, doctors and distribution networks presented earlier. Rahim, an owner of a clinic, offers not only medical services but also employment for medical professionals, cheap accommodation secure from police checks, alongside other small services necessary upon initial arrival in Tashkent. It is obvious that his financial and other social capacities are not comparable with Sayora's. Rahim has not enough resources to offer different kinds of opportunities for settling down, such as employment, paid work, free accommodation, marriage options, etc. Rahim has only limited options: for example a medical specialist who could make use of his network and find employment with medical services. Rahim also owns a house and a clinic so he can offer some kind of accommodation arrangements. Rahim did not consider himself rich in the sense that he had enough money to spend for himself and his family. He constantly complained about the wrong perception of his relatives and kin that he was rich and he was constantly asked to lend money. He described it as being his most critical problem, as the money he lent had never been returned in any form. He even mentioned that he had to distance himself from his relatives back in the village in Khorezm. On the contrary, Sayora makes good profits from maintaining strong contacts with 'back home' relatives and friends and new acquaintances. She easily finds and creates opportunities for those who ask her for help in Khorezm during her frequent visits there. She comes up with projects to create new jobs which widen her network of people, who are always ready to reimburse her by various forms of services and favours.

I started this chapter by presenting marriage institutions, and Sayora who played a crucial role in not only institutionalising marriage planning, but had also been very successful in building a Khorezmian community in Tashkent. Her statement '*man beda kichkina Khorazm oazisini tashkil atjakman*' (I want to organise a small oasis of Khorezm here) confirms the aims and purposes of her actions and activities partly described in this chapter. In this regard, big women or other types of 'leaders' are the main actors in the whole game.

Sayora can be compared to what Sahlins called a Big Man. Sayora is a Big Woman in Sahlins' sense (1972). Sayora wears different hats; she is a patron of various clients, a 'leader' of different Khorezmian networks, big woman, a religious teacher for all her Khorezmian 'friends' and a matchmaker in the Khorezmian community. In this chapter she comes in as a teacher in the brides' school, a leader, and coordinator of various networks, and also a big woman. As a big woman she has her own network of helpers from which she generates income in various forms, which she then invests in her status in other networks. By maintaining the school she raises her status among the parents who are 'very important' people of the same status as herself. There are, of course, other ways to raise her status, which includes organising events both at home and very often in the mountains in her country-house, where her network of helpers play a very crucial role in administrative organisation such as cooking, cleaning, serving and shopping. The money for organisation of all these events comes from the sales of the houses, where her construction team is vital, managing her income from greenhouses and other small businesses from some distance (from Tashkent to Khorezm). There are, of course, smaller groups of more intense relationships. *Krug*s are the smallest and most intensive networks for socialising. Sometimes these *krug*s involve also cash redistribution, but rather serve for more affective relationships such as friendship. Issues of trust have been brought up very often by Khorezmians as being important in the contexts of establishing relationships of various kinds. It also came up in the context of trust for a doctor. Although trust has been locally defined and often mentioned, there are of course other variables that play into the whole process of making decisions on choice of friends or in generally identifying oneself with a certain group.

In my view there are other issues involved in making decisions about staying inside the group instead of opting for assimilation into a larger society, once individuals have arrived in such a big city. The city offers an opportunity for migrants to become independent from all the binding obligations of kinship and other networks, as well as community at home. Nevertheless, Khorezmians already come to Tashkent with the plan of joining a Khorezmian community through established contacts prior to travel, which is a sure route into an 'ethnic trap'.[28] Ethnic networks offer social and financial security to a certain extent, but at the same time reciprocity and other binding conditions of ethnic solidarity require a considerable sacrifice of freedom in general, as well as freedom of choice. In the following chapter I discuss these issues in a more detailed manner.

The best example to illustrate networking as income generation was briefly mentioned in the case of distributors who sell cosmetic and healthcare products to the members of their networks. Recruitment as a distributor is an even better way to receive cash incentives from a company, which in turn creates bigger networks of sales. This type of network is more open, since non-Khorezmians can also be included, as opposed to other networks which are exclusively open only to Khorezmians. In the latter networks, services are based not only on generation of cash, but rather all kinds of services and favours are exchanged. This activity of selling cosmetic products can also be described as a purely business relationship. However, unlike a purely business relationship, a distributor requires more personal contact with her clients, and they would not or do not sell in the streets or bazaars as traders do. These types of distributors use their friendship visits or other events as an opportunity for trading their products and establishing clientele.

In the case of the private clinic and its associated medical network, it becomes clear how certain spaces are used: the clinic serves diverse purposes, or in other words, accommodates various ways to support newcomers from Khorezm to Tashkent through providing 'safe' accommodation and a means of new contacts, in addition to the medical services.

Getting a good medical check-up is vitally important for people who come from Khorezm region, due to poor health caused by environmental disaster in the region of the Aral Sea. Poor health was said to be one of the main reasons for relocation to Tashkent, alongside the economic situation in the region. Medical doctors from Khorezm who moved to Tashkent have used the growing number of Khorezmian migrants in Tashkent to create their 'own' clientele by staying connected with the migrant community, and referring each other's patient-clients to one another. The services are paid in different forms such as cash, food products or Khorezmian rice brought from Khorezm, or returned services and other favours. The payment is not 'officially' asked by doctors but rather offered voluntarily by patients themselves in the form of 'gifts' or other promises. Cash payments are asked only for the diagnostic services and medicine. Doctors may establish contacts with, for example, ultrasound specialists within their networks (but not necessarily) who owe them and who in return make an ultrasound diagnosis for free, so that the cash paid remains with the first doctor. These actors who have different capital and agency to manage and maintain networks contribute to the community-building of Khorezmians, as well as seeking primarily to further their personal interests.

In African examples from urban studies of ethnicity I find a number of similarities in the social organisation of various groups in newly formed cities. Cohen and others (in an edited volume by Cohen 1974) have shown that ethnicity has taken a different form in an urban context. Cohen (1974) even equates an ethnic formation to an interest group which emphasises the use of ethnicity for specific interests in the context of urban opportunities (Hannerz 1974; Mitchell 1974). Khorezmians, particularly certain actors, have managed to make use of ethnic networks and promote ethnic cohesion for economic interest and status advantage. As a result, certain kinds of multifunctional institutions have been created in order to accommodate those interests. Much work has been done on similar issues in urban African studies, which consider the role of the elite and their interest in promoting ethnicity and the formation of ethnic groups (Charsley 1974; Lloyd 1974; Schildkrout 1974). A closer look at the functions of these institutions reveal that they also fill the gaps of state provisional systems of social welfare and other structures and systems of state services.

To sum up, in this chapter I have considered the ways Khorezmian migrants have socially organised themselves as an ethnic community in the city of Tashkent. The case studies of networks, institutions of support and examples of *krug*s have shown that Khorezmians efficiently make use of their contacts, and organise their lives according to their common interests and their communities.

I have also argued that networking strategies are used to both generate personal income as well as promote group endogamy. These cases and examples not only show the unity of ethnic community, but also its inherent contradictions within the same community. These contradictions are constituted through the differences in generation and status based on seniority principles, which imply the hierarchical character of the roles and expectations assigned to the members of the networks and *krug*s. As regards the very making of relationships within various *krug*s, I have demonstrated the central aspects of those intrapersonal bonds: friendship, kinship, mutual self-interest, exclusivity, profession or ethnic insecurity, though most critically, perhaps that of trust and fellowship. In the next chapter I provide closer insights on these contradictions by analysing interpersonal relations based on power and dependence.

Notes

1 Rahim, 7 January 2006.
2 *Danish-bilish* is literally 'acquaintance-know'; the meaning is 'people one knows' or 'acquaintance'. See more details later in this chapter. See also my contribution on *tanish bilish* (Turaeva forthcoming), which explains it in a detailed manner in the encyclopaedia on informality edited by Ledeneva.
3 The events she organised were unusual, especially considering her status as *kelin*, who 'normally' would not have enough independence from her husband and in-laws to do anything beyond her household and family matters. The events she organised involved young unmarried and married women getting together for tea and discussing problems, or other social activities similar to those.
4 *Dim* is a Khorezmian version of Uzbek '*juda*' from Arab. '*jeddan*'/very much which is formed from the root word in Arabic '*jed*'/serious.
5 Sayora, 15 March 2006.
6 Sayora 8 April 2006.
7 Sayora 20 September 2006.
8 She bought those two-room flats on the first floor using her own savings, as she said. She also owned the flat above, which had three rooms. She rented it out to newly arrived kin or other Khorezmians until they found a place to live.

176 *Identification and belonging*

9 These things are usually done by women, such as matchmaking, searching for a girl for one's son.
10 From Arabic '*savab*'/reward also in a religious sense.
11 Interview with Sayora on 8 April 2006.
12 From Arabic '*niyat*'/intention.
13 See Chapter 7 for a more detailed discussion of the term.
14 Rotating savings and credit associations (roscas) are widely spread around the developing world under different names such as *Chit Funds* in India, *Susu* in West Africa, *Kye* in Korea (Besley 1994: 701). The classic anthropological studies of these associations are by Ardener (1964) and Geertz (1962; as cited in Besley 1994: 701).
15 Sardor, a Khorezmian man of 45, 28 April 2006.
16 People usually buy old cars but still for high prices, and their car (an old Russian '*Jiguli*' 07) cost them US$3,000. The money is usually saved over many years and at the time of purchase any deficit is borrowed from relatives or friends.
17 See Bell and Coleman (1999) for a more detailed analysis of friendship and examples of friendship ties from elsewhere for comparative perspective. See also Salter (2002), an edited volume on trust and kinship relations.
18 After he opened his own private clinic he left his job in the state clinic.
19 A local term used for an 'office'. This term is usually used by people of the older generation who had been of working or even studying age during the Soviet Union because this term is now replaced with *ofis*. Both terms, especially the latter, is very fancy to use and especially to have an *ofis* or *kabinet* automatically defines a person as somebody who has some kind of higher status and power in a government organisation (particularly the term *kabinet*) or even better in an international organisation (the term *ofis* would be appropriate in this context).
20 The sanitary epidemiological department check medical and other institutions which have to do with the general health of the population. They inspect the sanitary and hygiene conditions of medical service delivery institutions, as well as food production and outlets. It is general practice either to pay large sums and continue operating, or to comply with sanitary standards imposed by these departments. However, it is deemed practically impossible to meet these standards, considering the financial and technical options available in the country.
21 Reproductive health in Uzbekistan has culturally specific ways of dealing with these problems. The most popular and practised ways of dealing with it is going to traditional healers and to holy places and shrines.
22 See Chapter 3 for detailed information on the local regulation of registration in Tashkent, as well as about being 'legal' and 'illegal' in Tashkent.
23 *Medpunkt* is a small area, usually one-room or two-room, integrated in the administrative building of the village where one or two nurses operate. There is rarely a medical doctor as well, but usually doctors prefer working at the district hospitals. Working at a *medpunkt* is not desirable unless you were not accepted at the district hospitals. The reason is that the salary is miserable and 'under the table payments' are not usually made in these kind of places, because people who are seriously sick would go to a district hospital and would pay doctors there. In this place one can only get shots or intravenous drops, usually after they are prescribed in the district hospital.
24 Orzigul, 12 January 2006.
25 *Danish dohtirla jorala*, literally in Khorezmian is '*danish* doctor friends'. The term '*danish*' as I explained earlier is difficult to translate since it has several connotations, mainly 'strategic contact'.
26 Local markets do not offer good products for skin care and cosmetics, nor do bazaars where products get even worse as they have been standing around the whole day in the open sun; in a closed store they get worse than they were before by standing too long on the shelves. People have a common idea about most of the products coming from China as being fake, using the labels of popular brand names.

27 Interview with Nigora, 28 November 2005.
28 See Chapter 3 for more detailed migrants' stories of coming to Tashkent. I am grateful to Prof. Dr Schlee for giving me this term.

References

Ardener, Shirley, 1964. 'The comparative study of rotating credit associations', *Journal of the Anthropological Institute of Great Britain and Ireland*, 1964, 201–229.
Bell, S. and Coleman S. (eds), 1999. *The Anthropology of Friendship*. New York and Oxford: Berg.
Besley, T. 1994. 'Rotating savings and credit associations, credit markets and efficiency', *The Review of Economic Studies*, 61 (4), 701–719.
Charsley, S.R. 1974. 'The formation of ethnic groups', in C. Abner (ed.), *Urban Ethnicity*. London: Tavistock, pp. 337–368.
Cohen, A. (ed.), 1974. *Urban Ethnicity*. London: Tavistock.
Hannerz, U. 1974. 'Ethnicity and opportunity', in C. Abner (ed.), *Urban Ethnicity*. London: Tavistock, pp. 37–76.
Lewis, I.M. 1971. *Ecstatic Religion: An Anthropological Study of Spirit Possession and Shamanism*. Middlesex: Penguin Books.
Lloyd, P.C. 1974. 'Ethnicity and the structure of inequality in a Nigerian town in the mid-1950s', in C. Abner (ed.), *Urban Ethnicity*. London: Tavistock, pp. 223–250.
Mitchell J.C. 1974. 'Perceptions of ethnicity and ethnic behaviour: an empirical exploration', in C. Abner (ed.), *Urban Ethnicity*. London: Tavistock, pp. 1–36.
Sahlins, M. 1972. *Stone Age Economics*. London: Routledge.
Salter, F.K. (ed.), 2002. *Risky Transactions: Trust, Kinship, and Ethnicity*. New York: Berghahn Books.
Schildkrout, E. 1974. 'Ethnicity and generational differences among urban immigrants in Ghana', in C. Abner (ed.), *Urban Ethnicity*. London: Tavistock, pp. 187–222.
Schlee, G. 2008. *How Enemies are Made: Towards a Theory of Ethnic and Religious Conflicts*. New York: Berghahn Books.
Turaeva R. Forthcoming. 'Tanish-Bilish', in A. Ledeneva (ed.), *Global Encyclopaedia of Informality*. Cambridge: Cambridge University Press.

Part IV

Identification and interdependence

7 '*Ipsiz boglanib qalmaq*'[1] or bound without ropes

Interdependence in Khorezmian migrant communities in Tashkent

'*Ozbekni kichkinasi bolgaran Orisni gurjisi bolganing yahshi*'
[It is better to be Russians' small dog than a 'small Uzbek' among Uzbeks]

Having discussed networking strategies and other forms of social organisation of Khorezmians in Tashkent, I will consider the question of why Khorezmians remain together. What binds these Khorezmian networks and groups? As Boissevain (1974: 233) puts it: 'Coalitions, groups, classes and institutions are composed of people who, in different ways, are bound to each other.' In this chapter I will try to provide an answer to this question, looking deeper into the making of these various relations.

The chapter aims to explore the principle of binding relations within Khorezmians in Tashkent, and to show the internal contradictions within the Khorezmian community. Power, agency, dependence and autonomy are treated as variables in order to shed light on the making of unequal relations. As the title of this chapter suggests, I will look at the dynamics of relations of dependency and power.

As the saying in the epigraph to this chapter implies, there are *katta* (big) and *kichkina* (small) Uzbeks. *Kichkina* and *katta* are the adjectives that define one's status in Uzbek society, and can be applied in all spheres of human activity, from personal and social life, to all different levels of collective and political activities.[2] *Kichkina* refers to a person or an attribute of a person who has lower social status (depending on the context) and *katta* is one who has higher status. Particular duties and responsibilities are expected of individuals according to their perceived social status within a given community. Social status is closely related to economic status since any person with no financial possibilities will not be able to maintain his social status. Therefore *social* and *economic* can be used as synonyms in the given context. I will discuss more details of these statuses later in this chapter.

During the Soviet Union the adjective 'collective' carried an important meaning in all spheres of human activity, discouraging personal dependence on close individual networks. Humphrey and Sneath (1999: 142) stated that 'in the collective era [communist era] the plethora of bureaucratic procedures, and the need for authorisation for all sorts of matters, made connections [kinship relations] of vital importance'.[3] However, the interdependence of individuals during that period was not as strong as now, since the state had formerly granted social

182 *Identification and interdependence*

and financial securities. Individuals had more choices and freedom to create their own life, without the risk of various 'traps'. *Ethnic trap* as a term can best describe the dynamics of playing the ethnic card for short-term benefits and subsequently becoming bound within an ethnic community without further opportunity to escape. It is difficult to measure whether Khorezmians enjoy longer- or shorter-term benefits from their ethnic networks. Khorezmians do use their ethnic and kinship networks and fall into 'ethnic' or kinship traps, but to a certain extent this also improves their financial and social situation. They even find it more advantageous to be Khorezmians than members of other ethnic groups, saying, 'Others are not so united or have such solidarity [*ogzi birchiliki yok*]'. For the players of an ethnic card, however, this is not only a strategic means to gain profit, but also an inducement into the 'ethnic trap'. This combination makes the actor face the trader's dilemma (Evers 1994). The trader's dilemma is a situation in which a trader (or any actor who wants to benefit from something) has to make choices between his profits and favours for his or her kind or co-ethnic clients. In this dilemma, business-minded actors who want to make profits and still not lose face in their ethnic community face difficult choices.

In this chapter I provide a detailed explanation of the ways in which this dilemma is constantly faced by actors, though without a real solution. This implies that the solution to the dilemma is a non-solution, since they remain facing the dilemma until they have reached a certain status. The status enables the 'trader' to reach a positive balance in the situation, i.e. moving towards a more profitable point and at the same time gaining a better reputation within the community. Unequal relations require some degree of reciprocity in such interpersonal relations. The exchange is not fixed, but negotiable. Loyalty and trust are important in the relationships, as I will consider below. This chapter will present a view on this social world from the eyes of individual actors and their nearest proximate connections (dyads) in order to shed light on the smallest units of Khorezmian social organisation.

Kichkina and *katta* Khorezmians

How does one become *katta* or *kichkina* and what is it like to be seen in either category? Both of the terms are relative, depending on the person or community by which the individual is perceived. In one relationship or context a person can be *kichkina* and in another *katta* at the same time. There are two realms of social relations – superficial/surface/'short-term' (*bardi-galdi*/come-go, *yuzaki*/ superficial, *vaqtincha*/temporary) and more intensive or 'long-term' (*boshqacha, muhim*).[4] These are based on various reciprocities; balanced (*qaytarish garak*), generalised (*ot dushi*[Ru], *savab*, *sadaqa*) and negative (*paydalanish*[Kh]). In *bardi-galdi* (short-term) relations two kinds of reciprocities are chiefly involved – *qaytarish garak* (balanced) and *paydalanish* (negative reciprocity). In *muhim* (long-term, important) relations, *ot dushi*, *qaytarish garak* (balanced) reciprocities predominate. '*Qaytarish garak*' is literally 'must be returned' and could be compared to a balanced reciprocity; *ot dushi*/from the soul, in other words 'with pleasure' is synonymous to a balanced reciprocity with more emotional attachment involved; '*savab*' and '*sadaqa*' are part of religious almsgiving as an obligation of every Muslim (*har bir musulmon burchi*). *Paydanalanish*[5] is literally 'to make use of' and can be compared to negative reciprocity, and has a negative connotation which resembles free-riding. Free-riding is used here in the meaning of efforts to gain benefits at the expense of others without return in general, unlike the definition proposed by Hechter (1988: 9) which means 'to consume the good [public good] without contributing to its production'. Sahlins (1972: 94) wrote that 'reciprocity is always a "between" relation: however solidary, it can only perpetuate the separate economic identities of those who so exchange'.

There are two emic perspectives of conceptualising 'reciprocity' from the perspective of a giver and a taker. I deliberately avoid using the term 'receiver' instead of 'taker' since this word implies the aspect of acceptance, which is ambiguous in this context. A giver conceptualises the transaction based on two main ideas about the reciprocity and his relation to a taker. On the other hand a taker has his own theory about a transaction based on his interests, reciprocity and the relation to a giver as well as its future prospects. Reciprocity in this case is somewhat abstract and subjective understanding of the participants in the transaction of exchange. Taking Sahlins' definition of reciprocity as 'a relation in between', an emic perspective would find it difficult to arrive at a qualitative description of reciprocity as either generalised, negative or balanced, considering the contradictory understandings of reciprocity by a giver and taker. When the two different meanings of reciprocity do not match, conflicts of interests arise, as Halmurat also described it with regard to his co-ethnic clients in Chapter 3 of this book. His clients (often takers) entertain their own ideas of reciprocity with Halmurat, which at times may be compared with 'free-riding' or *paydalanish* (negative reciprocity), whereas the clients themselves do not see it as something negative and rather define this reciprocity as a balanced one, in the sense that they 'will also give back and, if not, then God will give Halmurat back'.[6]

Bardi-galdi relations are best illustrated by the example of Halmurat and his clients. Halmurat has innumerable contacts that he uses or the other way around. What binds this kind of relationship? This type of relationship is not only based on rational calculations.[7] There is another variable other than reciprocity that plays an important role here, known as '*mestnichestvo*[Ru]' (a well-studied term in Russian academic literature) and locally used as '*zemlyachestvo*[Ru]'. *Mestnichestvo* is from Russian and literally means 'place politics [my own interpretation]'. It is used mostly in Russian academic literature on Central Asia and described as the solidarity of people who are coming from the same locale. *Zemlyachestvo* is the derivative of a local term *zemlyak* (literally co-lander) which refers to a person who enjoys advantages of regional solidarity. Choice of particular contacts and affiliates, the provision of help or the development of friendship could usually be reduced to the same principle of regional solidarity in favour of a new associate who is *zemlyak*. In the stories or life stories, individuals and groups (*zemlyaki*) were cited as *zemlyak* or *zemlyaki* (plural) when the basis of the relationship was a common regional affiliation.

When Halmurat's services are paid for according to the existing rate, the client is no longer bound to him and may leave the relationship, though not always, as the client may anticipate future favours. Bound in this context means that 'the bound' (the client in this case) can be requested favours by 'the binder' (Halmurat) and sometimes the costs of these are not necessarily equitable. A simple example of such further exchange would be if the 'bound' person (one of Halmurat's clients) is a doctor. Halmurat, in turn, might ask him to make a full medical check of his mother or another of his relatives. Usually Halmurat would not pay for the doctor's services. This type of relation can also be described as the links or weak ties between various Khorezmian groups and networks which merge into a larger, imagined Khorezmian community in Tashkent (Anderson 2006).

Turning to *muhim*/important-type relations, I will first present individuals in order to introduce them and their views on their social world. Furthermore, I will shed light on their social relations. These serve as ideal types of relations that are found within a Khorezmian community in Tashkent. Along with introducing new individuals, I will also go back to the examples of social relations of those I have already introduced in earlier chapters of this book.

Rahima

Rahima, 31 years old, has an unfinished university education in Tashkent. She came to Tashkent in 1991 to study for the first time. She grew up with her three sisters and two brothers. Coming to Tashkent to study, she stayed with her two sisters and a brother, also students. Her brother and later two sisters stayed at their *aga*'s[8] (literally brother) place, and then moved to a separate two-room flat.

She had to leave her studies after she got married in 1992. She had married out of her village to another village (*begona yer*/strange place [as it was out of her village]). She gave birth to her son, and six years later to another. Rahima always looked unhappy, and when I talked to her and interviewed her she complained a great deal about her past life and her unfortunate marriage. She even implied that her husband might have used black magic to make her agree to their marriage. She also complained a lot about her parents-in-law, saying that they are 'uncivilised' (*madaniyatdan orkada*).[9] She complained that her parents-in-law did not let her go to Tashkent to continue her studies and forced her to quit. Her studies were very important for her as she very much dreamed of becoming a teacher and be *hatarda* ('keep the standard/level') which refers to a status of an educated intellectual, and therefore civilised. Difficulties in Rahima's life did not stop with her studies in Tashkent, but were followed by the difficulties of her pregnancy, and the combined hardships of working on the in-laws' plot (land for cultivation), housework and cooking added to by long absences by her husband. Her husband was travelling a lot, seeking work in Russia and later in Turkmenistan and Tashkent. She lived with her in-laws for five years in Khorezm until their own house was built nearby (next door in the same street). Her in-laws have one more son who was supposed to stay in the house with his family, which means that she was not obliged to live in the same house for the rest of her life. After she moved out of her in-laws' house, she was at least freed from the constant terror of her mother-in-law, although Rahima was expected to frequently appear at her mother-in-law's house and take part at the meals in order to continue her service to them as a proper *kelin*. Her husband was mostly away. It was only in 2004 that she could finally join her husband after a long separation, a favour from Sayora who invited her to come to Tashkent and live in her backyard house for free.

> Sayora offered us a chance to live in Tashkent and she explained to us what to do and she also said that it would be less profitable for my husband to work in Khorezm.... Before moving to Tashkent I once came here to see my husband with my little kid, which is when I met her. She said that I would be safe from difficulties if I moved to Tashkent, and she would always help us to improve things.

To my query over their new house in Khorezm she said

> We gave it to our neighbours for a while, because they had a large family. There were three *kelin*s living under one roof. In short, four families [the parents, their married children] lived in one house and I think it was difficult for them. I offered one of the *kelin*s my house and now she and her husband are living there. They are all from our *elat* [*mahalla*, small village].

Since Rahima lives in Tashkent she has her responsibilities designated by Sayora, including shopping and preparing lunch for the construction workers (shopping at a small, nearby stand which is owned by another Khorezmian in the same neighbourhood), taking care of Sayora's big dog, a cow and several chickens which are the source of fresh milk and eggs for Sayora's family. When she has 'hands free' she may be called to Sayora's house for help around the house. During special events, she is the first to be called upon for service in assisting cleaning, washing and other help. Another major task is making bread for Sayora's family and the construction workers. Baking bread is a highly labour-intensive and time-consuming process; a large amount of dough needs to be prepared, the fire is prepared in the oven (handmade out of mud and straw), and subsequent baking. When the dough is ready it must be divided into portions and rolled flat, and only after 15–20 minutes is it ready to be baked. The process of bread baking is onerous and requires many precautions and much attention. Preparing the dough is no less laborious, given the weight of the dough, requiring considerable strength to knead it into the required consistency.

Dilmurad

Dilmurad is 35 years old and was born in a village of a district in Khorezm region. He was born into a family of seven, three girls and two boys (all siblings are married and have their own families). He finished high school in his village. Later on he was persuaded by his parents to enter the Russian philology department at the University in Tashkent. His father was working in his shop and Dilmurad wanted to help his father so that he might later replace him there, but his father said that their village neighbours would gossip that he was unable to pay for his son's studies although he owned a shop. That was the main reason for his father's insistence on his studying in Tashkent.

When Dilmurad came to Tashkent for the first time, he stayed in a hostel with three co-villagers from Khorezm who were also his group mates. He studied full-time for two years, and in the third year became a part-time student because he got married. Later on he dropped his studies, since his family was building a new house, and there was a consequent lack of money.

He chose his wife himself (*özim tanlaganman*), and they studied at the same university. He was in love with his future wife, which is worth mentioning, since most marriages are 'normally' arranged. His parents had planned to arrange a young bride for him from their relatives – a daughter of his aunt (MS), since his aunt died and his parents' wanted to strengthen and restore relations. In fact, he married his wife against his parents' will. He lived for about five years with his wife in his parents' house together.[10] His two sisters married in the neighbourhood and lived not far from them. Only one was married in Urgench, the main town of Khorezm. His brother is married and lives in the parents' house. His brother is married to a girl from '*chetdan*' (literally 'from outside'), meaning a non-relative. His brother is unemployed and looks after the cattle in their house and plot of land.

Before coming to Tashkent, Dilmurad did all kinds of jobs. As he put it, 'there were no jobs left that I had not done'; but the main job was renovating houses. The only problem was very low wages. He mentioned that he even tried to sell rice in Tashkent, but returned bankrupt, explaining that it happened because he knew nothing about doing business. He told the story of that failure to me:

> When we moved to our new house my mother-in-law gave us a cow as a present. We sold it for 50,000 sums (about US$40) and I decided to try to do business. I came to Tashkent joining some other businessmen who had already been selling rice for a long time in Tashkent. I knew them because they were from our district centre.... I tried hard, but everything failed, though nobody stole from me or harmed me. We spent all the money on small items for the household that is all. It would be wrong if I said that I earned more money going to Tashkent for business.
>
> (Dilmurad, 35, 20 May 2006)

He came to Tashkent in 1998 as a craftsman because he said that work was better paid in Tashkent than in Khorezm. Before going to Tashkent some of his co-villagers were going to Russia to work and they asked him to join them, but his parents and his wife were against it, and his family said that it would be better if he worked in Tashkent. His work in Tashkent did not last long and he had to return to Khorezm and wait for the next job offer. In 2001–2002 there was a severe water shortage in Khorezm and the Shovot *kanal* dried up, the only source of water for the whole agricultural land of Khorezm. Dilmurad was forced to leave for Russia. He told me the story of how he went there.

> I built a house for one man in our village and he told me that he had been working in Russia. I was wondering where he had money from. He told me that I could earn a lot of money with my skills and he said that people did not appreciate my work enough in my village and paid very little. He offered me work in Russia and I agreed. We went there *somehow*. We made it there. There I earned about 180.000 sums [about US$150] for two and a half months, I do not remember all the details well as it was long ago but I could not stay there longer and had to come back home. [Then he continued with his story of going to Tashkent where he was finally established.] There was a wedding in our village and I was responsible for picking up musicians. My friend lent me his car, because the man who initially was responsible was a little drunk and my friend who was getting married asked me not to drink because I had a driver's license. After the wedding was over I brought the musicians home and there was the drunken man who was initially entrusted to take care of them. On the way back I talked with the man and I told him that I was going to Tashkent to work. He asked me if I knew anybody there, and I said no. He told me that he had a brother, Murad, who was a driver of a headman [a Khorezmian] in Tashkent and he suggested me to go to his brother so that he could introduce me to that headman. Later I came to Tashkent and met Murad and the headman there. The headman asked me to wait for some time until he found me a job. I stayed at his [headman's] house for 3–4 days and there were five other men living there who had already been working for him for a year. Their flat had four rooms, together with the living room. The men were all from our village. After three days Murad called me and took us to work. We started working in Sebzor district in Tashkent. We met Sayora two months later after we came to Tashkent when we were working on her new house. Murad is *Quda* (HB) of Sayora. I was working hard and she liked the way I worked. We established good contact with her. She is a very enthusiastic and energetic woman as she was closely involved when her house was being built. After her house was finished she asked me if I would be interested to work for her and she would help me to get established in Tashkent. I said that I did not know anybody in Tashkent, that it would be difficult with children as they go to school and I should talk with my family. After her house was finished her daughter's wedding was planned and I proposed that we spoke after the wedding. I went to Khorezm and came back after the wedding ceremonies were finished. I was not sure about moving to Tashkent with my family but Sayora said that I would not lose anything if I move to Tashkent because I was not selling my house in Khorezm. She promised to support me if I

would not betray her. She said that she had an interest in property business which means to buy old houses, rebuild and sell them. It meant very stable work and a good future for me and I did my best to make her trust me. My wife agreed to move. It was October or November 2004 when we moved to Tashkent and on 12 January we moved with all of our things and we left our house to one of our neighbours in Khorezm with his family which is a young married couple. They will take good care of it. My life became stable and secure after I met Sayora.

Sayora and Dilmurad

Below is the case study on the relationship between Sayora and Dilmurad. Besides her previous engagement in establishing a Khorezmian community and matchmaking services, discussed in Chapter 6, Sayora also owns a construction team and is actively involved in the property business in Tashkent. Sayora buys old houses of emigrating Russians and old Russians who want to get rid of their old, shabby houses and move to one-room comfortable flats. She renovates or rebuilds them and resells them. She has shown me the houses she owns and calculated the amount of income she gets from reselling them.

Sayora's construction team was put together with the help of Dilmurad, whose job was not only to lead the team but also recruit it from Khorezm. The construction team consisted of young men from 17 to 35 years of age. The number of workers in the team varies according to the season and orders or work available.

Sayora and her family moved into their new big house (mansion) built by a Khorezmian construction team which they recruited in Khorezm. Sayora took responsibility for controlling the whole construction project of her house as her husband had to work. That is where she got to know Dilmurad. When I asked Dilmurad what he does, he answered: 'I work under Sayora's arm [work for Sayora] (*Man Sayorani kolinda ishliman*).' Dilmurad 'did his best [*kolimnan galganini atdim*]' and 'served well [*yahshi hizmat*[11] *atdim*]' to gain Sayora's confidence. He has shown himself as a hardworking and skilful worker, as well as a loyal person, as he was doing extra work for Sayora and finding more people when it was necessary.

Sayora took care of short-term *propiska* for all the members of the construction workers team. According to Rahima, all of the workers were registered in one of the houses owned by Sayora in the same neighbourhood. A couple of times Dilmurad had discussions with Sayora about new members joining the team. Dilmurad would give references and describe a future candidate's profile. Sayora asked about the connection of Dilmurad to the future candidate; first his family background and then his skills and arrangements of payment. If she would be reluctant about a given candidate she would politely refuse by saying that he should wait a little, and when possible, she would let him know if there was the possibility of a job opening.

Were one to observe their interactions as they discussed the work or tasks assigned to Dilmurad, this would easily fall into employer–employee relations, since both did not show any expression of emotion, no exchange of thanks or any other personal exchange. However, Sayora is very closely involved in Dilmurad's private life, planning his free time and family matters. Dilmurad discusses his future plans with Sayora about when, where and how to build his house, his children's educations and kindergartens. He or his wife would have to discuss beforehand if it was permissible to go to Khorezm to visit their parents and relatives or if there were any special events there. Sayora closely took part in planning and organising any lifecycle events of Dilmurad's family, such as where and how to organise a circumcision party. By necessity, Dilmurad would share the agreed plan with his parents back in Khorezm, as if it were his own idea and plan in order not to simultaneously undermine his parents' authority. Sayora also finds girls for a marriage for unmarried members of her construction team. She proudly told me just before I left for Germany towards the end of my fieldwork that I was going to miss a wedding which she had organised and which would take place the coming spring. She said that she had found good girls for the boys (*bollara*) and was planning to decide the date of the marriage once she had talked to the parents of the two 'young men' in their village in Khorezm. I asked about the girls and she said

> Although they are not Khorezmians they are from good families with the same status as the families of the boys [*özlarina yarasha*]. You know these boys' parents entrusted me their boys and said that from the time they started to work for me they are in my will [*siza topshirdik bolamizni*] since it became difficult and their parents are very poor and cannot afford their sons' marriage so I do *savab* and organise their marriage myself in a very small circle [*kickgina hara chiroyli*/small and beautiful]. The girls – I found they are also from poor families and you know how difficult it is for 'people from here' (*bedakilara*)[12] to marry out their girls since their families have a big financial burden related to the marriage and many of their girls stay unmarried for just this reason. When the *sovchi* comes to them the parents send them back by saying they are not yet ready. The girls' parents cannot afford to collect their dowry that they already started to save when the girl was born. That is also the reason why the fathers are sad when a daughter is born. And in our tradition it is the other way around in terms of financial burden. In marriage, the parents of the boy have to pay mostly and have a good headache when the boy is born, as the payment for the marriage returns, since the girl-*kelin* comes to serve them for the rest of their lives [*hizmat atadi ömrini ahirinacha*].

Dilmurad and his wife (Rahima) are often in Sayora's house and participate in all family events, even in very small gatherings, both as family friends and part of the networks. He is accepted as a good friend and as a '*svoy*[Ru]/*ozlarimizniki*'[13] within Sayora's family as well as her kin members.

Dilmurad and Sayora are interdependent. Dilmurad depends on Sayora because she provides him with accommodation, a well-paid job and social security that consists of providing a legal status (*propiska*) and including him and his family in social events to boost his social status within the Khorezmian community. In addition to all of that the title of 'headman' of the construction team gives Dilmurad a certain status of being boss for his team members as well as status of *katta* among his friends and relatives back in Khorezm, granting him particular status within his community back home. This in turn further grants his and his wife's families and close relatives some kind of symbolic capital from which they can benefit in much the same way as families with contacts in Tashkent, as described in Chapter 3 of this book.

Thus Dilmurad fulfils all of Sayora's orders irrespective of the relevance to his direct responsibilities as a headman. These can vary from domestic shopping to serving tea to male guests in Sayora's house. Sayora depends on him in a different way, with a choice to abandon the relationship should it prove necessary. But rationally it is not likely that she will replace Dilmurad, as she has invested effort and finance in him, as well as trust, which is crucial and not easy to establish. If the headman is reliable and does a good job of managing his team, then Sayora must compromise sometimes in order not to lose a loyal worker.

Sayora and Rahima

Sayora met Rahima when she was visiting her husband in Tashkent, who had then been working for Sayora for about a year. Sayora liked her very much and offered to bring her to Tashkent so that she could live together with her husband. Sayora showed Rahima her house which was situated in the back of her own big house. The house was relatively small, with three adjacent small rooms, but, as Rahima stated, it was enough for her two children and husband. The garden was small and there was Sayora's cow, dog and several hens. Sayora had enough work for Rahima besides milking the cow twice a day, feeding her dog and hens and collecting the eggs. The bread oven was also in Rahima's future garden. Sayora was very proud to have fresh home-made milk and eggs (*domashniy*[Ru]). Rahima's responsibilities were to cook lunch for the construction workers and to help when necessary. This constituted payment in return for free accommodation and food for her family.

Mornings are very busy for Rahima because she has to milk the cow and by the time she has finished breakfast, sent the children to school and cleaned around her house she will be required to start cooking lunch for the workers, for which she must also have done the shopping. Often her husband can also pass the small vegetable stall and add this to his other shopping for Sayora. After Rahima has cooked lunch, things are more relaxed, unless Sayora prepares any further major tasks. Sayora has a big garden in one of her nearby houses where some work needs to be done. In the afternoon her children come from the school.

Sayora smiles at Rahima and politely asks if she needs something from her, and Sayora likes her very much and trusts her. Should Rahima need to see a doctor, Sayora is ready to organise a good one and pay the bills. Rahima appreciates that very much. Sayora always takes Rahima with her to her group tour of the mountains for a picnic. They go several times during the spring and summer time, usually about 15–20 people. I was only once in Sayora's mountain picnics. It was a big event and much help was needed to prepare food and tables, as well as cleaning up.

Sayora and Rahima do not exchange much conversation, as they are both very busy throughout the entire day. Rahima does not spend much time in Sayora's house unless Sayora asks her for some specific task. Rahima believes Sayora is decent enough to grant Rahima holidays or free time or other presents without her asking for them. When Rahima has some urgent task such as visiting her parents or relatives in Khorezm, she asks Sayora or lets her know about it in advance (*aldinan aytib koyaman*). Rahima is very glad to have moved to Tashkent and she does not complain about her 'working' relationship with Sayora, which is much better than her relationship with her mother-in-law who endlessly terrorised her back in the village, under worse conditions without any return.

Dilmurad and his team

The below case study concerns the type of interdependent relationship in which boundaries of kinship and patron–client relations overlap. Out of 14 team members in Dilmurad's construction team five are his kin members and there are three workers that are related to each other by kinship ties. The rest are from the same village and one met Dilmurad in Tashkent.

As I mentioned above, Dilmurad had initially been a construction worker himself. Now he is a headman and has enough power to recruit as well as fire construction workers, with the prior agreement of Sayora. If he needs more people for his team he calls his brother in Khorezm, who then recruits more workers from his network on Dilmurad's behalf. Sayora pays for the transport and organises 'accommodation'[14] for the newly arrived construction workers. His team members have to follow the rules set up by their headman, who usually advises them on where and when to go, and what clothes are appropriate.[15] There are no contracts, only some verbal agreements. At times there is no indication of exact salary at all, since young unemployed men are happy to start working somewhere like Tashkent, when the provision of transport, accommodation and food is already regarded as a kind of good fortune (*shungaam shukur atamiz boshda*/we praise God at least for that at the beginning).

Dilmurad says that it is complicated (*qiyin*/difficult) whenever close kinship relations are involved in the work because he is 'in between two fires [*ikki otni orasindaman*]: on the one side there are the relatives [*qarindash*], on the other there is the work and responsibilities'. He continued: 'But I try to be equal with my workers and if my relative tries to complain to his family I will talk to his family myself [*lichna*[Ru]/personally]'.

One of them (Utkir) is 'very problematic' as Dilmurad says, because he does not often obey orders and does not learn well. Dilmurad cannot let him go home as he is his kin. So they have lengthy discussions in which Dilmurad warns him that he will send him back home. Utkir is 19 years old and does not like the way he is treated by Dilmurad, the tone he uses when speaking with him and his many injunctions, such as not to go downtown in the evenings. He hopes to become a headman himself in the future and to stay in Tashkent. He said that he had not seen very much of Tashkent as yet, although he had already been there for six months.

Dilmurad is the boss of his construction workers and he dictates the rules 'in the house'. Whoever attempts to deviate from those rules will risk his current position and may have to return home unless he has other options in town. This particular relation of 'boss–employee' becomes complicated when kinship relations are involved, since Dilmurad would be pressurised by his elderly family members, accusing him of not complying with kinship rules, and of failing to take care of his kin. The situation of Dilmurad is one of 'trader's dilemma', in which he has to manage social distance between his kinship group and the conflicting need to perform his job well, a job from which he profits.

Dilmurad's dilemma of 'being between two fires' is an indicator of the importance of his kinship relations. In order to understand the importance of kinship relation, it is necessary to look closer at the dynamics of these relations. Below I will present the relation between a father and his sons.

Gafur and his eldest son

Here I will paste an extract from my fieldwork diary describing the environment of the family gathering 'governed' by Gafur (a father of four sons and a daughter). The extract describes an evening of the family's usual weekend gathering at Gafur's flat, and will provide basic ideas about some details of the content of this event. I took part several times in those family events during my fieldwork and also several times before starting my research. I was never formally invited there. I always just happened to be at Zumrad's (Gafur's second son's wife) place and she would take me along to the event at Gafur's home, usually on Sundays (every second Sunday). I knew some other members of this family including Gafur himself from before (my father's close friend's wife is a relative of Gafur).

We entered a three-room flat with a big living room that had no doors and which could be seen at first glance from the entrance. From that living room, Gafur could observe who was coming in and out of the flat. It was crowded with kids, Gafur's younger son (23), Gafur's young wife and his daughter-in-law of his third son who lives above the flat. Gafur's second son (Azim) has three children, his daughter has two and his third son has three. Gafur's first son is back at 'home' in Khorezm looking after houses in the village which belong to Gafur's family, as well as their fields in which they grow rice. I counted eight adults and eight children from 1 to 12 years of age. Gafur was sitting in his armchair, a low and old armchair covered with a colourful blanket of velvet fabric, typical for the rural regions of Khorezm. Gafur's armchair stands in the middle of the living room near the table, which is 25–30 cm high. He sits above it, and to reach something from the table he needs to lean down or ask someone's assistance. We came together with Zumrad, her three children and her husband (Gafur's second son). I was greeted very politely, after everybody greeted him on entering the living room. Zumrad introduced me as a daughter of Atajan (she said my father's name and asked him if he knew him). He didn't smile and very seriously greeted me back. We sat down at the table and he lifted his hands and made a traditional welcoming *patiya*[16] (*patiya oqidi*). After this, the women stood up and left to the kitchen and the men stayed. I felt uncomfortable, being the only woman left in the room. I decided to stay for a while. I was the only guest in the house, which would give me at least some time to remain at the table. Later, I could start helping around the kitchen, but still using my privileges of being a guest. Finally, I opted for the kitchen and chatted with the women there. While I was sitting with the men at the living room table I was ignored, and they talked about the state of things and the news. I waited until the sons had finished reporting to their father and awaited his response as well as his new orders for the coming week. Azim started to talk about his sales this week and reported on the truck driver who was supposed to bring honey from Khorezm. Gafur obviously ordered honey from Khorezm and asked his son, Azim, to take care of the bill, and to meet the truck driver delivering the honey (15 kg) at his flat. Azim reported the details of how he completed the task and asked if Gafur liked the honey. Further instructions were that Azim would have to find time to take Gafur's pregnant wife to hospital in the middle of the week, which was a burden for Azim. Gafur's first wife died a year and a half ago. Gafur brought a new young wife (he is 62 and she is 33) from Khorezm after one year (part of the funeral ceremonies) had passed.

The youngest son was not married, which was why he had no financial responsibilities. The third son was considered to be doing financially badly and he was not normally concerned with the financial duties of the family; that is, according to Azim's wife, who constantly complained of her husband's burdensome task of taking care of the whole family. The third son lives upstairs in a separate flat and mainly has his meals at his father's place. His wife, of course, helps around the house as a proper *kelin*.

From the description of the weekend evening gathering, one can imagine the duties and responsibilities of children and how parents, in this particular case a father, make use of this position. In the academic discussions about overlapping relations between kinship and patronage, authors describe paternalism as a relation of father to son, and at the same time that of patron.

Sons are bound to their fathers by the belief that their duties to their parents are sacred. Sacredness is underwritten by the myth which basically says: 'whatever one does in one's life it will return to you; if you take good care of your parents your children will care for you in the same manner'. This maintains that if a child mistreats or disobeys his parents, the same conduct will, in turn, later be levelled on him in adult life by his own progeny, an act of return from God. People are always reminded of the return of sins by bringing up examples from the cases of other families.

Gafur's second son (Azim) has to take the main responsibilities of the eldest son, since the actual eldest son lives far away in Khorezm. The responsibilities include, among others, caring for the entire family if any member has difficulties.

Azim sells rice in the bazaar together with his wife. Both Azim and Zumrad have separate locations in which to sell, and both have their own clients. Azim is a finance department graduate with working experience in banks. His wife, Zumrad, is a primary school teacher with a college education and previously worked in a primary school. Now they both have to sell rice as they cannot afford to work for the 'state' (*davlat ishi*/state work). Jointly, they earn a monthly minimum of US$300 and a maximum of US$900 equivalent, which is about ten times higher than any state salary. They say that their income is not bad, but they have three children and an extended family to take care of. Consequently, Azim is considered to be well-off by his extended family. His wife maintains that they must conceal their income. But it is not really possible, as most of their rice is supplied by their home village, and Gafur has access to that information. Thus, the relationship between Gafur and Azim is not limited to a son–father relation as understood by any Western notion of family relations. They both depend on each other financially, socially and morally, and at the same time are bound by family ties. This type of relationship has the highest degree of interdependence. First duty and feeling, then mythic fear alongside social pressure, are the main factors creating strong dependency in this case. Most of these factors are constructed within the traditions and religious belief that is nurtured from early childhood, which becomes an essential part of knowledge and belief about family and kinship relations. I will stop on these factors in a more detailed manner in the following section. Namely, I will shed light on the duties and responsibilities of individual family members and how this is nurtured from early childhood.

Socialising duties and responsibilities

Oyila

Since I emphasised duties and responsibilities as one of the main factors in the maintenance of the interdependent/dependent relationships, I will turn now to a brief introduction to the merging of these two notions and their development. Before doing so, I will briefly dwell on the definition of *oyila*, literally 'family', which needs to be clarified in order to understand some aspects of kinship relations, the duties and obligations of family members.

Oyila is translated as 'family' but its meaning and practical use corresponds to its original Arabic word *ayila*, which is an extended family (the extension is relative depending on the context) rather than a nuclear family. *Oyila* can be defined more specifically as a relatively smaller unit in the kinship networks consisting of two or more generations of 'husband(s)–wife/wives'. In *oyila* there should be elders (*kattala*/older ones or big ones and *qarrila*/elders) and young members with their families (*yoshla*/young ones). The 'nuclear family' in the Western sense is not a nuclear family in so far as it makes decisions and thinks as a 'family'. *Qarrila* (elders) and *kattala* (older sons) make important decisions for the whole *oyila*. 'Household' would not serve as an alternative since it is defined by the existence of basic rules regarding shared economy, which may also include 'extended family' or other relatives. The use and meaning of the term *oyila* varies from region to region and the term is usually defined within the context of its use. The use of the term *oyila* indicates the boundaries drawn along a close kinship group that varies from context to context, depending on the family history of a particular *oyila*. The same term can also be used sometimes in the meaning of 'family' in the Western understanding of it; at others, it includes the members of families living under one roof, or corresponds to a household which may include members who share financial means, but do not share the same residence. Some *oyila*s can also be a small or close kinship group that is known under one name.

Social age and expectation

What are the family duties, and how do they emerge? I will focus on duties which are directly connected to the making of dependency relations. Duties are expected to be taken seriously after reaching maturity. There are biological and social distinctions of age and maturity in social anthropological literature (Kertzer and Keith 1984). In the following I will define the social age system and the respective duties of each category of age system relevant for Khorezm.

The distinction of life periods is defined by the degree of maturity which is connected to certain lifecycle events or marked by certain achievements. Each of these age statuses are bound to particular obligations and duties. The distinction is gender-based, and different life periods are defined accordingly. There are approximately five periods or age statuses a person goes through in life. These are: (1) *bala*; (2) *yoshla*; (3) *ulli*; (4) *yoshi katta*; (5) *qarri*.

The period of childhood (*bola*) for boys lasts until he reaches 9–10 years of age and has finished primary school. Boys can play, and be spoiled, and can request things from their parents and relatives. It can be deduced from the discourse about children that when parents require something onerous from a child, the older members of the family will take the child's side, saying '*bola hali u ahir*' (but he is still a child). From teenage years onwards, a boy is considered to be 'young' (*yosh*) in the sense of being childish. When somebody complains about a young unmarried man who is no longer really young (around 23–24) in the sense of being childish, he can be defended by his parents saying 'he is still *yosh*/young'. After he gets married, he is considered to be responsible and must take the duties and rules seriously. This is when a man reaches a period of maturity (*ulli bola boldi*/he became big).

After he has several children he is expected to have different roles and different responsibilities and slowly start transforming himself into the rank of the elder (*yashi katta*). The time of entering into this rank is usually marked by the marriage of one or two of his offspring. Only after that can he expect to have his word taken seriously. At that time, he may enjoy the benefits of respect and obedience from the children and *kelin*s. This period is usually called the time when one can finally 'stretch one's legs and enjoy it' (*oyoqimni yozib hazzatib otiraman*). Here, some words on the duties of any father in a Khorezmian context are necessary. I already briefly noted the attitudes of Khorezmians and other Uzbeks in general towards housing and accommodation. There are, of course, different views on the size, type (a house or apartment flat), style and interior design of homes among Uzbeks in general. To own a house is a primary aim in adult life which, as much as my own local knowledge permits, can probably stand as a generalisation for all Central Asian communities. Usually, a Khorezmian father's duty is to build a house for each of his sons. Consequently, a son expects this of his father and, in turn, hopes to do the same for his own sons. But all these duties are only fulfilled if the appropriate respect is shown, and rules are followed by the children.

Girls are usually considered to be '*bola*' until they go to primary school. As early as primary school, girls are taught their responsibilities in the house. Usually once girls go to school, their parents or older members of the family will praise them: 'Now you are a big girl. You go to school.' They start learning housework early before school age, and as soon as they start to understand speech, they are asked to fetch and tidy, and are always praised for that. Thus when they go to school they are ready to accept obedience and their duties about the house.

Unlike boys, who are considered to reach maturity (*ulli*) after marriage, girls' periods of being '*yosh*' continue longer until they live separately from their in-law family and most likely when they have an already married son or daughter. Only then can they be considered mature (*ulli hatin*[17]). It is only after reaching 55 or 60 that they can be taken seriously by other elders and enter that rank, and enjoy the benefits of being an elder (*yashi katta*). This gender-based distribution of duties among children has implications for the degree of interdependence among family and kin members.

Concluding theoretical discussion: power relations and dependence theories

The above examples demonstrated the ways in which actors establish and maintain their social relationships within the Khorezmian community. I brought forward examples of relations based on power and unequal status. I will make use of the Foucauldian (1982) understanding of power as dispersed throughout social life. I would promote the task of relating power to several concepts such as authority, legitimacy, capital and status, all of which came out as important in analysing various interpersonal relationships. The examples included kinship relations and patron–client relations, in addition to the biographical details of the individuals involved, in order to present their perspectives on their lives and social interactions.

From the examples given in this chapter I showed that there are two realms of social relations within the Khorezmian community: shallow, short-term relations (weak ties) on the one hand, and long-term and important relations (strong ties) on the other. The former is based on particular reciprocities and ethnic solidarities shown in the example of Halmurat and his clients for *propiska* also described earlier in this book (in Chapter 3). The latter is more intensive and involves complex situations of crosscutting and overlapping ties in the social relations based on power and dependence. I focused more on the latter in this chapter, since I covered the former type of relations in earlier chapters of this book. Below, I will discuss this present ethnographic material in connection with the theoretical models and variables that might be relevant to my analysis.

Patrons and clients

The social relations based on power and dependence are mainly those relations between patrons and clients. This is particularly relevant in the Central Asian context. There is little research done in this field on the region. For instance, Ilkhamov (2007) deals with patronage and other informal networks in Uzbekistan focusing on governance structures; also Menon (1995) discusses the same issues, focusing on the security provisions and its importance in post-Soviet Central Asia, while Koroteyeva and Makarova (1998) deal with similar issues during Soviet and post-Soviet times. Northrop (2000) turns our attention to the importance of loyalty in similar social relations during the Soviet period. Discussing patron–client relationships, Eisenstadt and Roninger (1980: 48; 1984) bring up such variables as hierarchy, asymmetry, inequality, autonomy, spirituality, power, kinship and friendship. They (Eisenstadt and Roninger 1980: 48) state that:

> The stress on interpersonal relations and exchange became connected in the study of patronage with the upholding of several dimensions of social structure and action, seen as having been neglected both in classical functional anthropology and in the structural-functional approaches of sociology, as well as in the then current studies of modernisation. The most important dimensions were those of autonomy of power, the flow of resources and the structure of social relations in society, and on such aspects of interpersonal relations as hierarchy, asymmetry and inequality, and the autonomy of some aspects of symbolic dimension of human activity. The latter were seen as closely related in patron–client relations, to such concepts as honor, or spiritual dimensions of such interpersonal relations as friendship and ritual kinship.

The authors (Eisenstadt and Roninger 1980: 49) account for patron–client relations as being 'complex social arrangements' 'in their fullest expression', 'a distinct mode of regulating crucial aspects of institutional order' which are responsible for 'structuring of the flow of resources, exchange and power relations and their legitimation in society'.

198 *Identification and interdependence*

Recent debates on patron–client relations have implied that patron–client relations in certain geographical and cultural locales can be observed between kin members (Wolf 1966; Gellner and Waterbury 1977). Gellner and Waterbury (1977: 1) asserted that: 'patronage often borrows the language of kinship and also utilises the links of kin'. But they (Gellner and Waterbury 1977: 1) also wrote that 'a genuine kinship society is antithetical to patronage'. Eric Wolf (1966: 18) was explicit about the incorporation of patron–client relations in the lineage of certain societies 'with super-local unilineal descent groups' like China and the Near East. He (Wolf 1966: 18) asserted: 'we find the patron incorporated into the lineage, in the persons or persons manning the executive "gentry" positions in the lineage'. If a kin has a respected position and has access to resources, he can become a patron as seen in the relation between Gafur and his sons. Theoretically, one can argue that kin have responsibilities and duties to support each other. But the types of reciprocity and attitudes present in the actors are similar to patterns of patron–client relationships. How does it develop that kin who are potential patrons, i.e. in the position to offer support avoiding obligations of kinship rules, creating the relations between a patron and a client? If a patron has knowledge of negative outcome of his support/patronage which might end up being altruistic or with subsequent expanses on his (the patron's) side, he will seek reasons to find his way out of fulfilling his duty as a kinsman. This means a kinsperson in a position to offer something to another kin will avoid doing so unless the kinsperson seeking his support is consciously and voluntarily ready to reciprocate. This strategy is common knowledge for a 'client' relative, and why he or his family will choose the way expected by the patron of approaching the patron-kin by following the rules of clientele norms. It is likely that the 'client' will show the capacity and willingness to reimburse the 'support', not necessarily in the form of currency, but in the form of labour, loyalty, gifts or other services.

Opportunity or trap?

In the first instance, Khorezmian migrants usually seek social and economic support within their direct families. If there is no support available, they turn to their extended families. A last resort would be a friend or comrade from their neighbourhood or *zemlyak*[Ru].[18] The prospect of looking for jobs and opportunities within the state system outside of family or friends is believed to be impossible, due to the complex economic structural constraints and the dysfunctional character of the state system.

Dilmurad and his wife consider themselves to be luckier than those who arrived in Tashkent. Dilmurad, as many others before coming to Tashkent, established a contact who could assist in obtaining *propiska*, and finding jobs and a place to stay. Initially, and even later, it is difficult to establish oneself and it is expensive to live in Tashkent. If Dilmurad had not chosen to work for Sayora on a permanent basis he would have been required to search for other jobs or join some other construction team. An alternative would have been an offer to build or renovate, and only then recruit his own team from Khorezm, much as other headmen do.

If a Khorezmian decides to build his own house in Tashkent (cheaper than buying an existing house which is not built in a Khorezmian style), he recruits a construction team from Khorezm which is considerably cheaper. Even for small renovations, where one needs only one *usta* (master), it is cheaper to bring one from Khorezm than hiring one in Tashkent.

Dilmurad's current earnings include his monthly salary, accommodation and food provided by Sayora. But if a headman is 'independent' then he would earn from the income of the completed project with the help of a relatively cheap construction team brought from Khorezm. Expenses paid for accommodation, travel and food would finally be covered by a lump sum on completion of the project. Unlike his 'independent' colleagues, Dilmurad does not risk spending money on his team members, nor concern himself with their trouble with police. He is secured financially by Sayora with a stable salary, whereas the independent headman must always run the risk of either bankruptcy in the absence of contracts, or trouble with the state authorities.[19]

Outstanding ethnic entrepreneurs and other actors with status and capital become patrons and bosses for their clients. Power and agency are related concepts and are to be considered in the frame of structural constraints and structural possibilities (Westwood 2002). Economic and political processes create a particular context where structural constraints for individual action are created, which in turn opens up possibilities or options for other individuals such as Sayora. This kind of configuration creates unequal positions and situations where certain groups and individuals are more privileged than others.

At a group level the opportunities are open to titular groups (Tashkentis), which automatically creates a hierarchy of belonging. Belonging to a certain group becomes a matter of inclusion and exclusion. In this process, actors of status who possess a certain amount of capital play a crucial role. These particular structural constraints partly define agency of the actors with status and capital. As a result other individuals with restricted options and less agency fall under the power of those actors privileged by their status and capital.[20]

When I use the term *structure*, I borrow it from Giddens' (1986: xxxi) structuration theory, which defines it as 'rules and resources recursively implicated in social reproduction; institutionalised features of social systems have structural properties in the sense that relationships are stabilised across time and space'. Giddens (ibid.: xxvii) talks about 'constraining aspects of structural properties of social systems', but it is important to remember that there can also be benefits for other actors which are left aside. In the given context the 'structural constraints' are low payment or non-payment practices in state agencies, particular attitudes towards newcomers to Tashkent both by the state and Tashkentis, and contradictory attitudes towards ethnic solidarity in general. These constraints not only impede the actions of clients, lessening their options and agency, but also open up structural possibilities for such actors as Sayora, Halmurat, Gafur, and also Dilmurad (in relation to his team members) who have different status and

200 *Identification and interdependence*

capital. Their possibilities include the resources which they are in a position to control (employment, *propiska*, accommodation) and are in a position to redistribute among their clients. Sayora, Halmurat, Gafur and Dilmurad have a say over certain resources, and possess the capacity and knowledge to create their own 'markets', with their own rules and principles of redistribution. As one of my Tashkenti informants said: '*Hayot bu bozor* [Life is a market!]'. The term 'market' carries a wider meaning here than it usually does in the economic understanding of the term. The term 'market' allows the definition of a space where services are offered and negotiated, and transactions take place in a variety of forms and content. The rules are defined and predefined by both actors and structures where capital and status play important roles.

The agency of dependents is limited, but that does not mean it is absent. It would be erroneous to maintain that they are merely the passive recipients of the wills and intentions of those more influential and powerful than their own. Giddens (2000: 93) argues that power relations are '*two-way*' and 'are relations of autonomy and dependence, but even the most autonomous agent is in some degree dependent, and the most dependent actor or party in a relationship retains some autonomy'. Foucault (1982: 790) also pointed to the same observation by stating that the exercise of power is not possible without one important element, which is freedom. In other words '[p]ower is exercised only over free subjects, and only insofar as they are free'. This implies that the dependent actor has chosen to enter the dependent relationship with his or her own interests and benefits in mind.

In the above 'market', the options for those who have limited choices are in competition with others. Knowledge of possible benefits in the market is channelled through certain networks, the access to which is defined along kinship and ethnic belonging. A good client of Halmurat will use his contact (with Halmurat) as capital to sell to other Khorezmians who do not know Halmurat. Dilmurad is in possession of good opportunities for young men to provide construction jobs, or other work for those who want to come to Tashkent to make money. Sayora can offer a wide range of opportunities of different kinds; employment, *propiska*, accommodation, social security and even 'successful' marriage, among others. The opportunities are, of course, ethnicity-based. Clients have to decide if they want to enter the relations with co-ethnics or look for other opportunities elsewhere. In this situation it becomes a dilemma for an actor who has to choose between those offers and gaining the benefits without falling into the ethnic trap of dependency relations. This leads me to the next point or question about how people fall into the dependency relations and the problems involved within those types of social relations.

Trader's dilemma

Halmurat is approached by his client co-ethnics, requesting a *propiska* stamp in their passport, whereby Halmurat makes a profit. On the other hand, his clients play the ethnic card, appealing for ethnic solidarity in order to profit themselves (getting their *propiska* stamp) at the expense of Halmurat's interests and therefore opting for short-term relations. Some also reciprocate the transaction in order to ensure a long-term relation with Halmurat.

The latter is more intensive, and important relations are based on dependence, patronage and kinship. These relations involve duties and obligations directly related to the particular status and roles of the individuals involved. In both kinds of relations Khorezmians face the 'trader's dilemma' in choosing between making a profit, or expressing ethnic solidarity. The trader's dilemma is solved in those two types of relations differently. In the shallow/*yuzaki* kind of relations, profit often outweighs ethnic altruism and solidarity, since the relation is, relatively speaking, independent and sometimes not reciprocated. In other words, the trader opts for profit at the expense of ethnic altruism and solidarity. In this relation each has an option to leave this relation. In the second – *muhim/ boshqacha*, relations of patronage, kinship and ethnicity, the dependence is high due to overlapping ties of kinship, ethnicity and patronage: there is no easy option to leave this relation. In these types of relations the trader's dilemma remains unsolved, and actors fall into the ethnic trap of dependency relations. The solution to the dilemma is suggested as a non-solution where dependents manage the balance between profit and good terms with their respective patrons and other members of the community – at least until they themselves become 'established'[21] in Tashkent. Dependence and power of the patron may be analysed in terms of treating power and agency as variables and utilising the model of the trader's dilemma to explain the situation of the individuals who have fallen into the ethnic trap.

Examples from various regions of South-east Asia have shown that solutions to the trader's dilemma may be found through conversion and formation of a separate ethnic group in order to distance themselves from existing kinship groups (Evers 1994). In the above situation, an actor who has been offered benefits within a limited but secure system of income generation and socialisation drawn along kinship and ethnic lines has to make choices. The choices are limited because of the structural constraints discussed above. As a result of exclusionary practices of certain groups, individuals are left with limited choices offered within their own group. In times of uncertainty and in the absence of social security values, interests change accordingly. In other words, what is lacking becomes valuable. Social security is then more valuable than opting for obtaining more income, which also involves a certain degree of risk. Diminished income but a secure and stable future is an attractive offer in return for the solidarity and loyalty offered by ethnic and kinship networks and groups. Having chosen to use the resources offered by these networks, an actor has to play an ethnic card which offers solutions for the short term in order to start his new life in an unfamiliar location. The long-term prospect is difficult to predict, entering a new community with its own rules and principles of social organisation. In this context it is important to manage *social distance* in order to make 'individual profits'. Individual profit refers to the income which is not shared among one's extended family members or any other members of kinship, or others who are close to the individual. The term 'individual profits' is used in inverted commas because *individual* is not used here in the sense of ego but rather refers to the income of the nuclear family, which is also an ambivalent term.

The theory of the trader's dilemma is a classic example of managing social distance (Evers 1994). Evers (ibid.) describes the dilemma of a trader in a situation where the trader buys goods from his fellow villagers and sells to or buys from strangers outside of his group. In this situation the trader faces difficulty in making a profit, since he must deal with the 'moral economy' within his own group, and at the same time comply with an external economy, based on market principles and competition. Consequently the trader has to face the dilemma of making his own profit and at the same time keep the balance in his own group, who will otherwise accuse him of greed if he chooses to put high prices on sales or to pay low prices if he is buying from his own community. If he does not comply with the moral obligations and solidarity of his group he will be censured. Conversely, if he renounces his profit, he will become bankrupt. The solution proposed by the authors of this theory lies in the management of social and cultural distance by creating autonomous ethnic groups and traders' minorities, or doing business outside of the group.

In applying this theory to my data, the solutions proposed by the authors do not work very well considering the structural constraints and the context, although the trader's dilemma is very much faced by not only traders but others as well, since this theory can be applied to any situation of choice between ethnic group identification (collectiveness) and opting for freedom of opportunity in the open market among strangers. In the latter case, the risk of failure is, of course, very high, and socialisation within one's own group will be limited. Prices in the open market are subject to competition and the possibility of high gains may also be high. However, the existing structural constraints which limit participation on equal terms in competition drive the actors back to a reliance on their own networks, where they must face the trader's dilemma until they themselves have obtained a certain degree of status there. This implies that actors in a way continuously have to redefine the boundaries of their collective identification and manage the balance of social distance. This highlights very well the connection between bonding and identification, as Schlee (2008:16) points out in his theorisation of collective identification practices. Schlee (2002, 2008: 16), discussing patterns of identification, stated that they form 'systems of categories and taxonomies' with smaller and larger units. According to him (Schlee 2008: 16), there are rational and cognitive systems as well as emotional forces involved in the processes of identification. He states that in this process larger and smaller units need to be considered, referring to inner processes connected to emotional forces as bonding and outer representation of the same process involving larger units of analysis (Donahoe *et al.* 2009). As described in this chapter, *Muhim* types of relations may constitute a situation where actors have been unable to solve the trader's dilemma and have fallen into dependency traps. Furthermore, these relations often produce bonding of a kind that is typically understood as emotional attachment comparable with one between mother and child, and is usually connected to early socialisation. There is also a limited recognition of later socialisation and bond formation leading to particular forms of identification as a result of intense relationship which gives way to particular kinds of emotional relations and loyalty. Instances include military training participants and others. For example, Stockholm syndrome[22] can be an extreme version of the kind of emotional attachment and strong identification with the 'hostile' other. In order for this syndrome to develop there are three necessary conditions described by Fuselier (1999: 24), including time spent together, intensive contact and mutual support. The conditions are similar to those cases presented in this chapter where actors fall into total dependency on their patrons. In the cases of total dependency, such as between Sayora and her clients, as well as patron–client relations within kinship groups, bonding develops as a result of intense exchange, mutual support and dependence. The bonding does not necessarily have to involve positive emotions. It can also be composed of negative or mixed emotions. The necessary condition to define bonding is that it secures the relations, making them stable and lasting. Clients of Sayora, for example, expressed their loyalty to her and stated that they would not opt for an opportunity of better payment, saying that Sayora had provided for them in times of need, and that it would be inhumane (*odamgarcnilik bomidi*) to reward her in that manner.

To summarise, in this chapter I attempted to present the formation and dynamics of social relations of Khorezmian migrants in Tashkent, based on power and dependence. Following the examples in this chapter I would suggest the answer to the question 'What holds the Khorezmian community together when it is composed of different networks and groups?'. Among other issues considered here, this entails two main variables, *bonding* and *solidarity*. The two realms of social relations discussed in the chapter showed that there is an attempt and intent to gain more freedom (leaving the home village for metropolitan Tashkent) and to establish oneself independently, but numerous factors predetermine the traps people fall into (cf. Husan and Dilmurad).

After the demise of Soviet rule, the socio-economic and political situation in the country developed a more sophisticated system that devised increasing obstacles for ordinary people to freely engage in many spheres of social and political life. Social and ecological conditions, together with the composite knowledge and inner state of individuals, has created an environment which heavily influences the decision-making process. Actors find themselves facing the trader's dilemma.

Multiplicities of crosscutting and overlapping ties contribute to the increase of the degree of dependency: the solution to the trader's dilemma is a non-solution. The dependent acts according to the expectations of the agent who has control in that relation. However, it is not solely about power relations, involving finance and financial dominance: there are additional dependencies that do not necessarily involve finance, but are determined by loyalty, tradition and religious belief, in itself a complex psychological phenomenon.

Notes

1 A Khorezmian expression which means 'somebody is bound without any physical bonds'. The expression was used by several of my informants and other Khorezmians involved in conversations during informal talks, interviews and conversations among themselves.
2 Other works on the questions of power and status in another Central Asian context have been done – for example, Edmunds (1998), Collins (2006).
3 Clarifications in brackets are mine.
4 *Boshqacha* is literally 'another kind', the meaning of the adjective expresses particular things and matters that are close to the meaning of German '*etwas besonderes*' 'something special'. *Muhim* means important.
5 From Arabic '*faida*'/utility.
6 Alisher, 27, a Khorezmian client of the *propiska* office in Tashkent, Tashkent 2006.
7 I will use the term 'rational' as an etic term and where it is 'rational' from the actor's perspective I will indicate it as such. Although Coleman (1990: 18) stated that the term in social science should be used as an *emic* term by saying

> the theoretical aim of social science must be to conceive of that action [individual action] in a way that makes it rational from the point of view of the actor. Or put another way, much of what is ordinarily described as nonrational or irrational is merely so because the observers have not discovered the point of view of the actor, from which the action *is* rational [italics in original].

8 $Ağa^{Kh}$, aka^{Uz} is a kinship term indicating an elder brother, originally from Arabic '*Akh*'/brother.
9 The translation of the word '*madaniyat*' is very complex here because the etimiology of the word originates from Arabic '*madina*'/city which comes from '*maddi*' (solid object, material) plus the suffix '*-na*' indicating singular form. Its meaning comes close to both words, namely 'civilised' and 'cultured', which goes back to the Latin '*civica*'/city and '*cultivare*'/to cultivate. However, it has no etimiological relation to 'culture' which originates from Latin '*cultivare*'/to cultivate.
10 According to his wife it did not look like he stayed at home and was travelling all the time seeking jobs in different countries including Russia and Turkmenistan, and finally ended up in Tashkent.
11 From Arabic *hidme* (d(dh) > z consonant shift), meaning 'service'.
12 *Bedakila* is a pejorative term meaning people from here and at the same time meaning non-Khorezmians.
13 *Svoy/svoyak* is a Russian word translated as 'one's own' *Svoyak*, an irregular noun formed from the noun *svoy*, and *ozlarimizniki* is an Uzbek word translated as 'our own'.
14 Construction workers are accommodated either on the construction site or in nearby accommodation. Outside of Tashkent they often live in one of Sayora's unrenovated houses. In the larger construction sites I encountered many construction workers sleeping in a big hall filled with *raskladushka*s (a 0.5 m high aluminium travel bed) at the construction site.
15 The style of dress is especially instructed for security reasons as it is one of the first means to recognise an '*oblast'noy*' (regional/newcomer), especially for police surveillance in the metro stations, on the streets and in the bazaars. See more details on dress codes in Chapter 5. See Chapter 3 for more details of the trouble construction workers encounter with the police in the streets of Tashkent.
16 *Patiya* is a blessing which is a ritual with citing *sura*s from the Koran, usually made after meals, short ones at the table when everybody gathers and for all other blessings.
17 From Arabic '*U'lu*'/highest latitude, high and '*hatun*'/important lady.
18 Co-lander, co-regional. See the discussion of the term *zemlyak* in this chapter.

19 See Chapter 3 for Husan's (headman of a small construction team working independently) story of his team members getting into trouble with the police.
20 See Baldwin (1980) for conceptual analysis of relations between power and interdependence.
21 I have described the meaning of being 'established' in Tashkent in Chapter 3, and status of newcomers
22 Stockholm syndrome was coined by the criminologist and psychiatrist Nils Bejerot as a psychological diagnosis of hostages at Norrmalmstorg in Stockholm. In this event the hostages were taken by bank robbers from 23 August to 28 August 1973. As a result of the two weeks as hostages, victims developed sympathetic feelings for the hostage takers and went on to defend them in the subsequent court trial. I appreciate and attribute this comparison to Prof. Schlee, who brought it up when discussing this book.

References

Anderson, B. 2006 [1983]. *Imagined Communities: Reflections on the Rise and Spread of Nationalism*, revised edition. New York: Verso.
Baldwin, D. 1980. 'Interdependence and power: a conceptual analysis', *International Organisation*, 34 (4), 471–506.
Boissevain, J. 1974. *Friends of Friends: Networks, Manipulators and Coalitions*. Oxford: Basil Blackwell.
Coleman, J.S. 1990. *Foundations of Social Theory*. Cambridge, MA: Belknap Press.
Collins, K. 2006. *Clan Politics and Regime Transition in Central Asia*. Cambridge: Cambridge University Press.
Donahoe, B., Eidson, J., Feyissa, D., Fuest, V., Hoehne, M., Nieswand, B., Schlee, G. and Zenker, O. 2009. 'The formation and mobilisation of collective identities in situations of conflict and integration', Working Paper No. 116, Max Planck Institute for Social Anthropology, Halle Saale.
Edmunds, T. 1998. 'Power and powerlessness in Kazakstani society: ethnic problems in perspective', *Central Asian Survey*, 17 (3), 463–470.
Eisenstadt, S.N. and Roniger, L. 1980. 'Patron–client relations as a model of structuring social exchange', *Comparative Studies in Society and History*, 22 (1), 42–77.
Eisenstadt, S.N. and Roniger, L. 1984. *Patrons, Clients and Friends: Interpersonal Relations and the Structure of Trust in Society*. Cambridge: Cambridge University Press.
Evers, H.-D. 1994. 'The traders' dilemma: a theory of the social transformation of markets and society', in H. Evers and H. Schrader (eds), *The Moral Economy of Trade: Ethnicity and Developing Markets*. London and New York: Routledge.
Foucault, Michel. 1982. 'The subject and power', *Critical Inquiry*, 1982, 777–795.
Fuselier, D. 1999. 'Placing the Stockholm syndrome in perspective,'. *FBI Law Enforcement Bulletin*, July, 22–25.
Gellner, E. and Waterbury, J. 1977. *Patrons and Clients in Mediterranean Societies*. London: Center for Mediterranean Studies of the American Universities Field Staff.
Giddens, A. 1986. *The Constitution of Society: Outline of the Theory of Structuration*. Berkeley and Los Angeles, CA: University of California Press.
Giddens, A. 2000 [1979]. *Central Problems in Social Theory: Action, Structure and Contradition in Social Analysis*. Berkeley and Los Angeles, CA: University of California Press.
Hechter, M. 1988. *Principles of Group Solidarity*. Berkeley, CA: University of California Press.

Humphrey, C. and Sneath, D. (eds), 1999. *The End of Nomadism? Society, State, and the Environment in Inner Asia.* Durham, NC: Duke University Press.

Ilkhamov, A. 2007. 'Neopatrimonialism, interest groups and patronage networks: the impasses of the governance system in Uzbekistan', *Central Asian Survey*, 26 (1), 65–84.

Kertzer, D. and Keith, J. (eds) 1984. *Age and Anthropological Theory.* Ithaca, NY: Cornell University Press.

Koroteyeva, V. and Makarova, E. 1998. 'Money and social connections in the Soviet and post-Soviet Uzbek city', *Central Asian Survey*, 17 (4), 579–596.

Menon, R. 1995. 'In the shadow of the bear: security in post-Soviet Central Asia', *International Security*, 20 (1), 149–181.

Northrop, D. 2000. 'Languages of loyalty: gender; politics, and party supervision in Uzbekistan 1927–41', *The Russian Review*, 2000, 179–200.

Sahlins, M. 1972. *Stone Age Economics.* London: Routledge.

Schlee, G. 2002. *Imagined Differences: Hatred and the Construction of Identity.* Münster: Lit.

Schlee, G. 2008. *How Enemies are Made: Towards a Theory of Ethnic and Religious Conflicts.* New York: Berghahn Books.

Westwood, S. 2002. *Power and Social.* London: Routledge.

Wolf, E. 1966. *Kinship, Friendship, and Patron–Client Relations in Complex Societies: The Social Anthropology of Complex Societies.* New York: Harper & Row.

Epilogue

8 Identity theories revisited
Relations of 'I and We' vs 'We and They'

In this book I have explored the dynamics of inter-ethnic relations between Khorezmians and other Uzbek groups in Tashkent, the capital city of Uzbekistan. My main focus was on the communication aspects of identifications among the groups in question. I shed light on the ways in which collective identities are communicated to the relevant Others.

I argued that collective identification does not arise simply as a result of contact with the relevant Others. Rather, maintenance of collective identities is a dialectical process of communicating a collective identity to others and perception of those identities by Others. On one side of that dialectic there is a collective having its own internal rules and principles of organisation. On the other side, members of this collective produce representations of their collective identity in relation to members of other groups.

The difference between 'Us' and 'They' does not emerge solely from contacts with the relevant Other, but is also determined by external structures and processes related to state policies, economic situations, and the like. Also, past developments in the region (i.e. Uzbekistan) also influences the dynamics of identification. These external structures and factors also contribute to inequality among groups, and facilitate the differential access to power and resources which is directly connected to fierce competition within and between groups.

In order to analyse inter-ethnic contact I focused on the communication aspects of collective identifications, drawing on methodological and theoretical traditions of several disciplines such as sociolinguistics, economics and social anthropology. I made use of an interpretive approach in my analysis of communicative practices adopted from sociolinguistics (Gumperz 1997) in order to shed light on the exchange of meanings in the course of interaction and communication among sub-ethnic groups in Tashkent. In this concluding section of the book I will establish links between the topics I discussed in this book. This section of the book in no way aims to draw final conclusions about collective identification processes and their definitions; rather, it sheds considerable light on those aspects and variables which are important in the analysis of such processes as collective identification. These linkages complete an explanatory framework for studying collective identities I offered in this book.

We vs Others: *de jure* boundaries

As I outlined at the beginning of the book, state policies to control mobility (*propiska*) drew *de jure* boundaries among Uzbek regional groups (Chapter 3). *Propiska* divided Uzbeks into *priyezjiye* (newcomers) and *mestniye* (locals). This prompted autochthony discourses among these groups because *propiska* legally delineated belonging to a place of registration. Bureaucratic procedures for registering in certain places have been extremely difficult, such as in Tashkent city. This procedural discrimination of non-residents of Tashkent prompted further divisions among Uzbeks on the ground. Very high 'fees' (unofficial) for Tashkent *propiska* further distinguished non-residents of Tashkent between rich and poor. These official procedures of exclusion from basic civil rights such as free movement within one's own country and free residence had direct implications for further identity politics and inter-ethnic relations normally observed in the context of international migration. These are networks, illegal migration and underground economies, among others, studied in the field of international migration.

We vs Others: identification and communication

The objective of this study was to look at various aspects of the politics of identity and difference, by focusing on the communication aspects of this process. As I have shown in this book, this process is a continuous one which involves webs of relations and interactions within the groups discussed (Chapter 4). The findings of my sociolinguistic analysis of inter-ethnic communication in Chapter 4 show that the identification process is a strategic and instrumental one. Linguistic differences and their strategic employment imply particular attitudes on the part of speakers and interlocutors: their language choice and references for collective identification are illustrated in Figure 4.3. These findings support the theoretical arguments of Gumperz (1997, 1999) concerning the strategic use of we-codes and they-codes. I have also considered two important variables in my analysis of strategic action; one is conscious knowledge or 'being aware' and the other is 'intentionality' (Gumperz 1997: 16, 17) in the process of communicating one's identity. In my analysis of communication, I particularly focused on instances of miscommunication. One of the findings within this context indicates that there is another aspect of intent which is what I referred to as 'perceived intent', which contributes to *miscommunication* (Chapter 4). This stems from existing stereotypes and a-priori discourses on the interpretation of the intent of a speaker by the listener. I defined perceived intent as an aspect of perception which a listener perceives, interprets or understands to be the intent of the speaker. The relation between intent and perceived intent implies an understanding of the speech event, its heterogeneity and its possible inherent contradictions. If it is taken that intent implies something planned and directed to some purpose then it is perceived not always as intended or planned.

Language varieties and language prestige play no less important a role in this style of miscomprehension and in the politics of identity and difference, despite the fact that these varieties are officially part of the Uzbek language. The linguistic analysis of differences within Uzbek dialects demonstrated an approximate degree of possible misunderstanding between the most distant dialects of Uzbek, such as Khorezmian. Another finding in the sphere of language variety and prestige concerned existing linguistic hierarchies, which coincided with group hierarchies on the local level of everyday interaction. In this regard, I argued that hierarchies produced on the state level of linguistic and national politics do not make sense on the local level of everyday interaction, since the hierarchies differ.

Since I took an interactional approach in my studies of collective identification and analysis of the contact among sub-ethnic groups in Tashkent, my findings largely support Barth's ideas on boundaries and inter-ethnic relations. He argued that boundary maintenance is a continuous process where the relations between identity and difference are continuously renegotiated and in constant flux. In this context I showed the strategic actions in the ethnographic examples throughout this book, including networking strategies, marriage planning, the institutionalisation of various services and support, and the establishment of informal economic niches along ethnic lines.

I observed two distinct ways of collective identification in inter-ethnic relations between Khorezmians and non-Khorezmians. There is a prevailing discourse of autochthony concerning who does or does not belong to Tashkent, whereas Khorezmians have other arguments about their identity and difference from non-Khorezmians. Khorezmians stress their difference through their language and their history of having belonged to a separate khanate, and relate to their home (*oy yan*) in Khorezm rather than their current place of residence. The similarities in content of identity discourses and practices include physical appearance and dress code, which generally concern rural and urban distinctions. However, rural and urban understanding in Tashkent contends that only Tashkentis are properly urban and the rest are rural (*harib*).

Who are the We and who are the Others?

It is not new that discourses do not necessarily match with actual practice. People talk about the equality of all ethnic groups but the social reality was full of exclusionary practices and identity politics. I took up the existing discursive practices of difference-making and systematically studied their meanings in the mundanity of people's lives. The most decisive of these practices concerned marriage relations. For instance, Khorezmian parents tried to ensure that their children marry fellow Khorezmians. The same people would stress the equality of all people (*odam saylamaq*/to sort people). The same goes for the social events and gatherings of Khorezmians. The analysis of the social organisation of Khorezmians indicated that there are several forms of socialising within and between the groups in question. The category of people who participated in various social events depended on the importance of the event to the host family. 'Strangers' (*begona, chetdan*) would often be excluded, for example, from the most important events such as lifecycle celebrations. Classification of friends into different categories of importance was also telling about their attitudes towards themselves as a group and towards Others.

While I concentrated on identification processes of the Khorezmian community, I also gained some insights concerning other Uzbek groups and their ways of establishing similarities and making differences. These differences and hierarchy of different Uzbek groups and their taxonomy of the relations among Uzbeks derives from the informants themselves, and I tried to take all the collected perspectives into account, which sometimes resulted in two names for more or less the same group. I applied these working categories when studying inter-ethnic relations among these groups and came to the following understanding of collective identification. Collective identities are made out of infinity relations often based on power and dependence. There are internal divisions and other hierarchies that are relevant within what constitutes the We. Therefore, the We is not a homogeneous unit which represents itself to the Other. Thus, collective identities are shaped and changed in the processes of collective identification. Collective identification processes include two realms of social relations, namely the relations of '*I and We*' and the relations of '*We and They*'. Collective identification is a process where the relations within the realm of 'I and We' are in dialectic relationship with those relations within the realm of 'We and They'.

The relations of I and We: identification and bonding

The We-domain of relationships which are often affective was discussed in Part IV of this book. Systematic and in-depth studies of this realm showed that there are internal hierarchies and internal divisions, and often these relations are based on power and dependence (Chapter 7). While the We is a conceptual category, it is also important to remember that it consists of people and their social relationships; they can be bound to each other by bonds of sentiments. In this regard, Schlee's (2008: 16) suggestion to distinguish between bonding and identification was helpful. Schlee had Simon's definition of bonding relations in mind when suggesting the above distinction, namely that bonding refers to the more emotional attachment and early socialisation – usually of mother and child. I argue that bonding can also be created between strangers, or in Bourdieu's (1977: 196) understanding, between a 'creditor and [a] debtor, [a] master and *khammes*' as a result of intense relations of total dependence for a long period of time, initially established as mutual support in a critical situation. This can also be compared to Stockholm syndrome, as described in Chapter 7.

This line of thinking brought me further to an important distinction between two types of social relations among Khorezmians in Tashkent. These are what my informants called, 'deep' (*boshkacha*/another kind) (type A later) and 'shallow' (*yuzaki*/superficial) (type B later) relations (Chapter 7).

Social relationships involve trust. Trust is more likely to develop with fellow ethnics. These relationships have both utilitarian and non-utilitarian bases. After some social exchange these relationships turn into various kinds of dependencies.

These relations of dependence create a dilemma for a Khorezmian newcomer to Tashkent, who may choose to benefit from the services and support offered by these ethnic networks. In the relations of type A, the trader's dilemma described in Chapter 7, ethnic solidarity and loyalty to kinship ties and/or patron often prevail at the expense of individual profit. Conversely, in type B relations the weight is more on the side of profit against solidarity, and this weight is governed by reciprocity (Chapter 7).

To some extent, the trader's dilemma model proposed by Evers (1994) applied to the case of many Khorezmians. They face the dilemma that they have to choose between ethnic solidarity and profit, and as a result find themselves in complex relations of power and dependence. I proposed that the solution to this kind of dilemma was a non-solution for the actors, since they remain facing the dilemma until they reach a certain status, and are then in a position to offer benefit to others. In interpersonal relations, unequal relations require some amount of reciprocity. The exchange is not fixed, it is negotiable. Loyalty and trust are important in these relationships.

Taking into account all the above aspects and variables when studying collective identification and based on the material presented throughout this book, I make the following concluding propositions. First, language varieties and rhetorical strategies are important in the processes of communicating oneself to the Other, particularly in those regions which are composed of different language groups. In this respect, various ascribed categories versus self-identifications as a group or a collective differ. Second, the processes of collective identification are strongly based on security provisions in terms of financial, social situation and kinship position. Thirdly, collective identities are institutionalised by means of ethnic and kinship networks and of 'routinised practices' (Jenkins 1997: 26) maintaining transactions and order. This order is maintained through relations of power and dependence which create various dilemma situations and bonding. The institutional basis of collective identities is not constituted by state power, but exists in relatively independent forms with their own hierarchies and policies. State power only indirectly influences the ordering and policies within the realm of the social life of these networks and collectives.

To conclude, my research findings contribute to the studies of internal migration, state–citizen relations, sociolinguistic studies of collective identifications, power relations of dependence, economic theories of the trader's dilemma, strategic action and instrumentalism, the institutionalisation of collective identities and the institutionalisation of support and socialisation. My findings indicate that there is considerable research to be done, both in terms of the suggested thematic focus and towards filling the gaps in ethnographic research on Central Asia, which are still wide.

References

Bourdieu, P. 1977 [1972]. *Outline of a Theory of Practice.* Cambridge: Cambridge University Press.

Evers, H.-D. 1994. 'The traders' dilemma: a theory of the social transformation of markets and society', in H. Evers and H. Schrader (eds), *The Moral Economy of Trade: Ethnicity and Developing Markets*. London and New York: Routledge, pp. 7–14.

Gumperz, J.J. 1997 [1982]. *Language and Social Identity*. Cambridge: Cambridge University Press.

Gumperz, J.J. 1999 [1982]. *Discourse Strategies*. Cambridge: Cambridge University Press.

Jenkins, R. 1997. *Rethinking Ethnicity: Arguments and Explorations*. London, Thousand Oaks, CA and New Delhi: Sage.

Schlee, G. 2008. *How Enemies are Made: Towards a Theory of Ethnic and Religious Conflicts*. New York: Berghahn Books.

Index

Page numbers in **bold** denote figures.

Adat 27
'affirmative action' 34
Afghanistan 25–6, 29, 41n3
Al-Biruni 25
Al-Tabari 25
allochthons 4, 5, 125–7, 141, 142
allochthony 7, 142
analogy 34, 81n26
anthropological fieldwork 12
anthropological research 12
Arab conquest 25
Arabs 9, 24
Arian population 29
Aristotle 110
assimilation 3, 173
autochthons 4, 121, 125–7, 140, 141, 142, 143
autochthony 7, 121–2, 127, 138, 140–3, 146, 210, 211; language of 142
autonomy 31, 32, 181, 197, 200

Barth, Frederik 3–4, 7, 8, 10, 87–8, 122, 211
Basmachi movement 31, 32
bazaar(s) 1–2, 14, 56, 64, 66, 93, 98, 99, 126–7, 139, 141, 168, 174, 194; *mardikor* 72–4
belonging 7, 28, 29, 38, 122, 138–9 144, 146, 150–1, 199, 200, 210; deterritorialised modes of belonging 145; mode of 144, 145; national 50, 140; politics of 3, 127, 135–6, 142–3; systems 34, 64, 127
Bolsheviks 31–2, 35
bonding 8, 10–11, 203; and identification 8, 202, 212–13; theory of 5
boundaries 4, 6, 10, 12, 13, 16, 23, 48–9, 63, 78–9, 93, 115n40, 122–3, 125–6, 145–7, 191, 195, 202, 210–11
Bourdieu, Pierre 8, 93, 212
bribe(s) 15, 75, 76
Bukhara 4, 26, 28, 33, 41n8, 124, 135, 140, 145; khanate 29–30, 32
Bukhara People's Soviet Republic 32, 33

categorisation: of groups 4, 11, 40, 87–8, 121–2, 126, 138
centralisation: one-city-centralisation 34–5, 138
Chagatay 26; *see also* language
check point(s) 58–60
China 25, 29, 49
Chingiz Khan 24, 26, 28
Chingizid 27, 28
citizen(s): Soviet 36–8; Uzbek 4, 49–52, 66, 72, 79, 80n19
citizenship 4, 50, 78, 79, 124
clanship 28
class 64, 101, 152, 153, 181
classification: of groups 10, 11, 28; language 90
client(s) 65, 68–9, 71, 73, 74, 106, 139, 155, 169–71, 173–4, 194, 197, 199–200; *see also* patron–client relationship
co-ethnic 182–4, 200
code-switching 104; they-code(s) 6–7, 104, 210; we-code 104, 210
collectivisation 34, 35, 37. 40
communication 3, 5–7, 13, 88–9, 93–4, 95, 110–12, 209, 210; 'communicative competence' 89, 101
communism 35
communist party 31
conflict 3, 28, 34, 39, 122, 126, 127, 144, 183

216 Index

constructivist 8, 11
cross-cutting ties 8
cultural marker(s) 3; clothing 130–4; food 7, 61, 130, 134–5, 144; jewellery 133–4

dependence 5, 181, 200, 201, 203, 212, 213; interdependence 6, 7, 181, 196; theories 196–7
dependency 181, 194, 195, 200, 201–3
deportation 38, 40, 76–7; 'combing out' 77; illegal residents 49, 72–4, 77
dialect *see* language
'dialectic' 3, 16n5, 209, 212
dialectical process 3, 209
discourse(s) 23, 87, 103, 111, 112, 152; analysis 10, 121, 125; autochthony 7, 121–2, 125, 127–8, 138, 141–4, 146–7, 210, 211
Durman 28

early history 23–4, 147
ecology of languages 105
economic theories 5, 10, 213 (*see also* rational choice); trader's dilemma
emic 8–10, 89, 106–7, 183, 204n7
ethnic identity 11, 70, 122
ethnicity 8–9, 10–11, 33, 34, 79, 125, 142–3, 146, 174–5, 200, 201; sub-ethnic groups 9, 11, 121, 122–4, 138, 146, 209, 211; sub-ethnicity/sub-ethnicities 10–12, 121, 124–5
ethno-genesis 11
ethnography 5, 12, 17n8, 49, 65; of communication 5, 13; 'ethnography of speaking' 13
ethnos see Shirokogorov, Sergei M.; Gumilev, Lev
etic 9–10, 204n7
Evers, Hans-Dieter 182, 201, 202, 213; *see also* trader's dilemma
exclusion 88, 121, 135, 141, 199, 210

family 23, 36, 41n7, 53–6, 62–5, 70–2, 74, 77, 80n9, 80n19, 94, 96, 97, 102, 107, 130, 136–8, 140, 150, 152–3, 155–8, 164–6, 169–70, 172, 185–96, 198, 201–2, 211; in-law family 56, 57, 70, 94, 103, 153–4, 157, 184–5, 196
Fergana Valley 4, 31, 123, 128, 133, 135, 136, 140, 143
fieldwork 4, 12–16, 17n12, 68, 74, 89, 151, 155, 162, 165, 189, 192
Finke, Peter 17n8, 17n11, 24, 26, 27, 28, 29, 33, 115n43, 122, 123

Foucault, Michel 200
friendship 57, 78, 159, 162, 163, 164, 165, 173, 174, 175, 176n17, 183, 197

Geertz, Clifford 8, 10, 176n14
Gemeinsamkeit 3; *see also* Weber
Giddens, Anthony 199, 200
Glick-Schiller, Nina 78, 145
Golden Horde 26
governance 27, 197; centralised 4, 34; autonomous 31; Soviet 24, 31, 35, 36, 37, 41, 42n11, 50; Uzbek 50, 51, 66, 71, 80n19, 81n26, 122, 139, 141–3
government 4, 40, 124
great population movements 23, 24
Gumilev, Lev 8, 124, 125
Gumperz, John J. 5, 7, 89, 104, 111, 112, 209, 210

Handelman, Don 10
Hatan 28
'home' 7, 54, 56, 63, 105, 122, 125, 138, 144–5, 156, 192, 211
home blindness 14
Homo Sovietikus 29, 33–8, 50
hospitality 106

identification 6, 72, 108, 110, 115n41, 122, 132, 139, 203; collective 3, 5, 6–8, 48, 49, 100, 122, 135, 141, 146–7, 202, 209–13; ethnic 10 (*see also* Handelman, Don); processes 3, 6–8, 10, 48, 88, 110, 111, 209, 210, 212; representation 3, 6, 7, 124, 146, 202, 209; self-identification 123–5, 138, 143, 213
identity/identities: collective 3, 5–7, 9, 11, 48, 51, 100, 110, 111, 121, 122, 124, 146, 209, 212, 213; markers, 7, 24, 115n42 (*see also* language); national 3, 4, 17n8, 17n11, 34, 89, 114n18, 122, 123, 145; politics 3, 5, 7, 48, 49, 63, 121–3, 125, 130, 146, 210, 211; social identities 6; theory 6
ideology 33, 34, 37, 51, 121, 122, 146
in-laws; *see* family
inclusion and exclusion 88, 121, 135, 199
industrialisation 35, 36
informal businesses 5
institutionalisation 33, 211, 213
instrumentalism 8, 213
intelligentsia 31
inter-ethnic relations 3, 5, 7, 23, 24, 49, 209–12
'interlocutor' 88–9, 94

jihad 31
journey 48–9, 58, 59–60, 79

kadry 33
Karakalpakstan 24, 25. 124
Kazak (people) 28, 31, 32, 121, 131
Kazak Autonomous Soviet Socialist Republic (ASSR) 33
Kazakhstan 16n7, 17n8, 24, **30**, 40, 52, 75
khanates 23, 24, 28, 32, 211; Khiva Khanate 32; Uzbek Khanate 28
Khiva People's Soviet Republic 32
Khorezm 1–2, 4, 9, 10, 14, 16, 17n8, 25, 26, 28, 32, 33, 49, 50, 52–60, 62, 63, 65, 66, 91, 94, 97, 99, 101, 103, 105, 114n15, 114n20, 114n30, 122, 124, 129, 131, 134, 137, 139, 144–6, 153–6, 161, 164–74, 184–95, 199, 211
Khwarizm 25
kinship: group 28, 57, 64, 164, 192, 195, 201, 203; *kelin* 51, 56, 80n9, 137, 152–8, 160, 161, 163–4, 175n3 185, 189, 193, 196; networks 16, 80n9, 151, 153, 155, 159, 161, 163–5, 182, 194, 201, 213; relations 8, 41n7, 159, 176n17, 181, 191, 192, 194, 196; rules 27, 192, 198; terminology 41n7; ties 23, 57, 79, 150, 161, 164, 191, 213
Kiyat 28
Kokand 31
kolkhozes 40
kollektivizatsiya 37–8
Komsomol 38
Koreans 40
Kurlagut 28
Kushan Empire 25
Kushchi 28
Kypchak 26–8
Kyrgyzstan 16n7, 17n8, 17n12, 24, 52

language: *adabiycha* 88, 93–4, 96, 101–2, **109**; Chagatay 26–7, 90, 91, **92**; choice 7, 88–9, 96, 101, 103–4, 210; dialect *see* dialects 4, 88, 90–3, 100, 107–9, 211; East Iranian 25; Kazak 31, **91**, 105; Khorezmian (*Khorazm dialekt*) 3–4, 87–9, 91, 95, 98–9, 105, 107; Kypchak 26, 90, 91, **92**, 105, 131; literary Uzbek 88, 93; Oghuz 90–1, 105, 131; Russian 17n13, 80n13, 80n19, 81n27, 106, 107, 113n13, 114n17, 166, 168, 171, 183, 204n13; Tajik **91**; Tashkent 87–9. 91, 93, 95–109, 113n1, 113n2; 113n4, 113n11; *toshkencha* 87, 141; Turkic 26,

Index 217

90, 91, 113n12; Turkmen 91, 105; Uzbek 31, 90–2, 103, 113n12, 211; varieties 23, 89, 95, 104, 106, 107, 110, 146, 210–11, 213
latecomers 141
Lefebvre, Henri 146, 148n20
lifecycle events 55, 63, 94, 162, 189, 195, 212
lingua franca 93, 101
local registration 4, 48, 64, 68, 151, 168–9; *see also propiska*

Manghit 27, 28
marriage 33, 55, 77, 103, 125, 130, 140, 151, 154, 168, 172, 173, 184, 186, 189, 195–6, 200, 211; brices' schools 5, 16, 151, 152, 156, 173; inter-marriage 57, 108, 130, 137; strategies 7–8, 54, 56–7, 135–8, 151, 153, 158. 165
Mavaraunakhr 29
migrants 4, 5, 48–52, 63, 64, 66, 72–4, 76–9, 101, 138, 140–1, 143–5, 147, 150, 165, 173–5, 198, 203
migration 25, 40, 48, 51. 78; forced migration 38; illegal migration 49, 210; internal migration 5, 49, 78–9, 213; international migration 49, 51, 78–9, 210; out-migration 41; patterns 49, 79; transnational migration 5, 78; voluntary migration 38–9
miscommunication 7, 111, 112, 210
mobility 6, 12, 48–51, 66, 78, 105, 210
modernisation 33, 40, 197
modernity 23
Mongolia 24, 26, 28

nation(s) 23, 143; formation 29–34, 48; making of 34; nation theories of Stalin 32; 'Soviet nation' ideology 34; Uzbek 11, 23, 29, 34, 51, 90, 114n16, 121
'national collectivity' 33, 113n13
National Delimitation 32
National Security Service (SNB) 80n19
nationality 34, 88, 114n16
nationality policies 23, 123
Negro 2, 107, 121, 126
network(s) 8, 14, 15, 16, 32, 49, 51, 64–5, 74, 88, 94, 105, 137, 140–1, 150–3, 155, 159–60, 165–6, 169–5, 181, 182, 184, 191, 197, 200–3, 210, 213; kinship *see* kinship; trans-local 4
newcomers 62–4, 107, 113n11, 136, 140, 150, 155, 174, 199, 204n15, 210, 213

218 Index

nomads 24–6, 28, 29, 40

oblast 29, 25, 123, 140; Karakalpak Autonomous *Oblast'* 33; Kyrgyz Autonomous *Oblast'* 33
Oguz 27, 41n5
Oktyabryata 38
Öli-yuvuvchi 28
'Other' 2, 3, 5, 6–7, 9, 48, 108, 110–11, 121, 122, 124, 125–30, 136, 142, 143, 146, 147, 151, 209–13; *see also* collective; identity
Özbeg Khan 27

pan-Turkic 11, 31, 42n10
paralinguistic 110, 112
participant observation 13
passport(s) 50, 58– 60, 67–71, 73, 75, 77, 79n2, 79n4, 80n17, 81n20, 132, 168, 169, 200
patron–client relationships 8, 197, 198
patronage 193, 197–8, 201
physical boundaries 74, 145
Pioner 38
political field 4, 48, 49
post-Soviet 17n8, 23, 34, 49, 50, 79, 92, 142, 197
power 8, 26, 27, 28, 31, 42n11, 76, 81n26, 93, 94, 110, 140, 143, 146, 152, 164, 175, 176n19, 181, 191, 209, 212, 213; relations 8, 16, 196–204
prestige 63, 92, 103, 210, 211
primordialism 8; primordialist 8–10
propiska 4–6, 14, 16, 24, 48–51, 54, 56, 60, 64–8, 71–4, 76–9, 79n2, 79n3, 136, 140, 142, 151, 168, 172, 188, 190, 197, 198, 200–1, 210

Qandchi 28
Qarluq 25, 26, 28
Qashqadarya 4, 124, 140
Qungirot 27

rational choice 5, 10
reciprocity 16, 54, 137, 174, 182–3, 198, 213
regionals 80n13, 108, 122, 126, 128, 132–4, 141, 145
representation 3, 6, 7, 124, 132, 146, 202, 209
resettlement 24, 31, 38–41
residential arrangements 49, 63, 154
rhetoric 110–13
road 48, 58, 66, 73, 141

Ruskulov, Turar (Soviet politician) 32
Russia 29, 31, 52, 72, 163, 184, 186, 187, 204n10
'Russian colonisation' 24
Russian Empire 34
Russians 23, 29–31, 40, 42n10, 65, 114n17, 124, 154, 181, 188

Sahlins, Marshall 173, 183
Samarkand 26, 29, 124, 133, 134
Schlee, Günther 8, 9, 10, 11, 104, 115n42, 115n46, 152, 202, 205n22, 212
sedentary 23, 24, 28, 90
Semirechenskaya *oblast* 29
Shayban 26, 27, 28
Shaybanid 27, 28, 29
Shirokogorov, Sergei M. 8
Shurik 15
social organisation 4, 9, 11, 16, 27, 37, 41n7, 57, 111, 123, 148n17, 150–1, 174, 181, 182, 201, 211
social pressure 57, 194
socialism 35
solidarity 78, 174, 182, 183, 199, 200–3, 213
Soviet: citizen 36, 37, 38, 46; identity 29; nation 33, 34, 42, 50; rule 17n8, 17n12, 23–4, 31–3, 34, 35, 36, 38, **39**, 48, 50, 65, 203; social welfare 35, 36, 37; Union 17n12, 24, 27, 31–6, 38, 39, 42n14, 42n16, 49, 50–2, 92, 114n16, 127, 170, 176n19, 181
space 7–8, 13, 34, 41, 49, 51, 66, 78, 79n3, 88, 93, 98–101, 126, 127, 142–6, 148n20, 150, 157, 159, 167, 174, 199, 200
'speaker' 88–9, 110–13, 115n44, 141, 144, 145, 210
state 4, 6, 11, 15, 23, 25, 26, 33, 37, 48–51, 58, 64, 66, 72, 76, 77, 81n22, 81n26, 81n27, 93, 114n16, 122, 139, 140, 143, 144, 145, 166, 170, 175, 181–2, 194, 198, 199, 209, 210, 213
Stockholm syndrome 203, 205n22, 212
strategic marriage *see* marriage strategies
support 33, 37, 54, 57, 63, 65, 79, 106, 122, 123, 142, 161, 165–71, 174, 175, 198, 203, 211, 212, 213
Surkhandarya 4, 140

Tadjik *see* language
Tadjik Autonomous Soviet Socialist Republic (ASSR) 33
Tajikistan 16n7, 24
Tamerlane (Turkic ruler) 26–7
Tangut 28

Tashauz 59
'Them' 125
thick description 5, 58, 66
trade/trader 14, 16, 25, 28, 37–8, 42n10, 53, 66, 69, 93, 108, 143, 144, 147, 165, 174; rice trade/rice traders 55–7, 62, 64, 136, 139, 141, 150; shuttle traders 60, 61, 133
trader's dilemma 182, 192, 201–3, 213
transnationalism 78, 81n30
transport 13, 58, 60, 63, 191
tribal confederations 25, 27, 28, 121
Tsarist 24, 32, 41n7
'Turkestan' 29
Turkic *see* anguage
Turkic population 23, 31
Turkic tribes 26, 27, 29, 90
Turkicisation 25–7
Turkmen 28, 29, **30**, 31, 32, 124
Turkmen Autonomous Soviet Socialist Republic (ASSR) 33
Turkmenistan 1, 14, 16n7, 24, 42n14, 50, 59, 184, 204n10

Ulema 31, 41n8
urban 5, 7, 12, 17n8, 25, 40–1, 114n17, 133, 145, 148n21, 174, 175, 211
urbanisation 36, 78, 104
Urgench 1, 50, 55, 58–9, 105, 114n30, 139, 168, 186
Uyghur 25, 26, 28
Uzbek: groups 3, 4, 9, 11, 13, 23, 49, 88, 100, 106, 114n34, 122, 138, 209, 212; nation 11, 23, 29, 34, 48, 51, 90, 128; (*see also* nation); state 50, 121

Uzbek Autonomous Soviet Socialist Republic (ASSR) 33
Uzbekisation 90
Uzbekistan 2–5, 7, 9, 10, 12, 14, 15, 16n7, 17n8, 17n12, 17n13, 24, 40, 48–52, 60, 64, 66–9, 72, 73, 74, 76, 77, 78–9, 80n12, 80n19, 81n28, 87, 91–3, 101, 114n16, 122, 123–4, 127, 128, 131, 132, 134, 136, 138–9, 140, 142–3, 144, 145, 147n10, 165, 176n21, 197, 209
Uzbekness 123, 143, 146

village 12, 27, 38, 40, 42n16, 51, 53, 54, 55, 56, 57, 63, 64, 72–3, 74, 80n16, 102, 106, 107, 108, **109**, 145, 168, 169, 173, 176n23, 184, 185, 186, 187, 189, 191, 192, 194, 203

We and They 3, 7, 100–1, 109, 122, 127, 146, 212
'We-ness' 5; *see also* identity; collective; location-work 12
Weber, Max 3
welfare system 23, 34, 35, 37; Ministries of Welfare 36–7; Social Welfare System 35–6
women 13, 16, 17n12, 36, 42n12, 55–6, 61, 73, 94, 114n28, 131–3, 138, 147n15, 153, 154, 160, 161, 162, 163, 164, 167, 171, 173, 175n3, 176n9, 193

Yurchi 28

Zakaspiskaya *oblast'* 29
Zoroastrianism 25

Helping you to choose the right eBooks for your Library

Add Routledge titles to your library's digital collection today. Taylor and Francis ebooks contains over 50,000 titles in the Humanities, Social Sciences, Behavioural Sciences, Built Environment and Law.

Choose from a range of subject packages or create your own!

Benefits for you

- Free MARC records
- COUNTER-compliant usage statistics
- Flexible purchase and pricing options
- All titles DRM-free.

REQUEST YOUR FREE INSTITUTIONAL TRIAL TODAY

Free Trials Available
We offer free trials to qualifying academic, corporate and government customers.

Benefits for your user

- Off-site, anytime access via Athens or referring URL
- Print or copy pages or chapters
- Full content search
- Bookmark, highlight and annotate text
- Access to thousands of pages of quality research at the click of a button.

eCollections – Choose from over 30 subject eCollections, including:

Archaeology	Language Learning
Architecture	Law
Asian Studies	Literature
Business & Management	Media & Communication
Classical Studies	Middle East Studies
Construction	Music
Creative & Media Arts	Philosophy
Criminology & Criminal Justice	Planning
Economics	Politics
Education	Psychology & Mental Health
Energy	Religion
Engineering	Security
English Language & Linguistics	Social Work
Environment & Sustainability	Sociology
Geography	Sport
Health Studies	Theatre & Performance
History	Tourism, Hospitality & Events

For more information, pricing enquiries or to order a free trial, please contact your local sales team:
www.tandfebooks.com/page/sales

The home of Routledge books

www.tandfebooks.com